Fat Is a Feminist Issue
Fat Is a Feminist Issue II
What's Really Going On Here?
Towards Emotional Literacy

With Luise Eichenbaum

Understanding Women
What Do Women Want?
Between Women

Susie Orbach

The Impossibility of Sex

of Sex

Stories of the Intimate Relationship
Between Therapist and Patient

A TOUCHSTONE BOOK
PUBLISHED BY SIMON & SCHUSTER
New York   London   Toronto   Sydney   Singapore

TOUCHSTONE
Rockefeller Center
1230 Avenue of the Americas
New York, NY 10020

First Touchstone Edition 2002
TOUCHSTONE and colophon are registered trademarks
of Simon & Schuster, Inc.

For information about special discounts for bulk purchases,
please contact Simon & Schuster Special Sales:
1-800-456-6798 or business@simonandschuster.com

Designed by Brooke Koven
Set in Perpetua
Manufactured in the United States of America

10   9   8   7   6   5   4   3   2   1

The Library of Congress has cataloged the Scribner edition as follows:

Orbach, Susie, date.
The impossibility of sex : stories of the intimate relationship between
therapist and patient / Susie Orbach.
p.   cm.
Includes bibliographical references and index.
1. Therapist and patient—Case studies. I. Title.
RC480.8.O73 2000
616.89'14—dc21   99-056861

ISBN 0-684-86426-6
     0-684-86427-4 (Pbk)

For Sara Baerwald,
Caroline Pick
and
Gillian Slovo

Contents

IN THIS BOOK I have struggled with certain words without a satisfactory conclusion. I am unhappy about all the words used to describe the person who visits the therapist's consulting room. Is she or he a patient? Well, sometimes yes. Certain individuals like that word because it captures for them the sense that there is something wrong, an emotional illness. Is she or he a client? Again, sometimes yes. Certain individuals like that word because it connotes a kind of consultative process. Is she or he an analysand? Certain individuals like this word because it conveys something about the process of a therapy and it has a symmetry: analyst—analysand.

I myself find that all these words capture something about the therapy and the therapy process but are considerably less than perfect. In what follows I have chosen to use the words interchangeably, as I have also done with the words psychotherapist, therapist and analyst.

In the text, in the musings in italics, I have usually referred to the primary caregiver in the person's early life as the mother. I realize that this word choice is not always appropriate. There are fathers who have primary responsibility for their children from birth and there are relatives and nannies who fulfill this role. Rarely in my clinical experience of seeing adults has this role been an enterprise between two people in the way that it is becoming for some couples with children today. We have yet to see the effects of joint childrearing on adult psychologies so I have retained the notion of the mother or mother substitute, a notion that will have to be expanded as the generations now raising children make new arrangements between them.

I have also chosen for simplicity's sake to use the word "she" throughout for the personal pronoun rather than "she" or "he."

A Room with a View

EVERY WORKING DAY people come into my consulting room to talk. Although depression, anguish, disappointment, dread, fear or anxiety may have propelled them into therapy in the first place, the conversation soon opens up into a confidential exchange in which desire, hope and longing also fill the room.

Therapy is at its core an intimate relationship that explores some of the most profound questions we have to encounter as human beings. The issues of how one can trust, how disappointment tears the psyche, how love and hate are related, what sexuality means to the individual, how betrayal closes us off to other people and how we can dare to open ourselves again are all dramatized within the therapeutic relationship.

Therapy addresses these crucial issues in two ways. First, as one might expect, it examines how particular themes unfold in a patient's life. Second, it explores how the issues of trust, betrayal, disappointment, love, hate, sexuality and so on occur in and shape the relationship between therapist and patient. The relationship in the consulting room becomes a witness to, a stage for, as well as a participant in a unique form of human drama.

Over twenty-odd years I have listened to and engaged with women and men, couples and groups of people, sufficiently troubled about themselves to want to understand themselves anew. Successful women and men, highly educated, articulate and in demanding jobs, as well as students and the unemployed, young and old, people from different ethnic, national, religious and class backgrounds have entered my consulting room to talk about what they yearn for amidst lives that feel stopped or thwarted.

Listening to, talking to and engaging with people as a psychotherapist I have seen individual and family lives transform. I have witnessed and been inspired by people's capacity to change their lives, to resituate themselves within themselves so that their creative, intellectual and emotional capacities can develop. From the sidelines I have participated in the psychological struggles, the victories, and the strength they have found to activate lives that have personal purpose and value. Their struggles have forced them to confront the deeper questions about human nature, about the integrity of human beings, about the meaning of human connection, about what makes us laugh, cry, love, grieve, hate, hurt, embrace, heal.

The psychotherapist has a particular view from her room. Drawn into the world of her patients, trained to surrender to the drama that patients create, as well as to extract herself sufficiently to see what repetitively hurtful patterns are enacted, the therapist bobs in and out of the emotional turmoil that is at the heart of the human condition. The therapist is offered a special kind of opportunity to enter into the emotional experiences of another. She does so as a guest, touched and moved by the pain that besets her patients, but unlike them she is not trapped by these emotions.

The interest and fascination that people have in psychotherapy and psychoanalysis have encouraged me to try to write something about the experience of psychotherapy from the psychotherapist's perspective. It is common for clinicians to write books and academic papers about psychological theory, psychological development and the technical issues in the therapy relationship and I have done so myself.[1] But here I am trying to do something very different. By giving a flavor of what the practice of psychoanalytic psychotherapy is like from the psychotherapist's point of view, I want to convey particular aspects of doing psychotherapy: the challenges it poses, the intellectual and ethical problems a therapist encounters, the *feel* of the relationship developed between therapist and patient.

The popular view of the therapist, generated from novels and movies, is of a silent, implacable listener unaffected by the most shocking revelations. We are accustomed to thinking of the therapist's neutrality, of her imperviousness and of her attentiveness, but we may not be aware of how this equanimity comes about. In the stories that follow I try to show the kinds of psychological states that a therapist experiences during the process of a therapy and to demonstrate that it is through scrutinizing the ways in which she *is* affected and stirred up by her patients that she is enabled to fulfill her professional responsibilities.

Because each patient evokes differing responses from the therapist, each story has a different feeling and shape to it. Some patients evoke a need to theorize their experiences in order to make sense of them while others do not. So some stories contain more theoretical musings or tangential thoughts than others to elucidate the story from the point of view of the therapist. These thoughts are there not to illustrate psychological theory but to illustrate how certain issues provoke the thought process of a psychotherapist as she works. They are printed in italics to allow them to be easily distinguished.

In popular lore the psychotherapist is a detective fashioning from the patient's material a plausible narrative which, when tracked down, reveals the byways of the psychic journey. But while the detective form which Freud was such a master at employing is one way of telling about a therapy, it is not the method that I can use. Therapy today is not so much the putting together of details to produce the cathartic aha! as it is an exploration of the development of the therapy relationship and of the minuscule movements within the individual and between the two people engaged in the therapy.

Perhaps the drama of Freud's insightful moment is lost in modern therapy. Today's analyses tend not to consist of earth-shattering realization, insight or interpretation, but of the slow building up of conditions in which it is possible for the patient to understand herself afresh and to construct a meaningful relationship with the therapist in which the patient feels more fully accepted and understood. So, although there are moments of drama in these stories, for the most part what the therapist and the patient consider moments of seismic significance are of a different order. These can be the small moments of emotional settling, when what has been misplaced or sat awkwardly outside the patient's experience is incorporated in a new way into the individual's psyche. It can be a moment when something happens between therapist and patient which jolts the patient out of her habitual responses so that she can experience a new possibility rather than the repetition of an old pattern. My concern here has been to convey how the changes an individual makes, which might be imperceptible to an outsider to the therapy process, can have major significance for the patient.

It is with this aspect of the endeavor that I confront several difficulties as a writer. In wanting to translate on to the page my view of the core and substance of the clinical situation, I am challenged by the difficulties of translating from one aesthetic to another. The clinical conversation has its own aesthetic, its own grace. Held by a gossamer-like structure of the session times and the responsibilities each party brings to the encounter, the clinical conversation has a shape, a texture and a sensuality specific to itself. It is an aesthetic built up over hundreds of hours of purposeful conversing. Those twin arcs of a therapy, the pentimento and palimpsest, describe a form of great beauty and that beauty, that grace, cannot easily be rendered on the written page. Just as a beautiful sculpture describes in concrete form a set of feelings and ideas, or a poem inscribes and communicates a mood which demands that form of expression, so a therapy is the process of a deep intersubjective, interpersonal encounter. It loses or reduces, as does any aesthetic form, a great deal in translation. And yet I have still felt it worthwhile to try to put into written form something of the *experience* the psychotherapist can have both in and outside the consulting room as she reflects on her patient.

For the psychotherapeutic couple—therapist and patient, analyst and analysand—part of what makes for an effective therapy is the collaborative nature of the venture. The two people work to understand together the shape of the patient's life and difficulties. The therapist has particular knowledges and expertise but the therapeutic aspects of the therapy depend upon its being experienced as a joint discovery, even if the sequence of discovery is not simultaneous. The therapist may feel or even be sure she knows something of value about the patient which she needs to point out to her, but the value to the patient is in the discovery of something of meaning for herself. The therapy relationship becomes a place in which discovery can be made, discussed, verified and assimilated. The therapist's knowledge derives from an understanding of psychological processes combined with an acute sensitivity in knowing what to say and how to say it—and when to say nothing at all.

Over years of practice a therapist develops a confidence about the precise form of her engagement at any moment. Her theory and experience are sufficiently well integrated to be able—as with any skill—to do some things automatically while being alert to exceptions. Her confidence in what she *does* know gives the therapist the capacity to doubt, to question and to surrender to the problems when she *doesn't* know and *doesn't* yet understand what is happening to her patient. It is one of the truisms of many professions that it is the newcomers and the very experienced who can afford not to know without being shaken by it. Those in between often need to cling to theory and to the models passed on from their own therapies, supervisors and teachers about what to do and how exactly to do it. Years down the line they can catch up with a more relaxed reworking of the not-knowing they had as beginners.

These stories of therapeutic relationships with Adam, Belle, Joanna, Edgar, Jenny and Carol and Maria do not identically mirror the range of people I have seen (or supervised the therapy of) in terms of age, class, ethnic or national background. Neither are they meant to give a representative impression of my practice. Why I came up with these stories is surely possible to analyze! Without the work I have been privileged to do for more than twenty years, without the number of consultations, the work with trainees and with psychotherapists in cities as widespread as Frankfurt, New York and Auckland, I would not have a clinical base large enough to allow me to write. To all of you who have talked with me over the years, about yourselves or your clinical practices, thank you very much.

The Vampire Casanova

FELT TWITCHES in my vagina, pleasurable contractions. It was a sunny Sunday morning in spring, two years after I had stopped seeing Adam. I was chopping some fennel when he not so much entered my mind as tapped on my body, as he had so many times during the course of a five-year therapy. Adam was a chef and from time to time when I was preparing food, his presence would insinuate itself and I would be back in the physical ambiance of our therapy time together.

Adam was a fornicator, a lover, a stud; a man whose daily life was shaped by sexual desire and sexual conquest in a spiral of infatuation, seduction and vanquishing. There were never less than one love interest and two or three gorgeous "girls" on the go, not of course counting on the previously conquered, who would return for occasional trysts when they were in town or between boyfriends.

The year before he embarked on therapy the then 36-year-old

Adam developed a problem that jeopardized his perception of himself. He had started to ejaculate too soon. Desperate to make the problem go away, he came to therapy. "Too soon for whom?" I asked. "Too soon for me. You know, too soon for me to really give it to her. To fuck her real special. Like no one else. Take her places she's never been."

The imperative of his sexuality and the potency of his penis fascinated me. It was so present and insistent that I felt swept back twenty years to before my generation's encounter with feminism thought it had remade sexual relations both in and out of bed.

What did coming too soon mean to him? That it wasn't complete? That his orgasm was a squib rather than a release and a connection? Was he anxious? Did he have to concentrate too hard on giving to the woman? Was he insecure?

"All of those, sure," he said on his first session. "See, I really love women," he said, slowing down as he realized he was sobbing. "Take Sarah who I was with last week. Now she's something special." He paused another second. "While I was romancing her, I really believed, you know, that I loved her."

Before self-reflection could count, before he could register how hearing himself was a new experience, he pulled himself out of his pain and slowly spoke what would be ours to sort out over the next few years.

"I'm a physically passionate man," he said as he looked into my eyes and mimed Me Tarzan, You Jane. "It's just nature. But something is getting in the way of mine. So, figure it out, Doc. Come on. Without fucking what's the point. Fucking is my life."

The bluntness of his words and the flip between Southern American formality and crudeness jarred with the softness, almost a sweetness, in his persona. I wondered about the clash.

Adam began to tell his story. Although few feelings came through, the preliminary shape he gave his life had a certain coherence to it. He was born on Long Island in the working-class community of Huntington Station shortly before the end of the Second World War. His father and mother had been childhood sweethearts and she had become pregnant before he went off to serve in Europe. The photos Adam had of his father in uniform and the stories his mother told about him portrayed him as an eager, if somewhat naive, young man, ready to serve his country and see a bit of Gay Paree. War was a romantic moment rather than the reality of bombs, scarcity, cold and death. While he was stationed in England, Adam's father got involved with a Yorkshire woman, who also became pregnant. He promised to take her with him to the United States (Adam often wondered if his father had entered into a fraudulent marriage with her). On returning to New York, Adam's father moved in with his mother and him for a year but when it came out that he had fathered another child, there were terrible fights and eventually he left for California. He kept in sporadic touch with Adam for a few years, coming back once for a few months when Adam was six, but his father dropped out of his life after his eighth birthday when he turned from being a heroic husband and father to a maligned bigamist.

Adam grew up very close to his mother. He was her companion, her little man. At twelve he was making decisions for the two of them, carrying the money she earned as a beautician, telling her how much they could spend. They moved around a lot, from New York to Florida and then around the state, either to catch up with some new man she was after or chasing a job opportunity that did not quite pan out. He learned to make friends quickly and to let them go easily. He was distracted from the pain of his dislocations by the abundant dramas his mother wrought in their lives.

At seventeen, after finishing high school in Vero Beach, Florida, Adam went back to New York, tried butchering, his father's trade, then acting and moved on to selling art and doing exquisite dinner-party cooking. He found his way into a glitzy social scene and discovered how sexy he could be to neglected married women. Wonderful at paying them attention, knowing what they longed for and dressed like a man with twenty times his income, Adam became extremely desirable. In 1972 when he was twenty-seven he married Elizabeth, a wealthy divorcée.

Elizabeth misconstrued Adam's pursuit of her as true love (which it was at the time) and she was crushed by his philandering. She divorced him quickly, giving him enough money to start a restaurant. Designed by a friend, hung with paintings on loan from artists he used to represent, and given sufficient publicity as New York's coolest restaurant just at the time when food and eateries became a leisure pursuit of a large segment of New York's middle class, his restaurant soon took off. He became a respected chef and restaurateur. Meanwhile, his mother, who had moved to New York to be nearer to him after a failed love affair, died of cancer at the age of fifty-five.

Before Adam came to see me in 1980 his life was shaped by two preoccupations: being a celebrity chef—rushing around judging competitions, doing guest-chef stints in other restaurants, creating beautiful tables for photo shoots, writing a cookbook with his assistant—and having girlfriends, dozens and dozens of them.

His hectic life and pursuit of women worked well enough for him. He felt gratified by the attention he received, pleased to be the consummate lover and part of a glamorous set. There was plenty of excitement. He was always living in a mini-drama, often of his own making, where one or two of the women he was sleeping with would be on the verge of finding out about another. Concealment and the fear of discovery excited him enormously. I thought of the analyst Winnicott's observation: "It is a joy to be hidden but a disaster not to be found" and wondered what it foretold of what needed finding in therapy.

The scrapes Adam got himself into and the tension of his many work commitments helped him feel valued. He was clearly needed by others. If he had not hit this problem of early ejaculation, he never, he assured me, would be seeing me. "Everything was coming up roses till that point. Hell, I wouldn't have been here sitting with you, ma'am. I'd a been making you sweet sweet love." Extreme intensity exuded from him even in this play tease and I could sense how compelling the turn of his attention to a woman might be.

His discomfort in seeking help from a woman after many years of looking after women in one way or another was pronounced. He was awkward as he tried to give a fuller account of himself, to show some vulnerability, not to be the big guy who was always in charge.

Yet he settled well into therapy. He was relieved to be able to talk about his life, the ins and outs of his love affairs and the emotional patterns he wove. As we got to know each other better, more details emerged about sex and loving. He now frequently sought a different kind of sex, a more violent encounter teetering on the edge of bondage and rape. His sexual fantasy life had moved in that direction when he started to come too soon, and he had discovered that while masturbating he could sustain his excitement long enough with a violent fantasy to give him a satisfying orgasm. It did not work when he was actually with someone. With a woman, however much he wanted her, he felt precarious, anxious and that he "came too soon."

Adam was indeed a sensual man. I could feel it in greeting him. When I put out my hand to shake his on our first encounter, the presence of his hand stayed with me. After he left the consulting room, his smell was in my nose. When he stood up to leave it was as though the room were being emptied. When he talked about women, I could feel his love. Clichéd words which I might have tended to laugh at if they had come from a friend took on a lush, rich tone. He found women miraculous, beautiful, sexy, delicious and inviting; their movements, their smells, their pretty lingerie draped nature with tenderness. His open appreciation and joy gave me a new perspective on my gender's sexuality and I could almost see women from his perspective as wondrous, luscious, magical, holding secrets desperately worth penetrating.

He was nothing if he wasn't a lover, he said. He needed to pursue, to please, to have a woman's pleasure in his sexual capacities reflected back to him. He wanted to get to the heart of women, emotionally and sexually, so that they would be forever transformed by his touch. And they were. His intensity, interest and sexual certainty made it possible for his lovers to open up, to feel as though they were discovering their sexuality as adult women and to go where "they'd never been before." But despite his and their evident satisfaction and pleasure, Adam was always on to the next encounter, the next woman who could confirm him, who by opening her legs and her heart would make him feel he existed. Until his sexual problem.

The sexual problem that so dismayed Adam brought to a stop his habitual way of going about life, his way of understanding himself, his way of being with a woman, his way of giving and receiving love and his way of feeling good. All that he knew about himself was now thrown into question. In choosing psychoanalytic therapy, he was embarking on a journey to make some sense of the way he organized his emotional and sexual life, to question what motivated him, to fathom why his penis was forsaking him, to connect up, as he might say, with his emotional heartbeat.

While Adam was desperate to get his penis working for him again and had consulted physicians about techniques to forestall orgasm, he found that he was curiously relieved when I suggested that his "coming too soon" might hold clues about aspects of himself that as yet he did not recognize.

The issue of symptom relief has always been a thorny one for psychoanalysis. In Freud's work it was the symptom, principally the hysterical, non-organic symptom that disabled the individual in many different ways that psychoanalysis at first sought to comprehend. Anna O's tortured limbs, Cäcilie M's paralysis and the widespread phenomenon of physical anesthesia were the material that Freud and Breuer drew on in 1895 in their groundbreaking Studies on Hysteria. *Since that time psychoanalysis has swung between treating symptoms and interpreting them as metaphors, regarding them as manifestations of unconscious processes. Sometimes psychoanalytic patients have been relieved that in the analytic space they can speak of whatever enters their minds, that they need not slot everything about their experience into the narrow confines of their symptom. Sometimes they have been alarmed because their symptom, despite a most thorough analysis, remains entrenched. Clinicians walk an uneasy line between addressing the symptom per se, giving the person space to talk about it and how the symptom expresses, disables, enables and enunciates aspects of the individual, and at the same time offering the possibility that there are other ways of experiencing that the patient may not be allowing herself to acknowledge.*

• • •

Adam was quite interested to know what stories he had invented for himself about his magical phallus and why, if it was so magical, these powers had now deserted him. He could see at once that his self-conception as a lover was a lens through which all his experience passed and although part of him longed to be free of sexual anxiety and to return to the status quo, he was intrigued by the notion that there was something to know beyond his symptom and perhaps beyond his sexuality too.

It was not long into the therapy before Adam registered that I was a woman. Since his only repertoire with women was either to look after them or make love to them, seeing me as a woman put him in a quandary. Interested as he was that I be the doctor in a metaphorical white coat who would help him examine his life, he could not keep me in that category. He had to flirt.

It would be inaccurate to say that he would flirt when he was anxious or to fill the space or, as happens in normal social life, as a way of smoothing over those awkward moments that can occur between women and men. No. Such a description would strip Adam of his essence. Adam was flirtation incarnate: He could not help but flirt. When we first met, this flirtation had been expressed as charm. As his therapy continued, however, he beamed his seductiveness toward me and the analysis of it, including his active sexual pursuit of me, became a central feature of our sessions.

For a few months Adam and I explored the life of his penis. Through this valued part of himself he felt able to give and receive love, to make women desire and need him. His penis, he felt, let him convey to a woman that he was interested in her emotionally and sexually as she had never been noticed before. The intensity of his appeal, the promise he held out that he would reach and move her, spiritually and sexually, became irresistible. A woman who gave a hint of returning his interest would receive an emotional assault that not only had her longing for him but left her feeling that without his attention she was somehow lost.

As I listened to his accounts of seductions I felt acute sorrow for Adam in his fierce search to connect. I felt scared too for the woman he was currently after. I would not have wanted to be in her position. I could sense that he picked his women up in one place, twirled them around and then pulled them inside out, so that when they were dropped they had been through a sexual and emotional revolution that left them reeling as they tried to pick up the pieces of their pre-Adam selves. Although he played it as a game—game, set, match—it was the women who would be knocked out by him. He could always go on to the next conquest, the next woman who showed him how much she desired him.

In pursuit of a woman Adam was alive. Although he was aware that his encounters had a predictable pattern of pursuit, seduction and loss of interest, the chase worked for him. Adam's well-being, his sense of self, his raison d'être required a sexual quest, the challenge of teasing and coaxing the heart of a woman to open up so that he could capture her. When he secured the woman he was desperate for, there was a moment—sometimes a longish moment before his interest dissolved—when Adam felt loved and accepted.

He knew that he was sexually appealing. His distress over coming too soon humiliated him. It humiliated him that he had had to come to see me. By flirting in therapy he was bringing forward what he felt to be the best of him, inviting me to be entranced by those aspects of himself that he esteemed, so that as we entered into the not-so-nice bits, he was reassured that I could see his charm and accept him.

At first his flirting tickled me, somewhat as a teacher might feel at the predictable unfolding and development of a student she enjoyed. I had been flirted with in the consulting room before. I could anticipate that something of Adam's flirtatiousness would enter our relationship and, remembering Freud's injunction to analyze rather than take personally the professed love of a patient, I was not much worried about this entry of the erotic into the therapeutic space. It was not that Freud thought that the entreaties of a patient were disingenuous or unworthy but that we could learn much more about the patient through applying ourself to understanding the entreaties. Freud's caution to the analyst was that such seductions were an undeserving love, a transferred or transference love (from a parent to the analyst). Such love clothed that which must be uncovered if psychoanalysis was to be of value. The analyst need not be flattered by, or taken in by the sexual displays and exhortations of love emanating from his female patients. "He has no grounds for being proud of such a 'conquest,'" Freud warned.

So I was not surprised when Adam came on strong. He had been able to tell me that without the pursuit of a woman, he felt cavernously empty, as though he did not exist. I could imagine that at some point in our sessions I might briefly become the object of his desire. That, when or should this occur, I would be pointing out to him how his flirtation or desire could steer us in the direction of understanding what it concealed. I *was* surprised though by how strong and how explicit his appeal to me was.

"I have to make love to you," he said. "I need *you* more than I need therapy. It's killing me coming here session after session dreaming about you, thinking about you, smelling you—your sweet body smell and your perfume." He was really revving up now. "I imagine caressing you. My hands between your silky legs, my body aching, desperate to be with you. I know you feel it. I know you want me. I know you're just holding back because you're my doctor. I know you are."

No, Adam, that's not quite right is what I was thinking, but as he was declaring his desire and I was formulating my response I could feel my body tingle, Freud's injunction notwithstanding.

"You don't believe I'm for real because I told you about all those other girls. But this is different. You know it. You can feel it. I know you can. We'd both be missing something we've never had before if we said no to it. This is big. Something that comes round once."

I said nothing. I thought about Adam and his mother and how confusing it might have been for him to be her little man. I thought about how hard the renunciation of his childhood sexual desire for her might have been for him when she treated him so much as her partner rather than as her son. The togetherness he craved, the being reached and reaching out that were his refrain with women, could have been too tantalizingly for him. I wondered about her seductiveness, how much sexual play had passed from mother to son to bridge the gaps she felt in her sexual and emotional life.

My thoughts were intended as much to calm me down as they were to analyze the situation. This was not a little flirting around the edges but Adam's powerful declaration of desire. I was being given the treatment.

The problem for me was that I was not unmoved. I found Adam's entreaties attractive. I talked to myself in an attempt to slow down the emotional steamroller coming at me.

"I've never opened up like this," he continued in an approach modified to turn on a psychotherapist. "I've never been touched like this. No one has ever let me find myself before."

"Perhaps you're feeling some relief, sensing that it is possible to be understood more fully instead of having to rush in and out of relationships looking for some brief magical contact," I said, hoping that a bland comment could slow time and defuse the erotic.

Adam steamrollered on. "I know you think this is me doing my number but you've got to believe me. I've never bared myself before anyone else. All my honesty before was bullshit. My nakedness was a sham." I could feel him shifting into his Southern gentleman mode as he continued. "I thought I was bringing myself to the other person but it was a pretense. Listen to me, will you. Don't analyze this all away. I'm serious. Really serious. I want to, I have to, make love to you."

As Adam beamed his interest at me beyond the come-on line, his insistence, his passion, his desire was palpable. I was his prey. I could almost watch it happening in front of me except that I was part of who it was happening to. I could tell I was going to have a hard time with it. If I did not take it seriously, the therapy would be ruined but if I took it too seriously, the therapy would also be ruined. I was going to have to find the line to walk. Was I in danger, like his other women, of being tossed up, twirled around and then spat out?

I could sense him getting under my skin. I tried to analyze what was going on, to understand and to calm myself. This is nothing different in kind, I reminded myself, from the emotional places I have been to with other patients. It is different in quality because this is about sex and the erotic. I am feeling scared but if I do not get to what this is for him, if I do not take my experience as a sounding-board—a version of what he is feeling, needing or has felt—then as a therapist I am letting him down.

I said this to myself, hoping that by formulating it this way I would be able to keep my vision clear. I would be able to feel his attractiveness, what drove him and pulled women to him in a way that was useful to him. If I was not to believe this would happen in the course of my becoming awash in the effects of his seductiveness, then I would have had to stop being his therapist. And although I considered that option, it was too naive and clinically irresponsible. Adam was doing what he needed to be doing, what he could not help but do. If he could not act in his therapy the way he did in the world and so have this behavior understood, there was little hope that what troubled him could be grappled with.

The genuineness of his appeal landed on me much as it had landed on the dozens—no, the hundreds—of women he had bewitched before. While most of my channels were caught up in his appeals, an observing channel remained open. As I felt drawn by his allure, I was fascinated by how incredibly sincere and authentic it felt. It was as though his whole being exuded something utterly appealing. I saw and felt that I wanted to love him. The divide between the thought and what might happen felt precarious. He pulled on me in some irresistible way. The opportunist Casanova I had imagined him to be when he had talked earlier about his capacities as a romancer was effaced. Instead there sat before me a beguiling mixture of an eager virgin heart and a self-confident lover. So this is what hooks his women, I thought, even as I felt more than flattered and pleased by his attention.

I went to bed that night full of Adam. He stayed with me through the night so that when I awoke I was not sure whose bed I was in or who was in mine. My senses were sharpened as they can be in the throes of an infatuation. As I went about the pedestrian tasks of putting fresh flowers in the consulting room, reading the morning's mail and processing the news, I thought how wondrous life can be. When a friend phoned about some plans for the evening and heard an unfamiliar lilt in my eight A.M. voice her inquiry about my good mood made me try to get a hold of myself. Just where was this singing inside me coming from? Was I letting the countertransference—the feelings the therapist has for the patient—get a bit heady? I chuckled to myself. I was not prepared to give up the good feelings so hurriedly. So much of the psychotherapist's day is spent entering painful places, processing anxiety, buffeting the sorrow, anger, confusion and terror that patients bring. I went into the shower and as I let the water run on my body, I felt with pleasure its silkiness, the sensual flow of the water's pulse from the showerhead on to my body.

All at once the image of an enormous showerhead in a hotel bathroom I had glimpsed years before melded into a picture of Adam and me making love. He was trying to touch an erotic part of me that had never been awakened. I found myself smiling, even blushing, as I realized how exquisite, but also how ridiculous, it felt. I was in a state of sexual reverie, no doubt about that. Could I trust it to stay there? Every therapy is an adventure, I told myself. Unpacking it was part of the job, feeling it enough to know what was going on.

Ten percent of patients are vulnerable to sexual advances from their therapists. It is not only therapists leaping onto their patients that creates such a worrying picture, but also the danger that Freud highlighted of how an erotic transference encourages a therapist to act on rather than to analyze erotic feelings which can lead to an abuse of the therapeutic situation. To protect patients, therapists until recently felt it best to deny or sidestep their arousal but, if it continued, to rush back into therapy themselves and to case supervision to sort themselves out and to untangle the particulars of a case in which they felt the threat of becoming unprofessionally ensnared.

This undoubtedly helpful protocol is mandatory for a therapist for whom sexual arousal during the course of a therapy is not a single experience but a habitual trouble. However, alongside this minimum protection for the patient, a body of thought has begun to emerge over the last decade suggesting that a therapist who finds herself aroused might best help her patient if she can become less afraid of her responses and keep herself consciously aware of them long enough to think about them privately. Indeed Michael Tansey suggests[1] that it is precisely analysts' fear of their own sexual feelings toward their patients that needs to be addressed so that the erotic transference can be explored. If analysts cannot countenance such feelings within themselves but suppress or deny them or separate them from conscious awareness, there is a much higher chance of inappropriate sexuality being unwittingly enacted in the therapy. This danger is decreased if the analyst can think about erotic feelings for a patient (and what they signify) without fear of censure.

Although part of me envisioned professional reproof for the thoughts I was having, another part of me knew that I had to go on with this exploration and receive the feelings I was having as part of the treatment. Bodily sensations were as valid and useful as any others. It was just a question of holding on long enough and being alert enough to the idiosyncrasies of this arousal to untangle the bits that belonged to me personally from those that emanated from or were created between Adam and myself. The important thing, I told myself as I stepped out of the shower, was to be aware of any desire on my part to exploit the situation for my own sexual ends. Was being wanted in this way a buzz to a woman in a long-term relationship, used to great intensity but removed from the insistence of early sexual passion? If this was the case, and I knew I would have to question myself hard and honestly here, was I unconsciously encouraging a flirtation with Adam? Did I need him to confirm some aspect of my desirability?

Ugh. I did not much like that thought. If it was accurate I would have to take special care of what message I was sending Adam. Did I have a wish to be found desirable? Was this the chink of receptivity he had referred to in seeking women? I was not seeing Adam today. I had time to reflect on myself later. For now I focused on what I thought Adam was up to.

In one way Adam was taking up residence inside me in the manner he did with others. I accepted that this was his way of being attached. I recognized that in privately surrendering to his flirting I was wrapping myself up in his idiom. It was a way of speaking his language, of becoming close in the way that he could. That might be how he would be imprinted on me for now, just as other patients with a different psychic grammar would become emotionally imprinted in their unique ways. As I realized this I let his flirting stay with me. If this was the way he was finding a psychic home with me, so be it.

I went about my sessions that day grateful for the ones in which the engagement was more straightforward. That night I went through a list of the unexpected emotional journeys that I had been swept up in during years of being a therapist, journeys choked with difficult, powerful, unpleasant feelings.

I recalled the times when I felt hated. Unable to provide what a patient felt she needed from me, and unable to repair the horror of her past, I felt her hatred of her parent blending with her hatred of me and I became a useless, contemptible punching bag. The discomfort of that had been as hard to bear as the occasions when I felt dropped, jerked around or intensely needed.

I also remembered times when I felt clinically lost, when my brain scrambled, when I tumbled into another's psychic world not sure that I would find myself and my psychic footing again and having little to hold on to except a certain knowledge of the inevitability and the necessity of it all. I reminded myself that the therapist's lot is to be both in the place that is demanded by the patient while being able to recover oneself. I knew I needed to be affected, to be disturbed, to experience something of the patient's psychological state. I had always recovered myself and I had learned that it was an easier ride if I allowed myself to register rather than resist the pressure exerted on me in the therapy relationship. That way I was responding to only one emotional assault at a time. To have interfered by resisting would have doubled my confusion.

At least, I consoled myself, I had an inkling of what this emotional journey might entail. Adam had been so forthcoming about what he did with women, I had such a graphic picture of the way he picked them up and spewed them out, that I was well forewarned. If I were to surrender to his exhortation, not literally but inside myself, then I had a fair idea of the territory. It was not going to be a mystery.

The session following the weekend, Adam started right in. He had spent the weekend making love to Laura while thinking about me. Some love, I was thinking mockingly, rebuked by my own conceit. But before I could let myself off the hook, Adam's seduction took on a particular twist.

"The thing is this, Doc—and I know you can't believe that I'm getting into someone else's panties if I love you so much—the thing is, listen, please listen, 'cause this is weird. I could come right and I could be with this woman long enough because, because of what's happening between us."

In case I was slow to catch on, he repeated himself, refining it as he did so.

"Listen, I'm saying something about how you've helped me. Sex was what it was meant to be. The only thing was I wasn't making love to Laura. I was making love with you."

My mind rushed to interpret. Well, of course, that made a certain sense. Since he had lost his mother, his love felt unsafe. He might be engulfed by another woman. His attachment to his mother with its sexual taboo kept him relatively protected. He could love his mother and be sexual with other women. While it was not wholly satisfactory, at least he was not overwhelmed. He did not have to deal with his erotic feelings toward his mother (or hers to him). He could stay emotionally loyal to her, not desert her by ever really loving someone else. But when she died, this compromise had collapsed. He had had to sever the erotic lest he become smothered. Now I was a stand-in for his mother. His attachment to me mimicked aspects of his feelings for her, except that with me he could get a step closer to exploring the sexual.

I told Adam what I thought might be going on. I was not sure if I had a hold of something central for him or whether I was simply relieved at the clarity (however temporary) this brought me. At least my sexual feelings had evaporated and I was back on my feet.

Adam rejected my thoughts. Or rather he took them as a rebuff and, starting up his sexual motor, I got the full works once again.

"Hey, Doc, watch out! Don't hide behind the Freud stuff. I was trying to tell you that you're really helping me. Our love is making me better. Hey," he added, flipping to a direct physical approach. "Cute boots. You're looking great today."

I felt weary at the thought of the attempts I would be making over the rest of the fifty minutes to see what was under, inside and wrapped around this sexual bid for me and his focus on what might matter to or move a woman.

"Your attention to me, how I look, what I am wearing and how quasi-helpful I'm being, has a real intensity to it. It's as though you scan to get what will touch me and then pull me close to you."

"Yeah, Doc. Sure I do. That's what love means. You got a problem with that? You're one beautiful lady and I want you."

There was something about his Southern way of speaking that turned me right off. I was grateful for that and went back to the slog of trying to talk about his weekend with Laura and his feelings of attachment to me. I was not altogether successful because as long as I refused to speak through his metaphor, the distance between us grew. And while Adam would in time need to experience that space between us, I sensed that as yet he could not bear it. He could not approach the void. It was too difficult. He'd rather go for a tussle with me and continue to try to make the conversation sexual. To bring back the tease. To make our contact sing for him in that way.

He yanked one way and I yanked the other. Several sessions proceeded in this manner. He would make a flattering comment about my appearance or the way I said things. I would try to get behind or beyond those words to what else he might be saying. Enraged that I was not taking what he said at face value, he continued to beseech me, to tell me that the only reason he was coming to sessions was to court me and then we would fall into silence.

For ten months the therapy was on the edge. It teetered between his insistent, attempted seductions of me and my equally insistent position that we had to understand why he was so caught up with me, what he would be feeling if he were not, what we might be able to address in therapy if he could be with me without having to sexualize our encounter.

By challenging the sexual nature of his interest and attachment to me, I was denying the essence of him, he felt. While he battled to seduce me, I battled to make him face his emptiness. I felt cruel, almost callous, in my pursuit of what I felt he needed to do clinically.

Of course I discussed endlessly why Adam now found himself so caught up with me. Of course I tried to see what this "falling for me" was a panicky reaction to. Of course I repeatedly analyzed and suggested what I thought might be going on.

A lot of the time I stayed quiet. I needed to reflect on what he was saying, what I felt I was trying to say to him, and what I was feeling. My working hunch was that he was scared of contact with a woman that wasn't sexualized, that it made him too vulnerable, put him in touch with feelings of dependency, of rage and engulfment which lay at the core of the difficulty he had brought to therapy. I did not want to desexualize and reduce what he was expressing to infantile longings, but I felt strongly that if he could only get to those feelings, rather than divert himself with erotic play, we could address the difficulties he had faced growing up and transform the legacy they had left him—a legacy in which he was unable to own up to his rage and hatred of women, his fear of being dependent on them and his fear of being taken over by them.

I had an outline of how I thought the therapy might proceed if I could only get it on track. I juggled where I thought the treatment needed to go with my attempt to be open to where it was going. Resisting his insistence that we play in the erotic had merit, I felt, but I noticed that even our tug of war about where the work was to go had started to take on an erotic aspect too. In my rejection of his sexuality I feared I was dangerously close to the edge of sadism. Mindful of his recent interest in sadomasochistic sex, I wondered whether whatever I offered would be retranslated into the sexualized language he felt safe in.

The therapy continued in this manner. I wanted to find a way to extend his emotional repertoire so that other forms of contact could touch him. I made silent interpretations of his behavior. If I thought they would be useful I articulated them. Much of the time I was quietly trying to be with him, not be rattled by his sexual come-on and not reject him. I was caught in a bind for the way I could stay with him through the sexual onslaught was to do the very thing that infuriated him—transposing his sexual idiom into one I could work with. I hoped that by showing him it was possible to survive the anxiety I believe his sexuality covered up, he might find some confidence to approach it. I felt rather like a tired old schoolteacher insisting that the unruly children stay in their seats instead of running around the classroom. I was doggedly maintaining a boundary that was not to be crossed. But just as it would be for the pupils, what I held out for him was of doubtful pleasure or benefit. Running around was so much more fun.

The killjoy in me made me question myself further. Was I just a dreary middle-aged woman who would not play? Was I excessively rigid? Was I like those withholding therapists who refuse to enter into their patient's world and so leave the person stranded while they complacently rely on theory to keep them going? Maybe Adam was right. Life was dead boring without passion and *crises de coeur*. I had enjoyed the frisson between us just a few months back. Why was I pushing the richness of ordinary relating when it was manifestly so thin in comparison? Was I settling for emotional steadiness and some theory about how to live rather than embracing life?

I thought back to when I was younger, when my life had been much more on the edge, when I had been on the lookout for emotional adventure and was game for so many risks. Was I really sure I preferred my existence now or was I just rationalizing its staidness? Had I, without noticing the downside, dried up, deadened myself into defensively using my understanding of psychological processes to pin me down and keep me in one place? Did I look ruefully at women my age who were still adventurers before quickly comforting myself with a dose of smug maturity?

I did not really like this confrontation with myself. I felt I was sorted at a fundamental level. I did not want to be disturbed in this way by Adam. I did not like the challenge he was setting me. I knew the challenge was as much about him as it was about me. I knew that he needed to come up against me and find me steadfast. But I also knew that for me to be authentically firm, for me to genuinely get to what was behind his sexualization of our relationship, I had to experience and explore what he was throwing at me, not only his seductions but what his erotic play for me and my response to it said about my life.

One weekend I fell ill and went to bed with a fever in the afternoon. My family, taking care not to disturb me, left the house. In the unusual stillness I found myself fantasizing a different life, a life in which neither my family nor my work kept me tied down, a life that held a spontaneity different from the one I had become accustomed to. I found myself thinking about Adam and the hotel shower once again. I imagined telling my family I would be away the following weekend and then going to spend it with him.

The thoughts frightened me and, combined with my fever, made me not quite sure what was happening. I called a trusted friend and colleague to talk it over. A bit of supervision was what was required. Was this fantasy any different, I questioned myself, from the imaginings I had about another patient—to wrap her in a blanket and take her home? Was I insisting that Adam's erotic play was distracting us from more substantial issues because I was scared of being entangled?

I reminded myself yet again that a surrender to the psychological magnetism of a patient paradoxically strengthens the pull to recover oneself. I knew from experience that the less I opposed what might happen inside me, the speedier I would "refind" myself and be able to give back to Adam something useful that arose out of my emotional "surrender." I reassured myself that even as I slid along with Adam's seduction and became caught up in it, there would be a sliver of an observing eye looking and thinking about the experience I was having in a way that would be fruitful to him.

The next Monday there was a change in the session. Adam was not much interested in me. He was polite and solicitous but his energy was not relentlessly engaged in making me feel I was the only person who existed for him at that moment. Although I was extremely interested in the change in him, I was also disconcerted, since after the ten-month barrage I had finally allowed him to seep into me in the way he said he wanted to. Was there a concordance here between my taking him in sexually in my mind and his no longer needing me? Was this exactly what always happened with his lovers? He would lose interest when he had fully captured theirs. Once a woman really wanted him, his desire for her waned. It was the play that got him going, the conquest. A woman's surrender was her death knell. She would want him but he would no longer be interested in her.

The observing part of me smiled. It is often the case that when a therapist makes a shift inside herself because she has understood something about her feelings in relation to a patient, or allowed for some possibility, that wordlessly, almost miraculously, the atmosphere changes.[2] The part of me that had been caught up but had then finally let myself to go the hotel to have the affair let Adam off the hook. Once assured he was wanted, he could move on. By my wanting him, he had something of me inside him. He was not as empty and his desperation was stilled. For the present. Now the therapy could move forward. There was new information, new data to consider. The essential piece of him needing to be wanted, of having physically to conquer me, had now happened between us. What I was feeling might be a crucial insight into Adam's inner world, a part of himself that was either hidden under the pursuit or split off and projected onto his victim.

As Adam withdrew his interest from me, I was relieved to see that the sexual buzzing he had stimulated in me stopped. There was a slight sense of loss. I felt a little wan but my dominant feeling was one of relief. I felt eager for the new gear I hoped the therapy and our relationship might shift into.

But I was too quick to feel this was a breakthrough. Over the next few sessions as the sexual agenda expired in me, it got restimulated in him. I wondered whether I was going to be trapped in some paradoxical play in which if he did not come on to me sexually, I would have to be privately drawn to him. I was exasperated. Now he was flirting not only in every session but for almost all of the session. I could not quite place how I felt. There was something peculiar about being paid to receive sexual flattery for fifty minutes several times a week. There was also something harassing about it. More annoying was the fact that over the next few weeks Adam's sexuality found its way back to disturbing me and I found myself fantasizing once again.

Having been there once before, I wondered whether there would be a replay of what had occurred weeks earlier. Would it be that as soon as I took his sexual bid for me seriously, it would evaporate for him? Would I repeat the experience of both letdown and relief? Would Adam once more, after a few more sessions of sensing my withdrawal, come on again? I wondered how many rounds we might have to go like this, punching and blocking.

As I allowed myself to consider Adam as a lover, I felt his force, his strength and his desperateness. As I entered the fantasy, I dimly felt that I was not being invited to have a relationship with him, to create something with him. Sure, I was going to be given lots of attention but there was a deeper feeling: I was being asked to receive his intense hunger and desperation, to open myself up to be used by him. I shuddered. It was what I had formulated for myself theoretically but until this moment I had not really known or felt it. I had a glimpse of the way he picked up, hollowed out and rattled his women while staying slightly at a distance. Although he appeared present, sexually attentive and desperately wanting, a chilling absence stood where relating might have been expected. I wondered if this is what he had always felt with his mother. I wondered whether he had felt used, toyed with, rather than related to.

And yet while I could analyze the way he seemed to bore into me and even feel how disagreeable it was, it was not the only feeling. I was also drawn in, fascinated. Out of the desolation that I felt in surrendering to the fantasy, I felt the coldness at the heart of his seduction. My desire to reach him emotionally and transform what seemed like a steel rod at his core was aroused.

By now it was spring and Adam went away to judge food competitions in France for two weeks. During that time I kept a warm feeling for him and I missed him. Before he left I had felt something of the terror and isolation of his disturbance which would enable the work to proceed. I was looking forward to his return.

When he came back, he was incredibly offhand. Predictably, his interest in me was extinguished. Not only had I been aroused—which perhaps he had subliminally picked up—so he was not compelled to chase me, but more significant perhaps was how he dealt with his attachment to me in his absence. Without me there to represent it and literally embody it, our relationship was of no value to him. It was because he found his needs so overwhelming and so hard to tolerate that he had to be on the lookout to have them related to every second. Since he could not trust our attachment (or any other), he would transfer his hungers elsewhere to where he might get the sense that he was not flayed by them but was instead having them responded to. I was sure, and he confirmed it, that he had had umpteen liaisons while he was away.

My curiosity and my feelings about these other liaisons did not surprise me theoretically. But emotionally I felt betrayed. While I had been hanging on to our attachment enough to taste how abject his inner experience was, how desperately needy he was, how the steel core at the center of him made him unable to really love or use the love that came to him, and how much I hoped that our sessions could hold on to this truth, he had disappeared.

It was as though I had been scooped out and vampirized. My insides had been all stirred up with no place to go. I recognized myself in the description of my patients who had been at the receiving end of

Adam. Now I too felt that I was in need of something from Adam that I had not needed before, something he had tantalizingly promised would be met and which he was now withdrawing. I felt sick, foolish, ridiculed.

Fortunately I had the framework of therapy to steady myself. I set my energies to thinking about what I had experienced. I had an image of him climbing into me, creating a cavity through the center of me and then banging his fists on my skeleton from the inside. I felt colonized and as though he were eating me up. In the sessions his flirting, with its charm and sweetness, had been predominant. Now I felt him swooping in on me like a vulture.

I felt sick inside but also clearer about the work. I needed to find a way to bring out some of the feelings I had experienced with him to see whether they were a version of the horror he was always trying to escape from. My hunch had been that a dreadful emptiness sat inside him. What I was not clear on was where the vampirizing came from. He was so practiced in this behavior, so intent on sucking something out of the women he landed on and in, that I felt he might be trying to solve something that had happened repetitively to him early on, so that it had become the salient emotional experience for him. I conjectured that in his actions he was trying to gain a kind of mastery over the experience of having been swooped on by now becoming the agent rather than the victim of the swoop.

As my understanding stopped my sexual desire, Adam's flirting started up again. But with a distaste for what had happened last time, I was not to be rattled. I directed the conversation to the emptiness that lay behind his insistence and to the terrible dilemma he faced of wanting contact but not being able to use it when he got it. He kept trying to reach in and grab from me again what was so elusive for him. As I withstood his seductions I felt cruel and callous. But I felt I had to make that emptiness apparent between us before anything fundamental could change for him. If I softened it or covered it up, the chance for him to confront his bad feelings would be lost and we would be back in his repetitive cycle of search and destroy. As I refused his

entreaties and insisted that we talk about the emptiness or try not talking at all, I felt myself to be withholding.

I could see that he was in a great deal of pain and that it was
unbearable for him. Although my compassion was aroused, I felt quite
distant from him. I got a picture of him in terrible isolation, longing to
be touched but locked away. He reported several dreams that echoed
this theme. He was in a bank vault behind double steel doors; he was in
Lapland outside the igloos; he was on the Russian steppes during the
Second World War, searching for his father.

For all the care his mother had provided, I was forming a picture of
her withdrawal from him, perhaps when his father had returned from
Europe. Then, I guessed, Adam had turned to his father only to lose
both parents shortly afterward. We knew his mother had been distraught when her husband left but now I wondered whether she had
not become so deeply depressed that she had plundered Adam and his
childhood buoyancy as a way to keep going herself. As I suggested
these possibilities, they seemed to reach him.

He described himself falling into a black hole that would engulf
him. There was nothing there and yet he was taken over. This metaphor
from physics interested me because black holes suck everything into
them. Black holes emit no light, they absorb everything. Black holes
produce nothing. My experience of Adam's attempt to colonize me
rang true to his metaphor. He took, gutted and overwhelmed what was
in his emotional field but nothing filled him up. At the emotional core
of his experience he was desolate, devoid of meaning, frightened and
anxious.

Encountering such feelings of disintegration caused Adam to shake
involuntarily. The coming too soon, the shaking and the overwhelming
feelings of emptiness were the psychological equivalents of a tumbling
tower. There was psychic debris all over the place, large pieces of
rubble—some reusable, some extraneous, and lots of dust to clear. We
did not know what we would find. No wonder Adam repetitively
sought a new romance every time he even sensed this place inside himself. No wonder he was so quick to pry open the private places in

another. No wonder he was so anxious to create a beautiful aesthetic in his restaurant and cooking. He was desperate to feed, to connect, to find a home away from his inner wasteland.

With this desolation laid bare before us, it was inevitable that Adam would feel driven to flirt with me more. He wanted relief and before something new could develop, Adam would try to pop out of his depression by reverting to his habitual ways of relating. But these attempts were getting lamer and were accompanied now by great sadness. We stared into the life he had put together for himself and confronted his feelings of emptiness.

Throughout the summer I was not sure which way things would go. Would Adam have the courage to hang in there, to bear the bleakness? Could he live with the panic of nothingness? Could he tolerate the feelings of isolation long enough, knowing that I was standing by him but without experiencing my presence as an impingement? If he could do that, I knew he would be out of the woods. He would have faced something of what he feared. He could then grow from inside. His lovely attributes and qualities, which up until now were used in ways that ultimately stung others and failed to heal him, might feel generative and productive for him rather than weapons in his armory as he assaulted the world.

As autumn came my respect for Adam grew. He seemed to have understood what was required. He realized that falling for me or anyone else was, for the present, a diversion. He was swapping adventure and anxiety for a long, cold depression. His emptiness was deadening for him. He continued to work but without a woman to woo it felt routine and meaningless. Nothing built into anything. There were no highs, no little hills even, just unbroken pain and fear. Seeing him at work in his kitchen, his friends observed his attention to detail replacing his former exuberance. It was a sad time.

Although he was in terrible pain and very unsure of himself, he seemed to feel my presence and know that he could rely on me. Finally we were relating to each other, not spinning off into some confection. I felt moved by his pain and he could sense it. His depression and emptiness were in front of us rather than obscured. He was alone and frightened but he was not isolated. He had been reached.

For several months Adam continued to feel empty and depressed. He was in a hole but, hard as it was for him, it was the right place. It expressed rather than denied what he had felt for so long. Without his frantic swoops on others to divert himself, he learned to endure his emptiness. As he began to know and accept this state, it was transformed into a stillness which in time would turn into stability and reassurance.

Gradually the authenticity of our connection crystallized into something of use for him. He could absorb my seeing him in his bareness and was touched by my interest and attention to him. Slowly, slowly, connection rather than seduction could occur between us and between him and others. He became thoughtful and reflective. He was having the experience of being with an older woman without having to perform, without having to "give." He began to confront his terror of abandonment, his hatred of women, his need to have power over them and the ways in which he had done so. All these themes came to be played out between us but not as dramatically as the erotic fantasies that had permeated our relationship. I found it easy to accept and explore his hatred toward me, his fear that I could dump him, his desire to have power over me. That was all manageable. The bread and butter of a therapy. It was only around the erotic that I had had to face my own feelings so dramatically and to sort through why his seductiveness was so compelling. Meanwhile sex was still on his mind, as was his draw to women, but it was now beginning to be part of his life rather than what constituted it.

It was not clear sailing. He fretted that he would lose his charm, that the flashy skills he had parlayed around town would desert him. He could not quite see how who he had been and who he was coming to know himself to be could meld into one human being. There was a fault line running through him and he did not know how the two sides would fit together.

To me it seemed much clearer. Adam was developing from the

inside out, gathering up some of his old skills on a new foundation. I could see how much agony he was in, how confusing it was for him, how unstable he felt at having jettisoned so much without yet being able to trust that the new would be any good and would, in time, marry up with the aspects of his old self. I enjoyed his mind and the way he was thinking about himself, as it seemed so much more flexible. As he became less focused on charming others and crashing into their lives, he replaced his pursuit of women with a consideration of the variety of his needs and what would actually touch him.

As spring approached again, Adam met Karen, a thirty-four-year-old TV producer. For the first time since I had known him he had chosen a woman who had a measured response to him. Adam was scared not of sex but of his feelings for her. He wanted to nestle right in with her, to walk hand in hand, to stay close by. He was not used to straightforward affection like this; he was accustomed to drama, to seduction, to complication, to transgression. What frightened him now was the innocent and hopeful feel of their relationship.

"Can I trust myself, Doctor? Will I still feel the same way tomorrow? And the day after that?"

His concern about his ability to sustain loving feelings without the intrigue and the seesaw that were his signature was impressive. I felt encouraged. Knowing one's areas of difficulty goes a long way toward being able to renegotiate them.

Karen was a good match for him. She was not as afraid of intimacy as Adam was nor was she unpracticed at the long haul. Her husband, with whom she had had a good relationship, had died two years earlier. She and her six-year-old daughter were plodding along, trying to live between the cracks of their grief, surrounded by a supportive group of friends and family. Adam was a surprise to her. She had not thought that she was available for a new lover and perhaps it was her ability not to need him desperately and yet still be interested that enabled Adam to respond in a way that was fresh. They were caught up with each other excitedly rather than compulsively. He felt no desire to ravish her emotionally but just to lie with her, to talk with her and to play house with her and her daughter. They made love from a place so deep that he had not known it existed. Instead of the psychological and physical gymnastics he had employed before to reach into another, he now found himself effortlessly taken up with Karen. He did not need to fuck her as she had never been fucked before. Such a concept now jarred him. He lay with her, content, safe inside himself, safe with her and safe inside her.

They had a great half year together. Then Karen's daughter Jessie had an accident. It was a normal falling-off-your-bicycle-type of accident, except that Karen was not easily consoled. When Jessie was in the hospital, and during the physiotherapy treatments for her knee that followed, Karen was terribly distraught. She was deeply shaken, facing again the uncertainties of life. First she had lost a husband, now her daughter had hurt her leg. Karen's distress did not let up.

She leaned on Adam, who was at the ready with his heart and his shoulder. But he could not make Karen feel better and I could see how deeply this disturbed him. He had had his own private struggle when Jessie was first hurt and Karen had turned some of her attention away from him and toward Jessie. Despite his deep concern for the two of them, he felt abandoned. When Karen was spending all her time at the hospital, he found himself sauntering out of the kitchen to the bar of his restaurant to chat up some women, turning on his charm like a talent he had not used for a while. He was on automatic pilot seeking an old comfort. But within half an hour he felt wasted. He had been going through the motions of something that no longer landed him where he wanted to be. He discovered it was better to feel the loss of Karen than to create some diversion for himself.

Between two sessions Adam dreamed that Karen was leaving him. In the dream he watched as she went to his restaurant, emptied it of supplies, filched his recipes. He was confused and tormented. Why was she robbing him? It made no sense. The scene cut to her cooking his recipes and feeding an ailing aunt of his who had cancer. His aunt recovered. Karen said she would stay.

The dream startled Adam. This Karen was so out of character with

Karen herself that he took his dream as a message from his own hinterland. Why was he viewing her as a marauder, he wondered. Why was she able to stay with him when she had healed his aunt?

The dream helped us understand what we had not emotionally been able to grasp before. We now had confirmation for our hunch that as a boy he had been prematurely turned into a little man, encouraged to make life better for his mother by solving her problems. His energy and exuberance had been hijacked to keep her going but she had not been able to replenish his stocks. In his attempt to find his own way he had become someone who could service and charm. But this self was unstable because it did not have many resources of its own. For refueling he plundered others as his mother had plundered him. He had made himself essential to them so that he was wanted and needed. Faced with being unable to console Karen and feeling abandoned by her, he was thrown. In his dream he had revisited the distress of his childhood and the patterns of relating that had been shaped between him and his mother. But he found that Karen had healing powers, she was not just the women thief who had, for so long, peopled his unconscious.

This realization excited him. He had chosen a woman who really nourished him and whom he would not discard. This knowledge sat alongside his frustration that he could not make things better for Karen. It was humbling and hard for him. He felt uneasy relinquishing the illusion that he could turn things around for her. Not that Karen was expecting him to make it all better. She was level-headed and knew he could not. She was staying with her hurt, asking for no more than his support.

At first he experienced her need for support as a demand and in part it *was* a demand but not the kind of demand he was used to. Karen needed him to be patient and present while she struggled with the limits of her own protectiveness. She was not as available to him as before. But neither was she on the way out of the relationship. Adam had initially translated this difficult situation into the vernacular he knew for it resonated with his early abandonment by his father and his mother. When he felt dropped, he tried to still his anxiety by pillaging from the women at his bar. But it did not work. It made him feel worse. He moved back into himself and stayed with what he was actually feeling in order to manage the alarm that Karen's turn to her daughter had provoked in him.

His sensitivity to the dream and to the changes within him helped him accomplish the last piece of our work together. He learned to stand by while someone else was in pain, accompanying them through it but not fearing that he was being used. It made it possible for him and Karen to stay connected and close. He felt thwarted at not being able to repair the situation for her but he did not need to flee from her or from himself. He was now living his own emotional life and was quite able to deal with the real problems he encountered.

I returned to chopping the fennel, my mouth curving in a satisfied smile. What a whirlwind our journey had started with! How ephemeral all the erotic fantasizing had become and yet how absolutely crucial it turned out to have been to privately pursue what Adam had stimulated in me. In my engagement with what he, at that time, saw as the best of himself I came to understand the terror and bleakness at the heart of him. It gave me a view into where his difficulties lay.

I felt then, as I had often felt during our work together, that if his therapy had stopped midway, if I had been too frightened of the erotic feelings I was having or if he had walked away feeling misunderstood, that Adam would have been left, like many other men—a few of whom I have known in my practice and more I have heard about through my woman patients—a man bereft of himself. Men whose emptiness leads them to become psychological terrorists, feeding off the love they can produce for the women they romance and then drop. Men who have to play out and endlessly repeat the pursuit and van-quishing of others. Adam was no longer tied to that destiny. In facing the cold chill of his emptiness, he risked something more. His penis had led him away from a life that was no longer working into one that gave him more possibilities.

Belle

$\int$ HE WAS SHY and hesitant when she phoned for a consultation. I had no regular times free. But something about her fragility tugged at me and I arranged to see her the next Friday.

"Thank you, thank you," she said as I opened the door to a petite, waiflike thirty-something. "I'm desperate," she continued before she even made contact with the chair. "Nothing's working. I'm beyond a mess. My life isn't going anywhere."

She peeked her enormous turquoise eyes at me from under a dark shiny fringe. They were seductive, an immediate entreaty to respond to her. I did.

"Actually it's worse than that. I'm going round in circles. I'm at a dead end. I have to do something."

She was thirty-two. She had drifted since she left school. She could not wait to get away from her family. At seventeen she had come to

London, did a bit of nannying, then strayed into the music scene, a few low-level fashion spreads, some singing with an all-girl band. It was fine. Good even. A few relationships with much older men kept her going financially in the bad patches. Too much drugs, sex and rock 'n' roll kept her from thinking about a future. At any rate, who thought about a future in their twenties? Only nerds and suits. She was getting as far away from those as she could.

Her hesitancy on the phone and her appealing, delicate looks contrasted with this rather world-weary young woman who had experienced too much of the wrong end of life.

Belle had grown up near the port city of Dunedin on the southeast coast of South Island, New Zealand, the second of three daughters of a Scottish father and an English mother. Dunedin was deadly. Dad was a manager, an absent sort of presence in the family, which was run by Mum, an embittered critical woman who had been moved from London when her husband was asked to run the New Zealand office of a British firm. Mum had given up teaching when the children arrived and had never found her way back to anything she wanted to do. She was a misfit in Dunedin and missed London. Belle and her elder sister were rebels with energy, hanging out in the few coffee bars and discos that Dunedin had to offer, finally running off to the more metropolitan cities of Wellington and Auckland where there were more boys and more action, getting in on any adventure going until New Zealand itself proved too small.

"Anyway, I'm telling you all this stuff because it matters to shrinks and it's probably what's wrong with me, but to tell the truth my family is a long way away from me now and I never really think about Mum and Dad much. My big sister's over here and I never did get on with Marie, the baby."

Belle was a woman with drive but no sense of where to go. For one who appeared so fragile, she had gotten herself into situations that would have scared a more conventional young woman half to death. The scrapes, however, were not exactly incidental. They were how Belle lived. As she lurched from one crisis to another, the scrapes threaded together to give her a purpose. She existed through her survival of them.

Calamities could be found in all areas of her life. She had become accidentally pregnant more than once; she had lost her apartment several times; she was frequently broke and had had major fallings out with friends. She was always embroiled in some emergency and would train her soulful turquoise eyes on whomever she was close to at the time to bail her out. On her first visit to me, she had gotten lost, then dropped her car keys, so that when she arrived some thirty minutes late we had an emergency on our hands.

Belle assumed I would become involved in this drama and help her. It was a reasonable enough expectation. But the rules of engagement in therapy are different from those of ordinary social encounters. Having heard the brief account of her life and her crises, if I moved to help Belle as she was inviting me to, either by looking for her keys or by giving her my AAA card, I might be obstructing what therapy was trying to achieve. I might have fallen into her way of being rescued, short-circuiting an exploration of what was contained in her emergencies before we had established a different basis for our relationship.

It was tempting. Belle's apparent helplessness evoked my wish to clear up this latest mess of hers.[1] But as I had heard that messes were what she found herself in and out of incessantly, the challenge was to help her work out what she had created rather then smooth it away as if it had never happened. My approach ran the risk of delaying her with a frustration she was unaccustomed to. It also risked the possibility that she might not return for a further appointment.

The benefit of such an approach, if it worked, would be to give her a taste of therapeutic engagement. It might be more useful for her to feel the inconvenience of the lost keys than to solve her problem instantly. This was not an act of truculence on my part but a sense that there was something to be gotten hold of in her process of lurching from one dramatic emergency to another. As it stood at the moment, her emergencies seemed to constitute who she was. It was very early to be theorizing much about Belle, but these emergencies, I was formulating, were how she touched base with herself, how she bracketed the bits of life between A and B, the anchors mooring her.

So the lost keys sat between us. The foreshortened session increased the pressure I experienced to look after her. I sensed her frustration and a slight disbelief that I was not acting according to her expectations. People always helped her yet here I was, professionally designated to help, bypassing the emergency before us.

I could have tried to understand the specific meaning of the lost keys, picked it apart with her for its particular significance (She was ambivalent about coming? Her getting lost was a metaphor? She needed help finding the key to unlock who she was? and so on). Although that was a reasonable route, I was more interested in how her crises functioned as points of self-reference and moments of contact with others. I felt we had more to learn by not interpreting.

Those outside therapy will no doubt think I am laboring a point. What if I stopped being so precious and therapeutically scrupulous and just picked up the telephone to help her? Part of what I was assessing was whether Belle's responses to crises were repetitive and ritualized or whether, faced with the chance, she could adapt. What would happen if I did not rush in to rescue her? If my response was out of sync with what she anticipated, could she find a fresh reaction? How psychologically flexible was she and in what ways? Did she need her crises to follow a particular form? Would it intrigue and interest her to be responded to differently? Would she write it off and toss it away, or would she remold herself to whatever the situation required?

When a therapist meets a person in the consulting room for the first time, she is listening, feeling, sensing, evaluating and questioning her reactions. It's part of our training to look at several levels of experience at once—the intra-psychic, the defenses, the nature of the affect, the range of expression, the capacity to reflect—and to tune in, as Freud described it, to ourselves as though we were radio receivers to decode the signals we pick up. Comparing the patient's narrative to her biography and self-presentation, and constructing a tentative map of her inner world, are the therapist's equivalent of the physician's stethoscope, blood pressure pump and urine analysis. They are the equally crude but essential first markers in a process of getting to know a person that may stretch over several years. Because the patient's subjective experience is paramount in the treatment process, the therapist is looking for ways to assess the flexibility or rigidity of the patient's habitual responses. It is not that flexibility or rigidity has something to say per se, divorced from other factors. There are no consistent meanings or measures we can draw from them. Excessive adaptability is just as worrisome to the practitioner as inflexibility. Nevertheless how the individual is able to stretch, or is not, has significance and forms one of the axes in measuring whether therapy might be of use.

Hence my wish to take on the loss of Belle's keys in a way that was novel for her. Therapy is full of moments charged with potential meaning in which through a different kind of meeting, a challenge to the expected, the therapist offers the patient a different way of experiencing herself. These moments disrupt the habitual response in a context that encourages reflection. It is a gamble in the first session but, taking my lead from Belle's self-description as a drifter, I wanted to pose the option of her being purposeful to see where we might go with it.

Her response revealed something of how she was able, despite the waiflike appeal, to marshal her own resources. Feeling the loss of her keys did not remain with her long. When it became obvious that I was not rushing to help, she took out her mobile phone, called the police and told them she had been mugged just after getting out of her car and that her keys and bag had been taken. When she hung up she looked at me and said without a trace of visible guilt or self-questioning, "I added in the bag because that way I can file an insurance claim."

The unpredictability of what we encounter in the consulting room can keep us on our toes in a million different ways. Sometimes the things we are asked to witness are distasteful or awkward. A teenage patient abused as a child who dug into her anus and extracted feces on her fingernail, which she then picked at, is at one extreme. Involuntary head-banging or scratching at scabs is not uncommon. Hearing that one's patient has perpetrated a venomous verbal assault on a husband or a child or degraded a partner is common, as such an action is part of what has brought the patient into therapy. We have to notice our reactions, respond quietly inside ourselves to what we might find disturbing, daunting, or even repulsive, and then turn our attention back with compassion to the patient. Our training and raison d'être is to accept and explore rather than to reject or judge what is put before us. Through this kind of openness, that which needs understanding and confronting can receive it.

It is in this sense that we hear so much about the necessary neutrality of the therapist. People have often thought of therapeutic neutrality as a kind of indifference, an injunction against the therapist disclosing what she feels to the patient. But in contemporary psychoanalysis this neutrality is conceived of as an expression of receptivity and curiosity; a process in which the therapist reflectively observes her responses to her patient's behavior, processes them, and then turns her attention to the patient to see what is coming next. It is almost as if we had never before seen a tadpole turn into a frog and it surprises us. We privately register how it makes us feel, see what sense we can make of the two different states, and then turn back to find out what comes next.

As we turn our attention back to the patient with this kind of neutrality, we engage in the next stage of the process. We are open for therapeutic exchange. The thing that has shaken us is noticed. Now come the technical considerations. Do we refer to it, file it for future reference, invite the patient to comment on it, interpret it? Or, as I thought at that moment, as Belle and I were running past the time allotted for the consultation, refuse the case because it feels like too much trouble?

There is a pause toward the end of any first consultation when the therapist and potential patient are seeing whether they want to work together. This is not a trivial moment for either of them. If enough contact has been made, the individual seeking therapy will want to continue. She does not especially want to tell her story again to another person. If the balance between feeling excited, hopeful, cautious and scared is right and the hours and fees are workable, the potential patient is ready to commit herself. For the therapist, who knows much more about the therapeutic process than her expectant patient, the decision has a dif-

*ferent complexion. She has to assess whether she thinks she can be useful to the
person. Is the individual a candidate for therapy?*

Like or dislike is a consideration in deciding to take on a patient but
not in its commonplace way. Such perceptions form part of the psychic
picture the therapist is drawing. We may feel charmed, dismayed,
attracted, titillated, turned on or off by the individual before us. Belle
had already surprised me with her resourcefulness. She had responded
to my declining to help her by roping in the police and turning the crisis to her advantage by the phony insurance claim. At the same time I
could already sense a distaste aroused in me by her modus operandi. I
felt a certain resentment that I had become complicit in her lie so early
in our encounter. Before we went ahead, the question for me was
whether I could find the empathy to understand with her why lying
formed such a ready response to her scrapes.

Folded into my consideration of whether to offer Belle sessions
was whether I wanted to go through decoding and deconstructing
whatever this lying about the mugging, the crises and the drifting were
adaptations to. Where, I asked myself, would we find ourselves? Would
this be a rudderless therapy with session after session spent adrift?
Would she lie to me continually or attempt to rope me into her crises?
Or could I take heart from the fact that, unpleasant as it clearly was,
Belle had presented some of the uglier adaptations she had developed
and that with those before us, if we could grasp them, our initial work
was cut out and might even prove exciting?

For me to say yes to her there were initially three things I wanted
to hold on to to moor myself in this journey with her. The first was to
explore the purpose of her crises. Was my hunch about their function
valid: that they acted as a glue to hold her together? If so, what would
happen if the glue loosened? How might we want to dissolve that glue
and help her find a more fundamental form of ballast based on a more
continuous sense of having a self? Second, I wanted to explore the fantasies, conscious and unconscious, caught up in the creation of crises.
What did Belle imagine would happen? Was rescue by another impor-

tant? Was disaster an outcome that tantalized her? What was the importance of other people in the resolution of the crises? Did she need
them to help her or to witness what she was going through—to make
real an external representation of her inner emotional experience?
Third was the lie perpetrated on the mobile phone in my room. How
to address it? For address it I must.

As I talked myself into finding the hours for Belle, I was surprised
to feel a certain enthusiasm for our work together. Belle had laid out
before us what we needed to do, presenting in this first truncated consultation session something I sensed was central about her. We had
enough between us to work on for a good while if I could make sure
that responding to the next crisis and the one after that would not gob-
ble up all our energy. In a way she had done us a favor by pulling me
into her lying from the beginning. I did not have to wait for it to unfold
between us. It was there for us to address immediately.

Lies told in personal relationships are unpleasant. We may excuse a
white one because it saves face, but most people are uneasy with a
habitual or a purposeful liar because lying is an affront. To accept it tar-
nishes us. It makes us a cuckold by sweeping into our nest a bad egg not
of our making. Lies perpetrated in friendship or in the family are especially disapproved of and the offensive action is quickly pushed away so
as not to taint the recipient. But in commercial life concealment,
beguiling and tease are part of negotiation. The artifice is accepted by
the parties involved and disclosure and coyness form part of the armor
of business practice.

Psychotherapy walks an artful line between these responses. The
therapist has to recognize the lie as part of what the individual has in
her employ as a way of going about things and therefore should not be
offended as one might be in friendship. Equally, the therapist has to see
the lying as simultaneously an idiom of engagement and of disengage-
ment to which the therapy must respond with curiosity. Why, the therapist asks, does this individual need to lie? What solace and solution
does she find in her concoctions?

So I had no choice if I was going to begin to work with her. I had to respond to the lie I had witnessed. I could already feel an admiration for Belle, at her sheer ingenuity, the flexibility of mind ready to find advantage in situations most would have abandoned or been defeated by. Of course, as we came to see, for years the straightforward recognition of what could have been done had not been an option for her. She could not lose the keys and call a locksmith. That afforded no promise, no adventure, no way of showing herself and thus reassuring herself of her talents and charms, which she could only accept in this form. I could appreciate her strengths and wanted her to be able to feel them too, but addressing the lie was crucial since therapy is about finding a way to help people fold the talents and charms inside them, to nourish themselves.

I chose to do it sooner rather than later.

"Perhaps a place to start in our next session, Belle, is with your lie about the mugging and the stolen bag. That creative fiction of yours, it strikes me, slides you into the next crisis and gives you a kind of raison d'être. If we can find out why you need these crises, it might be helpful to you."

Belle seemed about to open her mouth when she interrupted herself. Her look went from self-righteous to slightly bashful. I thought I saw a tiny bit of relief register in her eyes. I wondered whether she would be back.

She returned the following Tuesday looking very different. Her outfit was smart, her dark hair pinned up, so that now I met a young woman-about-town rather than a fragile stray. She got straight to the point.

"I could tell you didn't approve of me on Friday. And I'm not going to justify myself. I don't think there is anything wrong with finding the best way out of a situation."

Her different appearance went along with a more forthright manner. I was not completely sure whether her sentences were a prelude or a conclusion. It felt as if she was anticipating a dispute with me, a mini-crisis through which she would reinforce herself with her winning words. My stillness left her words reverberating in the room.

She too held the stillness, not out of anxiety but out of interest in what she had said. She then shifted from defending herself to considering what she was saying.

"You know, Susie, I'm not sure what I think." A slight lilt at the end of the sentence confirmed her questioning of herself. "Strange," she continued, seeming surprised at what she was saying, "I've never not known what I think."

There was a crackling aliveness in the room. She held my gaze for a few minutes and then went back to the content of the first three sentences she had uttered.

I felt terribly pleased for her. Pausing to think and reflect is the molecular activity accompanying psychological change. Hearing oneself is a new form of knowledge. Allowing herself to realize she did not know what she thought was encouraging. In a way the significant moment in this session had occurred.[2] I was inclined to stay with the novelty of her reflection about not knowing. The forthrightness I had picked up from her when she came in had turned into interested self-questioning. She approached what was before us as a philosophy student and picked her way through arguments about the validity of lying. Reaching a full stop, she asked me what I thought, but before I could reply, she hurriedly said, "Oh, that's right. You aren't going to say, are you?" She smiled.

Her comment seemed to come not so much out of trying to please the therapist and stick by the therapeutic rules, which I had not actually laid out to her, but from an excitement that although she came for advice she was finding out something more interesting and fundamental. She quickly sensed that advice per se was not what she wanted. She was starting to reach for something different—the potential to open up to herself, reflect, understand. Something clicked into place in a way it never had before, revealing new vistas. It was a lovely moment.

The nature of change in therapy is not reducible. It is even hard to describe what constitutes change. Is it subjective? Yes. Is it about becoming conscious of oneself as a subject? Yes, the capacity for (intermittent) self-awareness is essential. How

much is it about feelings? A good deal. In Belle's case what seemed to be hap-
pening was that the hullabaloo she created around her, which stimulated feel-
ings of urgency that she must do something, was temporarily quieted inside the
therapy room. In place of this commotion, she was discovering a part of her that
seemed able to feel in a different way and, as a result, she was able to think from
a different basis.

The session continued. Belle wondered if I really had disapproved of her. She then asked herself a braver question. Did she disapprove of herself? She was showing an aptitude for therapy. Her curiosity about herself was appealing. So far I had not had to do much beyond enjoy her.

She then went on to question her position on self-justification. It was as though her psychological bravery was boundless. It is one thing to talk philosophy in the abstract but to come face to face with one's own deceit, and the accompanying self-justification, is impressive.

As the fifty minutes came to a close, I felt I had completed a mental marathon. I wondered whether Belle's new interest in self-examination at breakneck speed was a more benign version of the way she cranked herself up to both create and then solve her emergencies. It was possible. She could be converting that energy into a new relationship with herself. So be it. There would be enough time to unpack that one later.

As I made my notes, the difference I felt between the end of the consultation and the end of this session jumped out at me. On Friday I had met a woman in a whirlwind of crises and lies. Feeling a bit polluted and aggrieved at being roped in to her deceit, I was somewhat turned off. Now I was rather taken with Belle. That sweep from one attitude to another, a sweep that mirrored a dramatic change in her behavior, gave me pause. It did not feel disingenuous, but it did seem extraordinary, something I needed to register. It was not that I was witnessing a "flight into health," a commonplace experience for many patients in the early stages of therapy, when a very capable side of the person suddenly comes into play as though to give the individual inspiration as to what might be possible, as well as to protect her from the painful work of therapy by arousing in her a sense that she does not need psychotherapy and that all that was required was a sympathetic listening ear.

No, this was something of a different order. Either I was seeing the unfolding of a kind of intelligence that had been dammed up for an awfully long time in Belle or perhaps, it dawned on me, I was on the receiving end of a con. Or maybe it was a mixture of both.

I thought over what she had told me about her family to see whether that provided any clues. She had been pretty scathing about her father, a rather morose and distant man, who saw the family as something he supported but did not much engage himself with. He had felt pleased to get away from his own Scottish family, whom he described as dour. Belle had scoffed at his view since she felt this description fitted him too. She felt contempt for his gray life of going to work, coming home for dinner, mowing the lawn, watching TV, playing cards with Mum, being a Rotarian, knowing what he was doing day in day out, no adventure. His ambition was to retire to the North Island and breed horses. Belle reckoned that he did not have the spirit to pull it off.

Her mother came across as a difficult character: loving one day, brutally critical the next. The girls never knew what to expect and tried to overcome their fear of her by ignoring her. This infuriated their mother, who, after she had been cruel, would run after them looking for approval and forgiveness. Failing to find it, she would turn to shrieking instead. As for Belle's siblings, her elder sister Jill was doing some kind of banking in the City. She had not married and had innumerable friends and loads of money. They were not very close now. Marie was the only "normal child" according to Belle. She had married a sheep farmer, had two children and was planning to go back to being a primary school teacher. None of this stuff about her family was that important, Belle said. Her past was over. Left behind in New Zealand and good riddance to it.

In the bare bones of her story there was not much to work with.

The deadness she felt in her family and the unreliability of her mother might have created the conditions in which a life that was essentially her own creation (rather than one emerging from the cradle of a nourishing family) was what was on offer. Perhaps she had demonstrated such aptitude in the second session as a way to ensure that she would do this remaking of herself in the therapy, as she had done the job of bringing herself up, on her own. I could not tell yet. I would have to reflect on what occurred between us as time went on and whether she was able to allow me to "help" her with her changing.

I sighed and wondered what I would have made of her if I had met her outside the consulting room and the disquiet I had felt and then the admiration I had had toward her if they could just be experienced without having to be thought over so intensely. Here I was having to think about whether Belle's psychology had developed in such a way that the only route open to her was to con and cheat. I wondered—although I did not think for a moment it was conscious—whether Belle's whole life was a construct, with her lies, emergencies and cons standing in for experiences that might have generated more beneficial qualities from inside herself.

It did not feel like that. I did not feel I was being conned and if I was I could not work out, beyond a compulsion to do so, what the reason might be. The session had felt open and exciting but I would have to keep an open mind about the capacities Belle had shown us. There *was* a danger in taking them at face value for they were surely more complex than they appeared. I needed to ensure I would not be letting her down by becoming part of a trick she was able to play on herself that getting better was easy, rather than helping her find a way into the messy and chaotic bits that make up therapy.

For several sessions Belle's insights about herself galloped along. I began to relax into a very good feeling about her and the work we were doing together. It almost seemed too easy. I just had to drop in a remark or two and she would run with it. On the outside her life seemed to be taking a bit more shape. She had worked temporarily at a picture agency and had begun to think of becoming a photographers' agent. She did not consider apprenticing herself to an established agent but was making the connections that would make agenting a possibility if she was really serious.

She had a stable of acquaintances, not really friends to be intimate with but to hang out and party with. There was one man around her age with an acute crush on her with whom she had become quite close, although she could not stop herself from manipulating him. I would have trusted that all was well and that we were making good progress except for some lingering doubts I could not quite put my finger on. Was it her eagerness and adeptness at change—an adeptness that suggested fragility in a core self? Could she throw herself into any challenge because there was no self to defend? Was this why she continued to arrive for each session in a different physical persona—a Laura Ashley spring maiden one day, a professional woman the next, a working sculptor another, then a sexy movie star and so on? I found the physical discontinuities disconcerting. It did not feel as if it was merely the playful artifice so trumpeted by those who celebrate gender fluidity as performance.3 It was more disjointed.

I did not sense that Belle was trying to make a point by refusing to have a style. It came across rather as her being physically adrift, not quite knowing how to plot or dress herself. She would often remark on my shoes, jacket or sweater as though the clothes of a woman fifteen years older, dressed in professional attire, might be right for her. I noticed her remarks because they meshed in with a sensibility that seemed to be borrowing physical identities, first this one and then that one, as though she was attempting to concretize her inner instability through her physical presentation. Her antennae were out for clues from anywhere, but of course she did not know how to dress because she did not know who she was. A cocktail dress was as appropriate or as inappropriate as jeans.

It seemed she could go any which way in her physical search to develop herself. I had to be terribly careful that my presence did not force itself too much on her, so that in her attempt to anchor herself she would imitate me to the detriment of developing her self. Her struggle in therapy would be to consciously live through and be aware of the more difficult states of instability that her body was clearly expressing.

I registered this labile sense of her physicality as an unsureness about her body. I wondered whether she suffered the same relationship to her psyche as she did to her body. She had something of the physical feel of many women I had worked with whose eating problems hid bodies that could never be taken for granted but always had to be tinkered with, in one way or another, through the manipulation of appetite by starving, dieting or purging.

Although so much of what we are trying to do is to see the integrity of the psyche and the soma (indeed, Freud's earliest work with Breuer, Studies on Hysteria *in 1893, was particularly concerned with physical symptoms that had no discernible organic basis), there has been an ever-increasing emphasis on viewing non-organic and even organic physical symptoms as symbolic of mental distress. Nowadays such symptoms tend to be seen as stand-ins for what cannot be spoken of or as the expression of impaired psychological development. I would propose rather that they can be understood as the physical or concrete expression of a body instability or insecurity that might emanate from the physical aspects of the parent–child relationship.*

Of course this division is in part tautology. It is obvious that we are material and psychological beings and that one aspect cannot be understood without the other. But I have paid especial attention to the physical nature of the therapeutic relationship and to the feelings that are aroused in me as a psychotherapist at the physical level to rebalance what I feel is too often excluded from consideration. Such attention can provide vital clues to physical and emotional experience and to the development of the individual,[4] as well as guide us to innovations in clinical practice.

In Belle's case I was not having any striking physical responses in my body, much as I pondered the variety of her physical presentations and how disconcerting it was. What it suggested to me was that her body was as yet something not quite of her. Unsettled emotionally and unsettled physically, she was on a search for an identity or identities that could give form to who she experienced herself as being in any given moment. The lies and the conceit that had structured much of her sense of self could be understood as ways in which she was putting together a life and creating a story about herself. There was much more to it, as we shall see, but in essence it was not so much about being a liar as it was about creating stories for herself to live by. In the same way her various outfits had the feeling of creating a body and a physical personality to live by. No one style could stick because there was not much to stick to. On the inside she was no more a maiden than she was a career woman, an artist or a sex symbol. They were all equally useful or useless identities because they could not confirm an inner feeling of her physicality; they could be only glued onto a shaky corporeal and psychological self.

This brought me up against one of the clinical objectives I had following our initial consultation. I had met the first, which was to address the lie about how her keys came to be missing. The second and third had been to try to understand the purpose of her crises. My question then was whether her crises, both psychic and corporeal, which I believed she unconsciously instigated so that she could then solve them, were what held her together. That hunch was certainly borne out by what had transpired during our sessions so far. One emergency seemed to resolve itself, shortly to be followed by another. That was the base line being played and replayed as the constant. At the same time, however, running along the treble clef, another set of notes, not yet a tune nor simply a refrain, was beginning to sound itself. Belle showed an intensity and seriousness with trying to get to grips with herself.

Winnicott, the pediatrician analyst, provides us with profound insights into how human development proceeds both when it receives what is required and when it has to adapt to less than optimum parenting conditions. From his study of infancy and infant—mother relationships he proposes that infants whose offerings and initiatives——what he terms their gestures——are consistently unable to be received and valued by the parent will find another way to make contact by finding and developing an aspect of self that the parent recognizes and appreciates. In this way, he suggests, infants develop "false selves" that can prevent the development of what is felt to be central and unique to them, their "true selves". [5] The "true self" does not simply remain undeveloped. It becomes shrouded in shame. The individual senses that the reason she was unseen or rejected is that there is something deeply wrong with who she is. The multiple "false selves" that develop are never stable because they are disconnected from, or contingent on, the felt rejection of the "true self." Although they may contain equally valid and authentic aspects of the individual's personality, they are experienced as perilous in the worst case or unreliable at best.

The "false self" develops because the mother has been psychically out of step with her infant. The consequences of this psychological mismatching, Winnicott proposes, are deep. The infant fails to be secure in her very existence. She cannot take living and just being for granted. Rather, she exists—comes alive—on the basis of responding to interference. When she is grossly interfered with, what Winnicott terms "impinged on," then she marshals the psychic energy to feel legitimate and defend herself. Winnicott further theorizes that recovery from impingements may become so central to the individual's sense of existence that she could be said to create emergencies and crises in order to have a sense of continuity. [6]

Belle was, as I said, a receptive and responsive patient. She took to her therapy and to the task of self-reflection like a proverbial duck to water. She was subtle in her self-appraisal and copious in her emotional responsiveness, and as far as our relationship went she gave me every cue that she valued our time and work together. If our beginning had been different, I would not have been anything but delighted with how the therapy was progressing. But the lie in the first session stayed implanted in me. It alerted me to the possibility that there might be things that were being concealed or could not be talked about, or that in some way or another my enjoyment of her and her therapeutic progress might embody a kind of collusion. What kind I was not sure. She seemed to trust me a bit too readily, so that I felt I had to maintain an openness to the idea that we might not quite be getting where we needed to be. That her need to feel all right in my eyes was encouraging us not to see certain things.

There was a slight false note that I registered. When anyone left Belle by marrying or leaving the country, the extent to which she subsequently denied the friend's importance to her seemed odd. The extent to which she was understanding about my vacations was also odd. It was as though she could not bear to need anyone. It was not that we did not discuss partings or separations. We did. But while the anticipation of waiting from one session to the next was sometimes excruciating for her, trying to talk about my vacation breaks did not get us anywhere. Belle's response was to show her interest in where I was going and her concern that I should have a wonderful or exotic time. In contrast to how difficult a three-day wait to see me sometimes was, there were no feelings of abandonment or worry over a month's or six weeks' separation.

Her friends' departures, however, formed quite a bit of our dialogue. Belle could weep about or castigate the person who had left her if I could make convincing links between the narrative she was constructing, the emergencies she was creating, and the feelings she might have about being left. But while their leaving could be discussed, and while there was intensity and purposeful application to the work at hand, there was a way in which no one's parting or separation could really be felt despite her apparent show of emotion. In some fundamental way Belle could not quite allow herself to attach herself to another; she could not bear to acknowledge her needs and dependencies on another; she could not bear for anyone on whom she relied to mean much to her. Perhaps she could "trust" me so readily because she was nowhere near the feelings of distrust she must surely have for someone who could easily lie and fool another.

How could I say this? How could I assess the quality of her regrets, her capacity to trust and pass judgment on whether she was feeling what she needed to be feeling sufficiently? What authority gives the psychotherapeutic worker the right to evaluate the depth and veracity of another's emotional life? What evidence do we supply? What measure do we apply?

This contentious question for psychoanalysis is rarely answered satisfactorily as there is no empirical data to draw on. Clinicians must continually rely on their subjective experience. It is through the therapist's use of her individual self as a register that such assessments are made. They can be inaccurate, of course, but they can also be useful and in Belle's case I was not about to disregard what I registered. Belle dismissed how much people gave her and their commitment to her. She had a capacity to stir up in others a great desire to meet her, look after her or make things better for her. She always drew people to her—those who had helped her after she first moved to Britain, the men who had bailed her out of difficulties, her friends who had lived through her anguish over abortions and rootlessness—and these people gave tremendously of themselves. For all her saying how marvelous they were, she could not acknowledge their value and their meaning. In time she would betray them or feel betrayed by them. Disaster surrounded the endings of nearly all her relationships, so they were never there to rely on or to go back to—or finally to matter.

Of course she gave too and it made her feel good to do so. She was always finding special presents, arranging sweet surprises, showing thoughtfulness and care for her friends and acquaintances, so that her ability to discard people who touched her (and whom she touched) alarmed me. I wondered whether there was a loss (New Zealand, parents, grandparents, a special childhood friend?) that was repeating itself for her that led her to drop friends in order to reassure herself that she could go without, that she could master loss. It was the manner of their dropping that concerned me. For it seemed that when someone got under her skin, when she really felt desperately in need of the person, she was chagrined. She did not like to see or feel herself as empty and in need of others to fill her up or attach herself to. It panicked her and it was part of why she hustled. She needed to make herself busy lest a gap she could not cope with open up and reveal the terrible emptiness inside her. So if someone became too important, she needed to claw back what she had invested in them and in this disengaging show herself she could go without, thus experiencing a short-term high.

While I recognized this pattern from many people I had worked with, it was particularly pronounced in Belle. I believed that if she could intercept the pattern and live through whatever psychic urge she had to throw away the particular individual who was meaning too much to her, she might be able to connect the dots between her crises and emergencies and begin to create a sense of continuity for herself and in herself. It was living in the present with its ordinariness, its pedestrian conflicts, its lumps and bumps, that eluded her, for it was in the ordinariness that she failed to exist. To this end I worked with her to hold on to two friends, the man with the crush on her and a woman photographer. Although she continued to dump them in her head many times when they disappointed her, or when she felt appalled by how much she relied on them, she did manage to keep the friendships going.

I suppose that seeing her need over and over again to jettison those she became attached to, I should have realized that this phenomenon would entrap me too. One day Belle would realize that I did really mean something to her and so she would have to discard me. Perhaps somewhat too optimistically, I hoped that therapy could be the place to reverse this pattern, that together we would be able to struggle through her difficulties around attachment.

Some time into therapy, Belle was able to stop doing all the work on her own and to acknowledge her need of me a bit more, not simply as a technician who held steady while she worked on exploring herself but as someone whom she really counted on to be with her in her feelings and her struggles. She would look at me intently, almost drinking in my presence, as though she felt for the first time another's respect for her. It clearly perplexed her that someone, I, was genuinely interested in her. She was not used to it. In one way or another she had nullified the attention she had received from others so that it did not quite count, except for when it counted too much and she had to get out of the relationship. Hesitantly she allowed herself to feel that she was of interest, of value, in just being herself. Of course, she did not do this without resistance, without declaiming that I did this for everyone "on that couch" or that I did it only because I was paid. But even she found her excuse lame; she could feel my interest, pleasure and concern in her. I dared to hope that she was on her way to being a person from the inside, that the stuck-on quality of her physical and psychological personas was giving way as she found that there was someone at home and that she would not evaporate.

Belle generated fewer and fewer emergencies and she did not come in bulging with a full agenda. She could even be still enough to know what was on her mind or in her heart and let the session unfold as it may. Where before lies had constituted the way she put herself together, now in a few friendships and in her work she was able to cope with a certain amount of uncertainty and not knowing. Although I was still aware of her abilities as a con and liar, it was very much in the background of my mind as these activities no longer occupied center stage.

Belle's two friendships with the photographer and the man who had a crush on her seemed to be going well. She did not relate to either of them on the basis of needing to be rescued and I felt encouraged that she was able to have direct feelings and be very angry in the consulting room when they failed her in one way or another.

To be sure her anger was not a pretty sight. She would rail at them, spit venomous rage, diminish them with her contempt. Although there was an ugliness to her dismissal of her loved and valued ones, we could view such outbursts as necessary and even positive steps on the way to sorting through her feelings about her need for others. To have to dismiss so brutally and so forcefully, I could point out, was a signal we could now use to understand her struggle to accept her need for and reliance on others. This was an act of entering the human race, of being part of the give-and-take of being dependent on others, who in turn are dependent on you, and through this interdependence, she might experience how the capacity for an autonomous sense of self can thrive.

She did not drop these two friends. She was experimenting with daring to let others really mean something to her. I was surprised then when an unexpected death in my family set our therapy work on a collision course we were not to recover from.

During a Tuesday session, about twenty months into therapy, I told Belle that I would have to be away for ten days and that we would miss two sessions, possibly three. She took the news with barely a shrug, let alone registering hurt, disappointment, fear, anger or relief—all possible reactions to an unanticipated break. Slightly offhand—and perhaps that should have been the clue—she asked why and when I told her she said it was convenient for her anyway because she had lots of work coming up that week.

Breaks had been managed before by her interest in where I was going. During the first year of the therapy there were times when she could not conceive of being out of touch and we had made arrangements for her to keep in contact by telephone while I was away. At other times it had been all right for her. When it had not been, there was a way I could accept the phone calls and intrusion into my private space because Belle felt psychologically homeless. In taking her on for therapy I had had to allow her almost to seep into me. It was as though there was an urgent need for an emotional home where she could nestle in and bed down. In the beginning months of her therapy she had occupied my mind when I was not with her. I had understood this as my picking up on her desperation for a place, an attachment, a connection, for being looked after and almost for being in the body and mind of a much larger person, similar to a mother who carries a physical and emotional awareness of her baby even when they are separated.

I went away to attend the funeral and matters connected with the death. Absorbed in my own grief and concerned for my fellow mourners, I was not much mindful of Belle or my other patients. When I rang to confirm my return and the resumption of sessions, I reached her machine and left word that I hoped to see her in my office the following Tuesday. It had been two weeks.

When she did not show up, at first I worried that she had not received the message on her answering machine. It was unlike her to miss a session—I was not sure I could remember it ever having happened before. I veered between berating myself for not speaking to her in person about the resumption of sessions and reflecting on what might be going on for her. My first concern was whether she was all right. I phoned to ask and to remind her that I was back.[7] She picked up the phone, was warm in the first moment and then said rather nonchalantly that she had received the message but she had forgotten. It was too late for her to come now, so we rescheduled for the next day.

On Wednesday she did not turn up. I was perplexed. As it was an unusual meeting time, I was tempted to call her again but that did not seem quite right. I was disappointed and sorry not to see her and even a little annoyed since rearranging this make-up session had caused scheduling gymnastics I do not much relish. But so be it. It was the end of the month. I sent out my bills and waited for Friday.

Friday arrived. By now I had not seen Belle for two and a half weeks. That was a long break in an intense therapeutic relationship. Some unease lingered over the nonchalance of the Tuesday phone call. I wondered what I, we, were in for. When she failed to show up at eleven, our usual time, I was surprised. More than that, I was thrown. My mind went into overdrive, not to worry about what might have happened to her by way of a crisis but to review what had occurred between us. If she had also missed sessions earlier on in her therapy I would not have been so surprised but coming now, after months and months of what seemed productive work, her miss unsettled me.

The strange thing was that at the same time as I was puzzled, it was also as though I had been expecting it all along. I had a split experience of Belle: one that held much admiration and respect for how she was developing and engaging with her struggles, and another that kept me apart and questioning, not aloof or distant, but biding my time to see whether what we appeared to be doing was real or some kind of fake. It was a strange feeling to be having but I had lived with that tension before and judged that it had something to do with Belle's own experience—wanting to move forward to a new sense of self and yet holding herself in suspension and disbelief, as though the amount of change required to transform herself from a hustler who knew how to get out quick to a connected person was just too much.

At eleven fifteen the telephone rang. Deep in my reflections, I was somewhat startled. It was Belle. She said she had had to leave London to do a job. She was in Berlin. She was sorry she had not been able to let me know. She'd see me on Tuesday.

As I replaced the receiver the words that I had heard but which were held waiting to be digested repeated themselves to me. I tried to process them, but it was as though there were no receptors for them. They hung between me and her, orphaned: *I'm in Berlin.* Mesmerized and before I could catch what I was doing, I dialed 1471. The automated operator informed me that the last call I had received came from Belle's home telephone number. I gulped and tried to turn my attention purposefully to what I had just heard and also to what it was that had made me suspicious in the first place.

I did not like the notion of myself as a checker-upper, a disbeliever, a sneak. As I had these thoughts I wondered what Belle must be experiencing to have to get herself out of our appointment in this manner. Why was she unable to say "I can't come"? What had been going on in this two-week absence to render our relationship a place of deceit?

But at the same time as I felt interested in what these answers might yield, the part of me that had always been expecting something untoward felt some relief. An aspect of my emotional experience of Belle was being confirmed. There was something not right in her and between us. We were as close as she had managed to let anyone become and yet, and yet, something had punctured the trust she was holding on to, so that what we were left with was that the new growth, the top layer of her that was reflective and thoughtful, was disintegrating before it could be consolidated into something substantial and before it could penetrate the layers of manufacture, stratagem and artfulness that had been a survival mechanism for most of her life.

I felt much as I had in our first session—repelled and yet drawn. I was excited that the lie had come up between us. It meant that she was reacting in therapy as she would elsewhere and that, as with the first lie I had witnessed, there was something important to work with. If she would only come to her session then we could find out why she had lied this time or whether, as I feared, there had been lies between us all along that I had not seen and taken up and had colluded with. I felt energized. The therapy was forcing me to take one of those leaps that feel very scary, but can be the means of making a new kind of relationship.

I was not only excited. There was something else too. I felt angry and dismissed, as though I were being ridiculed. Our relationship and what we had done together seemed to have been callously thrown off. Belle was keeping with the pattern of therapy by phoning but her lie was telling me something else which seemed to shred our relationship and undermine our work together. This dual experience of her was disagreeable. I disliked the way in which I was always on two roads at once with Belle—the distrusting and the trusting. It was tantalizing and disturbing.

I was pretty shaken up. I knew checking up on her indicated something about how I must have continued to tolerate deceit between us because otherwise I would not have found myself dialing the operator. It was not a number I had ever called before. (Indeed I did not even know that I knew it. But I had been impelled to dial it as if in a trance.) I felt sullied and angry and concerned. The only thing I could do for the present was reflect on my feelings. What had I missed? When had I colluded with her? What had I let pass? What had I not wanted to address?

The dominant feeling was one of hurt, with humiliation a close second. I felt slapped down and ridiculed. I had been holding on to an ersatz relationship. My heart was chilled, not just because of the hurt but by the horror of Belle's experience, the way she could so easily devalue a relationship—the urgency with which a relationship had to be jettisoned when something in it went wrong for her. I had seen her throw away people before and I had always known that this was a possibility between us, but I had hoped that our ability to understand her fears of dependency, and her capacity to tolerate disappointment with her friends, had made that unlikely. At the very least I felt we would be able to talk.

On the weekend I mulled over what I would say to her when we next met. My intention in all the sentences I formed for myself was to allow her to tell me about the deceit and for us to acknowledge that she could have a conflict—whatever it might be—that could simply be accepted. But of course she could not do this, that was the problem. The lie was not so much intentional as expedient, a slipping back to a known way of coping. My hunch was that she had found herself in an awkward corner because she could not imagine telling me what was on her mind. I wanted her, in the first instance, to be able to have and then to discuss those feelings without the necessity of resolving them immediately.

I wanted Belle to be able to tell me about the lie because I knew its utterance between us was significant. The lies that she proffered to keep people interested in her (so much more interesting to be mugged than to lose car keys) made those very same people less valuable to her when they believed her fabrications. Their belief in her stories turned them into gullible fools whom she privately, or at least unconsciously, mocked.

I had long thought that the reason our therapy had started off so well was that we *had* been able to address the first lie I heard her tell. We had not skipped over it or denied it or just let it be. I had seen Belle lie and had accepted that aspect of her without subscribing to the notion that lying was the only way for her to live. She had been intrigued by being met at that level so that we were able to go on to see the creative uses of her lie, the ways she parlayed lying as a way to manage feelings of emptiness, of not knowing and of wanting to get away from herself. My eyes on her lie had been a relief to her. They had given her the sense that lying existed for a reason and was functional up to a point but that the point was rapidly receding.

Now it seemed that a lie was covering up something between us which had led to her leaving. I had seen her, as I said, leave relationships before in rather destructive ways and I did not want her to get the idea that lying was going to be a useful way into or out of our relationship. I wanted her to have the experience of acknowledging her conflict to herself and then having the choice about whether she wanted to understand the conflict or not.

Mingling with my hurt and humiliation was concern for Belle. I wondered how much of what I was experiencing was a paraphrase of her emotional state. I could only speculate and make pictures in the air, for until I could talk to her, I did not know what had changed her heart or her attitude toward our relationship. But I had to start with what I had, my feelings and my actions.

My going away, I ventured, had felt like a slap in the face to her. It might have shown that her reliance on our relationship touched her far more than she wanted and that she had felt humiliated by how much it meant to her. Her need of me, I speculated, enraged her. To soothe herself, she reframed my concern for her as a con and a lie. It was *I* who had tricked her into believing she could be genuinely valued and valuable. That was clearly a swindle perpetrated by an emotional pretender.

As I formulated this sequence which accorded very neatly with my feelings, I remembered Belle telling me that at some point in the not too distant past she had occasionally slept with men for money. It was not a direct exchange and it was not regularized, so there was a way she was able to fool herself about it. But to my mind and hers when she spoke of the monetary gifts she had had bestowed on her, there was no doubt as to what had transpired.

If I was right and the sequence of events was as I had postulated, then the queasy feeling I was having at being ripped off and demeaned had an equivalence in Belle's prostitution. My acts of professional care and interest, which reflected deep feelings of concern and warmth for Belle, had an equivalent in her emotional landscape.

We had spent much time on her thwarted love, on how her mother especially had disappointed her, had not let her love her and how hopelessly Belle had tried to capture and hold her mother's interest. Her dislike of her mother and her cynicism toward their relationship were as much a shield she held against her knowledge of her love of her mother as they were weapons against her mother directly. She had scorned her mother and her efforts, dismissed her as a hysterical and useless person who could not work and did not know how to stand up for herself.

During the course of the months of therapy we had come upon the time her mother had left when Belle was six, because she could no longer bear the deadness of New Zealand. She went to London to stay with a friend for two weeks, leaving her daughters in the care of their father but, in reality, to care for themselves. But they had been too little to be left without explanations. With only their father's anxiety to wrap themselves up in, Belle had become quite terrified. Unable to go to school or to leave the house, she slept for almost the whole time that her mother was away. When her mother returned to the family home, Belle picked herself up in a pseudo-embrace of life. Everything was in its rightful place again, but something had ruptured for Belle and she could not find a way to restore it to herself.

As we had talked about it at the time, the rupture emblematized the impossibility of trust and certainty. Paradoxically, these had become so imperative because Belle had experienced so little of either between her mother and herself. It was the absence of reliably good contact *before* her disappearance that made her mother's brief absence impossible for her. It underscored her mother's deficiencies and undermined what Belle had thought she was holding on to in the relationship. "If we really mattered to her so much and were the only reason she was hanging in there with Dad in New Zealand, how could she leave?" Belle had wailed to me.

The complexities of adults' needs and their conflicts were not what Belle could have been expected to understand in her heart, especially since it felt so knotted up with the love and affection she craved from her mother. Her mother's two-week departure had been a dividing point between when things had been just about manageable and when they became unendurable for Belle.

When we talked about this time, I explored with Belle the protective coating she had assembled to withstand her need of her mother and the way in which her absence had come to stand for all that was wrong. I had contested her adherence to this story and the possible outcomes. "Absence doesn't necessarily mean desertion, Belle," I explained. "Absence may be hard but hating or cutting off the needed person is not necessarily a solution."

How I heard my words echo back now. The symmetry was too neat: her mother's two-week disappearance, my unforeseen two-week break. I had not taken it seriously. More striking even was her mother's need to get away from the deadness of New Zealand and my awareness that when I was preoccupied with the death of an important person in my life, Belle had not entered my awareness. I had not taken her with me. She was no longer so orphaned that she psychically accompanied me everywhere. I had "let her go," expected her to be all right. Perhaps this had been the case with Belle's mother too when she took her two-week trip home. Perhaps Belle had felt terribly dropped, not thought about. Now another symmetry entered my mind. The timing of my departure was twenty months into the therapy and the age gap between Belle and her younger sister was also twenty months. That must have been another disappearance. Her mother could have been distracted when Marie was born and turned whatever little attention Belle had received toward the baby.

A mother's capacity to sense her child's state of mind and to accept it, whatever it is, is the means by which the child organizes her experiences and feels safe in infancy and childhood. Although it is impossible to describe with any certainty the process by which a mother (or caring adult) helps transform the often chaotic and terrifying emotional states the child experiences and tries to rid herself of when she is distressed, most psychoanalytic theorists subscribe to the idea that the child imparts to the mother a version of her upset (and her joy) so that the mother feels these feelings as if they were her own. Because they are not, because their stimulation in her is only temporary, she also has the capacity to process feelings that may be difficult for the child and then return them to the child in a reassuring manner.

This process is the means by which deep contact is made between mother and child and forms a prototype for intimate understanding between adults. It is of course this process that is at work in therapy. The therapist makes herself available for the projected feeling and by living with a version of it, by being as close to being in another person's skin as is possible to be, appreciates some of what is so difficult for the patient. If the infant, the child or the vulnerable adult fails to feel contained in this way, she can experience dreadful states of chaos, emptiness or disintegration. In therapy the therapist, less disabled by such states of mind than the patient, finds a way to help the patient reprocess and assimilate the disturbing feelings she has tried to cast off.

While these processes—which go far beyond empathy—can be observed and experienced, it is impossible to explain how thoughts and feelings cross over from one person to another. Analysts and psychotherapists talk as though there were a literal field between two people, a kind of physical exchange in which feelings are aroused, transferred or lodged in the other. But the fact is that we are not able to explain quite what is happening when these processes are at work. The phrase "projective identification" is the psychoanalysts' terminology for spelling out (as Thomas Ogden tried to do so painstakingly in his 1982 book of the same name[8]) the multiple processes at work in this engendering and transferring of feeling states from one to another. But despite our inability to grasp these processes completely, developmental psychologists and psychoanalysts have understood, as parents know well, how crucial it is for the mother to carry her baby's needs in her mind. Winnicott talks about primary maternal preoccupation, Wilfred Bion about reverie and Daniel Stern about attunement. These concepts are attempts to put into language the unique process by which an individual (usually the mother) can exquisitely carry in mind and heart the feelings of another (the baby), enabling the baby to feel recognized and real.

Belle had felt dropped by her mother's departure because her mother's depression had previously meant that their relationship felt precarious to Belle. I wondered whether with my departure to the funeral she had similarly sensed my turning away from her because this time, unlike with other leavings in which I had been careful to let her be intensively in touch if she needed it, I had unconsciously conveyed a lack of concern, an abandonment of her.

What would I have done differently, I wondered, if I had been aware of the symmetry of the two-week break and of the twenty months? What would I have said differently? What could I have offered Belle that would have allowed her to stay with her missing me rather than move into indifference and deceit?

Belle did not show up on Tuesday. This time a breathless message from a friend that Belle would not be able to come to her session reached me just before our meeting. I wondered what it had cost her to get her friend to make the call. As I felt my irritation rise, I registered again how much I had been expecting something like this. Belle's aptitude for therapy had been a surprise to me, now her mockery and disdain of it and of our relationship hurt terribly, but they were a confirmation of the other agenda that had always been with us.

I felt somewhat the fool. Why had I thought I could reach her in a meaningful and transforming way? How had I let myself be lulled into hoping she was doing what she appeared to be doing in therapy? What arrogance had made me think that I had touched and reached her in a way that could let her jettison her modus operandi?

Her absence stirred a wish in me to see her again. I felt kicked out and expelled. Her rejection was a brutal cut that made me sad: sad about her being thrown back on her habitual ways and sad for not being able to do what I now felt would have been a crucial piece of work—to address her difficulties around dependence and need.

Therapeutic failures are devastating. Although Freud wrote unselfconsciously about them, seeing them as valuable lessons for the psychoanalyst to draw upon, I myself was not so sanguine. I experienced pain, anger, regret and humiliation. I could make quite plausible explanations to myself about this therapeutic failure but the feelings that went with them were not so easily or neatly categorized.

Several years later I opened a *Harpers & Queen* magazine and there with her new and glitzy husband—a high-profile lawyer in banking—

was Belle. Seeing her so fresh-faced and vulnerable took me right back to the peculiarly poignant feelings of concern and rage that were now sedimented in me. I wanted to feel neutral, for it not to matter, for Belle to have been someone whom I had much enjoyed, admired and fretted over. I did not want the sour taste that sat side by side with my other feelings. I wanted to banish the ugliness, make a new story, construct a different ending to our therapy.

Of course this is what Belle did. The unpalatable taste of her emotional stories made her want to render them into something else again, to construct scenarios that left behind the pain and anguish. But while she could do this by creating her personas and learning enough psychological intelligence to keep her going a little further on, I could not. I was left with the pain of disappointing her, of not being able to be with the vulnerable Belle through this last real emergency long enough to help her create something new and sustaining for herself.

Footsteps in the Dark

THERE CAME A TIME, about eighteen months into Joanna's therapy, that on closing the consulting-room door behind us I would feel saturated by dread. The air seemed to undulate, distorting the play of light, so that the room broke up into unfamiliar patches of brightness and dullness. I felt woozy, as if my blood pressure was very low. It was quite hard to see Joanna's facial features clearly: her large, often lively black eyes and rosebud lips came in and out of focus as she seemed to rock toward me.

In the dread was just the slightest sense of menace. I waited to see what Joanna had to say and how she would say it. I hoped her words would dissipate this atmosphere of foreboding. Her life had become dark lately, as though she had fallen somewhere she did not want to be but could not climb out of. She felt dragged into a dank, emotional place she could not quite name and with her went I.

For the preceding year and a half Joanna had been an enormously engaging, even entertaining, patient. She looked forward to her sessions and would come in breathless and eager. She had charmed me with her intelligence, wry wit and savvy. But all this was in abeyance now as the menace sat between us. As I waited for her to speak, for that which was so present to find a form in language, I pondered on what was endangering her now. What was the nature of the darkness that she brought to us?

Joanna had come to therapy when she was thirty-four. She was the personnel director of a large company, but despite her clear abilities, her competence, her popularity and her evident joy in many aspects of her life, she despaired of ever having a permanent relationship in which she might have children. She was alarmed that she was growing older by the minute without having found the right person. She had had several long-term relationships with men whom she felt she had "worn down" with her insecurity. She had never doubted her capacity to attract lovers and to have men fall in love with her. But in this lay her dilemma. Her very confidence in providing what she felt a man wanted from her made her mistrustful of any relationship she was in. She felt responsible for creating the relationship—picked because she could magnetize the man, and yet she was not quite chosen by him. Perhaps, she worried, the man was in some sense her puppet, that too much of his desire for her was of *her* making. One day he would wake up and realize he did not want her and that he had been conned.

With her most recent lover, Jeremy, she demanded ever greater demonstrations of love and fidelity until, perplexed by what he had failed to do and how he had failed to love her in the right way, he had withdrawn into himself.

Jeremy's withdrawal made Joanna crazy. Abandoned and lost, she threw herself at him and on him, kicking and punching him until he would either hit her or cry or do both. Then she would feel great relief that she had been able to move him, to force out of him a raw and unpredictable response, a response that proved to her that she had indeed got under his skin and inside him.

Joanna was ashamed of this behavior and the attendant states that she entered. She wanted a stable relationship but could not see it happening. She had no difficulty falling in love but she felt doomed to destroy whatever intimacy she created.

When first she told me this, I wondered how this dynamic would come to play out between us. Could she use our relationship to explore her insecurity and discover what was so untrustworthy about herself? Would she feel that she was seducing me? That I did not care for her and that she had created my feelings for her? Would she feel that she had charmed me into liking her and that this would rebound on her, that we too would come unstuck in a destructive denouement?

Taking a kind of mental deep breath, I wondered whether this might be the therapy, the very center of the encounter, she would create for us. Like her lovers, I too could be seduced into great affection for her. What would happen when I mattered enough to her that she would come to worry about what *she* meant to *me*? What would happen when her insecurity entered into our relationship? Would those violent, pleading feelings enter our relationship too? Might she try to disrupt it, to undo it, to undermine it? Would I know how to respond in a way that allowed her to believe in our relationship?

In offering her therapy I had implicitly promised her that I would go with her into the deepest, most shameful and painful areas of difficulty; that along with listening to her accounts of hurt and anguish, I might well become one of the players on her stage, entering into the drama that she had created and bringing my own sense of how to be one of the characters.

Helping her think and sort through her conflicts, her unconscious desires, the psychic tactics of her internal saboteurs, her identifications and her projections—that would be the easy part. For that I had my book learning, my experience and the empathy that I felt for her. It was the possible enactment of her difficulties in our relationship that would be a challenge: who she needed me to be for her, who she might cast me as and how I might resist that casting.[1] How charm might give way to catastrophe.

. . .

Of course who the therapist needs to be for anyone in therapy is a complicated matter. Monitoring the shifts in that desire is part of the skill of the therapist. The patient requires the therapist to be a feeling and compassionate person. But while this is what might make it possible for a patient to begin to speak about what troubles her, this aspect of the therapy relationship is soon accompanied by the expectations that both parties have of each other. There is no human relationship without expectations brought from one's previous experiences of people. We human beings work on many different levels simultaneously and while part of us greets each new person afresh, allowing ourselves to be charmed or not by their personality, at another level each new relationship is imbued with the emotional imprint of our previous relationships. Indeed we often go further, so that we are unable to see who the new person is because we view her according to our experience of her predecessors. Our vision is itself constructed by the emotional scenarios we have already played in.

As we are creatures of memory, of learning and development, the inevitable presence of emotional responses and expectations from past relationships is both instructive and unfortunate. It allows us to anticipate the way things might go. It guides us as to when to relax and trust, and when to be wary. But at the same time it can prevent us from seeing who the other person really is, what is possible in a situation, how we might be transformed and changed by it, or how we might ourselves have an impact on it. Instead, we have a tendency to render the new situation as an imitation of a situation we have been in before.

The ubiquitous presence of past experience, which is what psychoanalysis terms transference, is part of what the psychotherapist studies during therapy. We look to see who the patient is asking us to be, who she casts us as, and why this happens at particular moments in therapy. We look at who the patient wishes us to be or dreads our becoming and how she construes our behavior in the light of her earlier experiences. And we ask ourselves if we can withstand becoming the person she psychologically turns us into. It requires our recognition of the pressure to transform as well as our refusal to be transformed. If psychotherapists decline to recognize who the patient attempts to make us, then we are of little value in therapy. But if we are only able to be who the patient wishes us to be in the transference, then we are also of no use.

Psychotherapy and psychoanalysis work to help the individual greet new experience as genuinely new so that it is not simply transposed into what is already known and familiar but is an opportunity for development and growth. When we are stuck in repetition, our psyche is inflexible and impervious, unable to be enlivened and enchanted by what is original and fresh.

So I was indeed charmed by Joanna. Her ways of speaking and her take on the world were refreshing and thoughtful. She was acute about herself and aware enough to say that she was being crazy when her feelings swamped her in a fairly innocuous situation. At one level she knew quite well what was amiss with her. She did not negate or shun it. The clinical picture seemed reasonably straightforward. Her insecurity had an intensity that interested me and which I knew I did not quite have the measure of. But as we became closer and she also felt able to show more of herself to her friends and colleagues, I felt this insecurity might be able to be understood and that we might engage with her sense of being a seducer and destroyer.

Joanna, one of five children in a poor family, had grown up in a London slum, where the ethos of what was good for the family ruled. It was not that the individual did not count, it was just that with five children, an infirm grandmother and an elderly maiden aunt to care for under one small roof, her parents had not had much time to focus on what each child might need. The children were encouraged to see themselves as a team and get on with it and, in the style of much immigrant culture, they did. Joanna seemed to have come out of that experience with a knack for addressing an individual's need for attention. She was a natural at her job in personnel. Her employers sought her opinion on restructuring the organization as she could deftly demonstrate how to encourage and stimulate the individual members of a team to be at their most productive and cooperative.

Joanna's family was excitable and argumentative. Her Italian mother was volatile. Quick to temper, she would yell at the children one moment, or slap their bottoms, and the next minute hug them to her with little show of remorse. The behavior of Joanna's Greek father was more violent and even less fathomable. He would suddenly become enraged with one of the children for no apparent reason and the child would be threatened with the same strap his father had used on him.

On many occasions Joanna had seen or heard her father's violence toward her mother. She would hear the screams and then sobs and curl up in fright with her sisters. Petrified and riveted by the violence, she made up stories about why it was happening. She did not like it but as she grew older she would accompany boyfriends to violent movies, and find herself identifying with both perpetrators and victims. The movies left her emotionally wrung out but not to the extent that she did not go again. Clearly they mirrored something inside her. Perhaps this was the dread, the menace in the room. Perhaps violence was on the agenda.

It was, but not in the way I expected.

I wondered whether the violence Joanna had witnessed and experienced from her father, and that she had enacted toward her previous lovers and Jeremy, would come into play between us because she felt thwarted, let down or misunderstood by me. When I speculated that she was angry with my easy acceptance and enjoyment of her, which left her feeling unable to show the more violent aspects of herself to me in therapy, I found that I was all wrong.

Unbeknownst to me, and contrary to my interpretive wanderings through the jungle of my responses to Joanna, her menace stemmed from an entirely different source.

It is axiomatic that whatever one anticipates in therapy is never quite what happens. The analyst Wilfred Bion's much quoted aphorism that one must enter each session "without memory or desire" reminds us how provisional our understandings must be. While his statement has an idealist edge, for analysis is above all the endeavor that recognizes the impossibility of denying what has previously occurred, nevertheless his insistence that the therapist must be open to what has not occurred before allows for the new to be thought about and for something previously unthought, unknown or unprecedented to develop in the therapeutic space. Therapy is truly alive when both patient and analyst are understanding anew.

For several weeks before the sense of menace descended, Joanna had been deeply affected by a diagnosis of breast cancer given to her friend Nulla. She feared for her friend, for what awaited her, for the difficult, almost impossible decisions she would have to make, for the sickness she would suffer. Cancer, this gobbler-up and divider of healthy cells, which swoops down and claims the lives of women in an apparently arbitrary way,[2] is an easy stimulus for a woman's fears and fantasies about her sexuality, her fecundity and her mortality.[3] The stealthy killer padding its way through a body can in a single moment tear up the known and replace it with the unknown. If one feels well but is in fact really ill, then fissures are created in one's certainties which are deeply unsettling. In Joanna's case, her friend's cancer had brought up issues that had lain undisturbed for years, allowing what was once hidden to be seen and grasped.

Joanna's involvement with Nulla's illness was understandable enough in itself. But there was a hint of frenzy around the horror her friend would face during her treatment, especially in the confined space of the body scanner. I did not register it though, or rather I did not especially explore it. I took it as a given that cancer in a close friend produces anxiety.

Heedless of the clues, I was confounded by the heaviness that pervaded the therapeutic space. Joanna was not talking. I waited. The explanations I was suggesting to myself about her relative silence and the doom-like quality in the room failed to convince me. I could find nothing useful to say to Joanna. There was no way out of the impasse and no way in either. I could not work out what had triggered the change in her. My lack of comprehension compounded the dread. This was no heart-stopping fear, no ringing alarm bells, no supercharged adrenaline hit. It was the discomfort of unknown and unexpected menace.

. . .

When a therapist is in doubt about what is occurring for the patient or between them, she may make tentative suggestions as a way to initiate a conversation around experience that is formless or hard to describe. The tentative offering can develop and be refined or it can be discarded. The therapist's demonstration of her capacity to ruminate, to think openly without a destination, brings to the therapeutic encounter something frequently missing from the way we usually think. Circular or repetitive thought can be creatively broken and those disparate fragments of experience that are so often excluded because we do not know how to think about them can then be linked by a new sense of meaning.

I felt as if I had nothing to say. Indeed I could not think. My mind froze. I felt lost and muddled. My thoughts did not seem to go anywhere or connect with anything. I felt quite desperate. I was failing Joanna. I could not help. She had gone somewhere I could not reach. With some relief, I realized that this feeling in itself was a possible place to start.

"Joanna," I said, "I'm not sure this can help us but I want to try to put into words what is occurring to me now."

For a millisecond I thought I saw hope in her eyes, willing me to reach her, but before I could grab onto that connection, the energy in her eyes vanished and she looked at me blankly. Although I was worried about what was happening, the atmosphere in the room shifted. I could now see her clearly as the wavering air became still.

"For the last few of our meetings I have been aware of a kind of dread in the room, a heavy fearfulness I haven't been able to understand. As this has persisted it has made me feel rather lost and muddled. I wonder whether these feelings of mine, these perceptions, can be of any value to us."

The dread and sense of menace did not lift as I hoped they might. Instead the confusion deepened and I felt further out on a limb. But I had spoken so I knew I could speak again. "I'm feeling rather far away from you," I continued. "I feel rather stranded and as though I'm in one bubble and you are in another. Does this make any sense to you?"

Delicacy is required when a psychotherapist attempts to move forward in a situation that feels stuck. She needs to be able to convey a sense of confidence that understanding will come even though it is in short supply at present and that its absence need not alarm. In a way the last thing Joanna needed was for me not to understand. In another way it was our route into understanding.

"I think there is something I'm not yet able to get a sufficient hold of to understand," I added before I shut up and waited. Theoretically I knew that if I put out what I was feeling to Joanna, there was a fair chance that we could move forward. It might be that what I was feeling was a version of what she was feeling but could not speak about. If that were so, there would be a certain relief for her, for both of us. If I was accurately naming what she could not yet speak of, it might lessen her isolation.

Eerily, Joanna seemed to stare at me and past me at the same time. She seemed to have left us completely. My pulse began to quicken. Had my lack of understanding made her feel crazier, more isolated? Had I somehow pushed her over an edge I did not know she was perched on? The menace multiplied and I felt on guard. What did she hear when I tried to articulate the confusion I felt? I began to regret my words, wished I had kept quiet. Stayed with her in the menace until I could understand it. Why was I so quick to think I had to put the unexplainable into words?

Joanna's stare now focused on me, holding me like a rabbit skidding into unexpected headlights on a country road. Without moving her eyes from mine, her right hand moved down to her bag. She took out a knife.

It was a small knife with an orange handle and a blade made for cutting steak.

Not knowing what I felt beyond alarm, my mind flew back to an internship I had done years earlier at an outpatient clinic in New York. There, patients on probation and sent for psychotherapy by the courts were required to surrender their guns and knives at reception. Now why did I not have that rule? But of course I did not have to. People came to me voluntarily and I was not used to thinking of weapons being brought to a therapy session. Besides, I was in England.

Then I wondered if I was imagining it. Had the fear in the room conjured up the knife? Was this really a knife? Or was it that same play of light which had distorted the room earlier, now glinting on the frames of Joanna's glasses? Was I paranoid? What was being conveyed? Was it real or symbolic? Was there a knife in the room and, if so, what was I going to say or do? If there was, it was far too late for me to be saying something as studied or pompous as "Let's talk about any violent thoughts or fantasies that are preoccupying you, Joanna. I'm sure you'll appreciate that while we can talk about such thoughts, acting on them would not be appropriate!" Textbook psychotherapy is all very well, I silently muttered to myself, but what good does it do now? Help!

And of course this cry from inside me was my way out and my way in. The alarm I felt, my sense of being out of my depth and my inner cry for help were my feelings and possibly also Joanna's. Wanting help for myself was no answer. I would have to try something else. I did not have a choice. I could not leave the room. I could not tell her to put the knife away exactly but I could not ignore it. I would have to try to use words, imprecise ones, clumsy ones, for they were all I had.

"Joanna," I started, "you've taken out a knife. I'm not sure why or what it means but perhaps you're trying to let us know what kind of alarm you feel, what kind of helpless state you are in?"

Joanna seemed to register my words. Time slowed. She looked at me and then rolled up her left sleeve. On her lower left arm were scratched two sets of crossing parallel lines, the blood dried to a tracery of fine scabs with a cross in the middle. "Play with me," she said sweetly, making a motion to hand me the knife.

Joanna's demeanor had dramatically changed. From menace and dread to a flash of beseeching hope, to staring off, to a rabbit caught in headlights, we had now arrived at a place that made me think of Joanna as a six-year-old: a scared, lovely, expectant six-year-old. Except that she had a small sharp knife in her hand. I really did not know what to do. Like every cliché in the book, my heart was racing and my mind was swimming. I knew I had to steady myself before I reacted. If I ignored her offer to hand over the knife I would be in really crazy territory. If I took it, I could not be sure what I was colluding with.

I took the knife and put it down beside me. I was not inexperienced with patients who cut themselves. I had encountered enough women in my practice and that of therapists I supervised to discover and reflect on the many impulses that led people to wound themselves. But analyzing a reported event is very different from being drawn into the middle of one. Psychoanalysis is very good on meaning. It is very good at helping one wait until the space clears to think. But this was no time to wait.

At any moment in therapy the therapist is making decisions about what to pursue. How should she think about what she is presented with? How might she help a patient stay with a feeling or stretch the space between her responses so she can be better understood? She has to decide whether to focus on the patient's narrative, to transpose what is heard as a comment on the therapeutic relationship, to scrutinize her own responses to what is being said or not said, and so on. Sometimes this process is conscious but more commonly there is an effortless flow between the various forms of knowing. When and if the therapist tumbles Alicelike down the hole into the world created by her patient, she tastes, smells and feels some of the patient's experience and in this way has information at a different level, a more hands-on sense of the patient's state. This entry into the patient's world is extremely valuable. It is through the therapist's ability to tolerate, master or think about the dilemmas that a patient experiences from the perspective of having had a taste of them that she can help the patient reach for a solution.

As I sat with Joanna at this moment, two things were happening simultaneously. Part of me was thinking, what game does she want me to play with her? What was a tic-tac-toe pattern doing carved on her forearm? Where has she regressed to? But another part just entered into what she had offered and started to play with her as though this was the most usual thing in the world.

I picked up a pad and a pen from the side table where I had placed the knife, drew my chair closer to hers, put two sets of intersecting parallel lines on the paper and asked her whether she wanted to be O's or X's. It was a few minutes into the game before I quite knew what to do with the activity in my mind. If I now had a severely regressed Joanna I was unsure of my capacities to be a child or play psychotherapist. I had very little to guide me or steady me as we swapped the pen back and forth.

As the game continued and we found a warm, even giggly, rhythm between us, I glanced at the clock and realized forty-eight minutes had gone by. I felt uneasy about the session ending at this point. I was unsure whether Joanna would feel that she could re-enter the therapy room as an adult. More than that, I was even more unsure about how I was going to comment on what had transpired. I wanted to mention the knife that now sat on my table but I did not feel I had enough time to think clearly about what I wanted to say. I wanted to talk about the Joanna I had been playing with and the menace that had preceded her appearance. I wanted to put together the jumbled parts of the session but I knew it was not possible. I went for simplicity.

"Joanna," I began, "it's time for us to stop for today."

"Oh, yes," she replied, shaking herself out of her reverie.

"See you on Thursday," I said.

"Right, see you on Thursday. Same time, same place," she said and walked off almost jauntily.

Drained, I exhaled, shook my head and went to my computer to make some notes, hoping that in writing I could make some sense of what might be happening for Joanna.

The orange knife with the small blade was still on my table. I knew I had to remove it before my next session but for some reason I hesitated to pick it up. In part it scared me. In part it fascinated me. It was a clue to the hidden world of someone I cared very deeply about. I needed to understand why she had brought it, about the marks on her arm, the state she had entered into, the menace that had preceded it.[4]

In the few minutes left before my next session, I picked up the knife and winced. It made me very uneasy. The sharp blade was a few inches long. But as I held it, I began to see it as a rather friendly-looking knife, a sort of paring knife. I found myself running my hand over its blade. Instead of alarming me, I found it rather soothing. It did not seem a violent instrument. With what had Joanna imbued the knife? I set it aside again and covered it with a notepad. I could not think about it just now.

The state of mind that Joanna had entered into and was to inhabit, intermittently and not infrequently, during the next months' sessions can be thought of as akin to, but a lot less severe than, the more dramatic personality disorders brought to popular attention in the book and the film *Sybil*. In that story aspects of the self, which have been cut off and seem to embody a different sort of personality, suddenly appear and "take over" from the central or main personality.

The psyche in its executive function as the register and manager of what we feel and experience encounters a mass of phenomena that refuse to be made much sense of. If the pain associated with an event or events is too great, it can become separated out and separated off from the individual's conscious knowledge and in time "forgotten," appearing only in dreams or slips of the tongue. We all rely on the capacity to "forget" or tuck certain things away. What is repressed or "forgotten" then influences and motivates aspects of our daily life in ways we are unaware of.

But when what happens to a person is beyond the bearable, beyond the forgettable, when the distress caused is so great and incomprehensible that it cannot simply be "forgotten" or excluded, there is instead a psychic amputation in which the unthinkable, the unfeelable, is torn away from the psyche. It becomes severed, dissociated.

Dissociation involves a different kind of splitting from repression's. There is a cleaving of the ego[5] in which psychological energy is removed from conscious and unconscious processes and is used to dam up and freeze intolerable experiences. Once banished, these experiences become ossified. They are not thought about or felt. They are walled off to prevent them from threatening to overwhelm the person as they did when they were first experienced.[6]

· · ·

But while theory about dissociated states interested me, of more immediate concern was what to do about the knife that still sat on my table. I ran through the gamut of possibilities. I could say nothing at Joanna's next session and wait to see if she mentioned the knife. But what if she did not? I could wait to see what she talked about and find a link between her narrative and the knife. Or I could raise the subject straightforwardly. But how? The more I tried to think my way around what to say and how to say it, the more I realized I just did not understand enough. But to avoid the knife would be to emphasize the split-off dissociated part of Joanna that had only found a way to come to therapy as a "separate" self. My first task was to get to know the wide-eyed girl with a knife, playing tic-tac-toe.

Joanna came to the next session as though nothing strange had occurred when we were last together. She talked about Nulla. Without my prompting, she began to think that there was something a bit odd about the nature of her preoccupation. Her concern with Nulla's treatment dovetailed with her interest in human biology. She loved the details of the human body and was fascinated by popular accounts of new medical technology. She remembered how, as a little girl, she had desperately wanted to be a doctor but she did not come from the kind of background or have the kind of schooling that made that a possibility for her. As she talked, she became increasingly aware that elements of her interest in medicine and the body bordered on the macabre. Her association with the macabre then led her to discuss a violent movie she had just seen and the curious mixture of excitement and cool detachment it had aroused in her.

I was always impressed with Joanna's capacity to question her responses in a thoughtful manner. I admired her self-reflectiveness and the honesty with which she was prepared to discuss the less than flattering aspects of herself. But now, in addition to admiration, I was intrigued because I had not considered that Joanna, who was so prepared to know about herself, might or could cohabit with a dissociated-self state. A considerable amount of her psychic energy must be going into binding up that state. I was surprised by how much was left over for the exploration of the more conscious parts of herself.

Her discussion of the film and of her interest in the medically macabre hung in the room. She talked so graphically about contaminated blood and blood transfusions that I felt my lower left arm wince and imagined deep red-blue droplets of blood dripping down to my wrist. I knew I was looking for a way in to discuss the last session, so I was not surprised by my physical empathy for the wounds that she had inflicted upon herself. I hesitated to speak, for while I wanted to bring up what had occurred last session, acting on my desire might interrupt some associations she might more valuably make for herself.

We stayed for a while with the movie and the way in which she felt a kind of peace while the most ghastly violations were enacted on the screen. She described being simultaneously aroused and calmed.

My mind went to some research that had investigated the physical and emotional aftereffects of trauma on eight Vietnam War veterans. It produced a surprising result. After the traumatized veterans had been shown a combat movie for fifteen minutes their perception of their pain was significantly reduced.[7] The movie images of violence created a state of hyperarousal, which in turn activated a soothing analgesic effect equivalent to the sedating effect of morphine in seven of the eight men.[8] Calming was achieved not through relaxation but through increasing stress.

An image of Joanna's left forearm flashed in front of me. Previously I might have pursued a discussion about the gruesome film to explore with her the appeal of various characters in it. Now, however, I was eager to find out whether the cuts on her arm had been a response to some extreme state that she had been unable to master. Our understanding of her father's violence had until now played a cameo rather than a starring role in Joanna's life. I wondered if that was about to change, whether the violence she had witnessed, borne and survived was to prove to be of more significance than we had so far given it. Had the violence entered her relationship with her father when she was very young so that her capacity to modulate physiological arousal was impaired? Had I misinterpreted her energy and efficiency at work? Did it mask a kind of addiction to a hyperarousal, similar to that of the Vietnam veterans, which she required in order to release the soothing action of her endogenous opioids? Did her violent encounters with her boyfriends offer her some relief, not just because she could stir them to do things they felt were out of character but because the rush she got from the violence stimulated the production of a calming analgesic?

If this were part of it, then her bringing this split-off part of herself to the therapy showed a certain emotional intelligence. She was finding a way to tell me about it. Indeed she was doing more: she was conveying to me at an almost visceral level something about how she managed surprise and alarm. Inside myself, although a part of me felt ambushed by the knife in the room, another part was deeply calm, in a kind of stoned slow motion in which every nuance seemed to reach my senses. I felt I was undergoing some of Joanna's experience. She had succeeded in communicating it to me.

"Joanna," I started, "could it be that the film, your interest in the macabre and the details of your friend's operation and treatment are linked in some disturbing and yet stimulating way?"

Before I could refine what I was wanting to say, Joanna stopped me. She sat forward, stretched her hands out and up in front of herself, spread her fingers in a fan and wailed. She looked like a little girl pressing her palms against a windowpane, helpless.

Bewildered and somewhat concerned about tipping her further into wherever she might be, I asked Joanna whom she was staring at so intently. "My parents, of course," she said, as if it was the most natural thing in the world to say and part of something I already knew. "My parents. They came to visit but they wouldn't let them in. I hated that. I hated seeing them like that."

There are moments in almost every therapy when the known suddenly evaporates and the psychotherapist feels she is about to stumble.

She worries about having missed some crucial detail—the age of a sibling, the name of a best friend, the significance of a particular incident. This was one of those moments and I squirmed inside. I thought I had paid close attention to Joanna's history but now it appeared I had missed something very crucial. Or had I? I was not quite sure. I reviewed the sequence of states we had been through together, hoping it would make some kind of sense. I thought about who she was when she first came to therapy: vivacious, eager, engaged. A beautiful, witty, able young woman struggling to feel her strengths, understand her insecurities and find a saner way of living with herself. Then the menace had come and I recalled how unexpected it had been, what a marked change it had brought to our relationship, how our easy exchange was replaced by dread. I reminded myself of the isolation, the confusions in the room, my sense of not being able to reach Joanna in any meaningful way. And then of the startling way the menace had been interrupted, how on the way to asking me to play tic-tac-toe Joanna had shown me her wounded arm, passed me the knife and taken on the appearance of a frightened girl. Nothing threaded through into any clarity.

This reference to her parents visiting and not being let in did not seem to fit anywhere. It was as unfamiliar to me as the Joanna I was now meeting.

"When, Joanna?" I said as gently and neutrally as I could. I was concerned now to open up a dialogue, to talk. If she felt I did not know what she was talking about I might have lost this chance.

"When I was in the hospital, the fever hospital, when Daniella and I were little." She looked at me and returned to her adult posture. Then she wept.

Fever hospital, of course. She *had* told me about having scarlet fever as a child but it had never assumed any significance between us. I was almost tempted to have the eureka! experience that framed the caricatures of psychoanalysis of yesteryear in which the identification of the trauma pigeonholed what had been incomprehensible perfectly into place. It was attractive. A picture of Joanna in one of the sprawling cottage-type hospitals built in England in Victorian times came to mind. The isolation units that were either in a general hospital or in a separate hospital developed after the 1834 Poor Laws were in constant use until the mid 1950s, when antibiotics and vaccines ended the need for quarantine. Imagining Joanna aged six locked away in one of these for weeks made me feel very sad for her.

Before John Bowlby's[9] ideas about early attachment became widespread, and the negative effects of separating young children from their parents when there was illness in the family were known, a child diagnosed with scarlet fever or diphtheria might see a doctor one moment and then an hour or two later be taken off by strangers in an ambulance to some distant, starched-white place that their parents would have difficulty visiting. There they would spend many weeks on a ward with several other children who were strangers. The adult care-givers, the nurses and doctors, were often nice enough, but they too were strangers. The child was plucked from home, set down in an unknown place, aware that there was something wrong but given nothing to smooth her entry into this new environment.

Such a separation was traumatic on several levels. To be separated from home at the age of four, five, six, seven is not easy (who, at any age, likes an unanticipated separation, after all?). To be separated when one is ill can create tremendous anxiety. To have the separation explained to you as being in your best interest makes little sense. To be in an unfamiliar setting with your pajamas and teddy bear as the only familiar objects, while strangers prod, feed and do strange things to you makes for a reality that may be very frightening and con-fusing. Everyone is focused on how good it is that you are being saved but, as with the child evacuees sent away from cities during the Second World War or the German Jewish children put on Kindertransport, *there is little attempt to understand and speak about the loss, the trauma, the terror that might sur-round displacement.*

Woven into upper-class and upper-middle-class British culture is the expe-rience of early separation from parents at boarding-school. This institution which fosters boys from a very early age has wrought a particular emotional pattern in which the pain of separation becomes something that the child learns to master rather than to grieve over. Boys taken from home as early as seven were and are encouraged to grin and bear it, and to convert their loss into bonding with the other boys in a hale and hearty show.

This ethos seeped into the isolation hospitals. There was an implicit demand that the children put on a happy face and shunt the pain off somewhere else rather than ease it by acknowledging it. There was an emphasis on "smiling for the nurses" or "cheering up," as though the doctors, nurses and aides could not bear to see the children's pain. Home was talked about, of course, as a wonderful place to go, but the agony of missing your bed, your mum and dad, your friends, dog, brothers, sisters, Gran, Auntie, your favorite food did not get much of a hearing. As part of a cultural patterning that insisted painful things were best left unsaid, children's sadness was only obliquely referred to and the trauma of an unanticipated and lengthy separation was compounded by not being spoken of.

When children returned home, the heartbreak that had been suffered by the children and parents alike—the latter feeling powerless to care for their children at home or save them from being taken away—conspired to maintain the silence: "Best not talk about it, dear. It will only upset her." The fever hospital was often handled as if it had never really happened. Even the teddy bear that a child had taken into the hospital and which represented some kind of continuity before and after the rupture was fumigated and often fell to pieces so that it was unable to accompany the child home.[10] The hospital experience became sealed off. The parents did not bring it up because it upset them too much while children were diverted into thinking that everything was nice now that things were back to normal.

They very often were not. And they were not for Joanna. The emotional and traumatic experience of the isolation unit, and the state of mind that Joanna was in while she was there, went underground. There had not been any way for her to talk about or think about that experience even with her sisters, and it was only in her fascination with medical matters and her interest in violent and sometimes macabre films, especially medical horror films, that indirectly breathed any life into that experience.

I immediately felt hope when Joanna mentioned the fever hospital.

I had the beginning of an explanation for the disruption and emotional terror of our last few sessions. The atmosphere of menace pervading our time together, the sense of dread as if something terrible was about to happen, the fear I think we both felt, my experience of being so outside of her and unable to reach her in any way, all now began to make some sense. As for Nulla's hospitalization, Joanna's panic about what it would be like for Nulla in the body scanner and her interest in mastering the medical became clearer.

By way of emphasizing the importance of these events, I asked Joanna more about her hands pressed against the glass, daily life in the unit, her parents' visits, the frequency of contact with them and her return home. I did not want this experience to be shut away prematurely by her again. We could talk, and think about and feel it together—to address the isolation and fear she felt then and had carried with her until now.

Although we were talking about extremely painful events, the room was now filled with feelings we could both comprehend and manage. Over the next five sessions the entire story emerged.

Joanna had a particularly strong image of her mother sobbing as she and Daniella got into the giant white ambulance and of the ambulance driver telling her, "Don't make Mummy worry. You are going to have a jolly time with other children while Doctor makes you better."

In recounting that sentence fierce anger shot from her eyes. Joanna had been overcome with terror and a sense of everything disintegrating. When the ambulance doors closed Daniella had started sobbing and as Joanna went to comfort her sister, she got a hold of herself. Joanna knew there *was* something to worry about. It was not all right and it was not going to be but she knew she would have to be brave.

Surviving the journey and the first week in the hospital was hard. Everything was so unfamiliar. She drifted into that state between sleep and wakefulness where jumbled-up thoughts that cannot quite be tracked sit inside a muffled brain. There is a safety in that form of consciousness. Time passes measured by the thermometer, the trays of unappetizing food, the radio program you wait for (only to float off to sleep five minutes later), the prods of the nurses and the opening and closing of blinds.

At the end of the first week Joanna awoke from her listless reverie and started staring out through the windowpanes. It was the day for visitors and she had an image of her ebullient family coming to visit them with armfuls of pasta and cakes. Her tension loosened in anticipation. She could feel herself begin to relax rather than retreat. But by midafternoon they had not arrived. Her expectant mood snapped. She went from dejected to frightened to frantic. In a frenzy she concocted scenarios to explain their absence. Another child was ill, there were no buses between home and the hospital, her auntie had had another fit. Joanna had been sure their family would come and she could not fit her certainty together in their absence.

Another week passed. Now she busied herself on the ward, made a best friend, endlessly played tic-tac-toe and jacks while fantasizing that she was Sleeping Beauty waiting to be rescued. Meanwhile Daniella was doing badly. She was lethargic and withdrawn and Joanna tried to comfort her, to be as buoyant as possible. Surely their parents would come next week.

On visiting day Joanna led her sister to the glass panes that separated their ward from the public space. The two girls balanced their elbows on their knees and waited. "Cheer up, cherubs," said the cleaner as she sneaked them a few cookies. "They'll come, you'll see. Don't you worry now." In her heart Joanna knew that her parents would come, she had no doubts. Mummy had always met the girls coming home from school and taken them to and from their ballet lessons. There had never been any question of waiting, let alone being stranded.

The girls turned to each other to reassure themselves. Joanna saw the fear and despair in Daniella. She diverted her own worry into comforting her, devising little games to play while they were waiting, thinking about who would be coming and what they would be wearing.

Two hours later, when no family members had shown up, she led her sobbing sister back to the ward, put her into her bed and went to her own, disconsolate.

The third weekend, their father arrived. Joanna and Daniella ran to greet him without having registered that they would be separated by a glass wall. He came with balloons and Italian confections and pretty knitted cardigans, a tantalizing picture of joy and caring on the other side of this barrier. Joanna sobbed and sobbed. She wanted to be so grown up and manage everything well but she could not. Her father played being cheery. He made funny faces and mimed. From the other side of the glass he blew kisses and hugs and clutched his breaking heart in operatic style. But as he took a great big, freshly ironed handkerchief out of his breast pocket, his jest turned to pain and he wept. When Joanna saw her father distraught, she took her sister's hand, ran back to the ward and then flopped down on her bed.

Three weeks later the girls went home. By that time there had been two more glass-divided visits, this time from both parents. These visits were what kept the girls going but at the same time they emphasized the desperateness of their situation. From behind the glass barrier, Joanna could not reach out or be reached. Stoically, she smiled and mimed back at her parents. When they left, she would run to her bed and weep.

The return home began to explain certain things. The first week they had been in the hospital Grandma had died. The second week the other children had been ill. Joanna's mother, who was in shock from all the loss, had been sedated by the doctor. There had been no one other than their father to care for the three children, no one to visit Joanna and Daniella.

But while the facts explained their parents' absence, something had dramatically changed for Joanna. Things were just not right at home. Her mother now dressed only in black and took on the demeanor of her Sicilian mother. She muttered and dragged herself around the home with heavy sighs and curses about the *dottore Inglese*. There was grief in the house but something else was different too. At first the closest Joanna could come to describing it was by saying it was as though a jigsaw blade had cut a pattern through the family and when they went to put the jigsaw puzzle back together again, there were a few missing pieces. The use of the blade imagery interested me.

I filed that and also Joanna's reference to the repetitive play of tic-tac-toe in the hospital. They were too obvious to point out and if Joanna had not made the links I did not want a facile foreclosure on what had transpired. I was more eager to understand what had changed, what now infused the household and the relationships in the family, to tease out, if possible, the parental agonies that had created in Joanna a sense that things were not right.

We lived through a number of sessions in which family life before the scarlet fever became idealized. Joanna wondered whether her father had been violent before then. She desperately wanted the hospital stay to demarcate her experience. She saw light before hospital and anxiety afterward. There was no surprise there. Our psychology often constellates around a perceived trauma, an event which we carry in our mind as being *the* significant event of childhood that upset the apple cart. And while such ideas are generally out of favor with contemporary analysts, who view the context in which distress is felt and handled, or mishandled repeatedly, as being more telling, nevertheless the need of the individual to have a fixed point, a moment at which before was good and after was bad, had a psychological resonance for Joanna.

Of course often such fixed points of memories are held on to precisely to conceal what was too painful to feel before. Like Freud's screen memories which protected the individual from a memory more terrible, the idealization of the past, of a time in childhood when things were just perfect, reassures the individual. There is hope because there was a time before the expulsion of Adam and Eve from Eden. The psychotherapist's job here requires special care. For she must create the space in which it is possible to talk about the atmosphere after the Fall and then find ways to invite the patient to ruminate about life before it, so that the patient might query together whether the difference could really have been so dramatic. Focusing on the "after being bad" and the "before being good" is also a

way to shift what could not be faced in the before to the after, where it seems
more manageable. Bad experience gets reclassified. But if that is inaccurate, then
we are reinforcing a kind of fiction with the patient, a fiction which prevents her
from connecting with the real emotional sensibilities in the family situation and
which holds her in a split experience rather than aiding her to bring more com-
plexity and texture to both the before and the after.

In Joanna's case there was some truth to her perception of a before and
an after. Her father's violence *had* started after the fever hospital; her
mother *had* metamorphosed following Joanna and Daniella's return
from the hospital. What had been brought into question for her parents
was a sense of whether they could bring up their children well and also
protect them. They were deeply shaken and their insecurity was exac-
erbated by the death of Joanna's grandmother, which now took on epic
proportions.

Joanna, who had learned to look after Daniella in the hospital, now
learned to look after her mother. What this meant was stuffing away
her feelings, being little Miss No Trouble, little Miss Clever, little Miss
Efficient and little Miss Cheerful. She did well at school, never got into
any kind of trouble that her mother or father might hear about, and
was as quiet and helpful as she could be.

But she had a secret life.

After classes finished she would go up to the art room and start
fiddling about with the nibs used for carving linoleum blocks. She
found the action of digging out a narrow trench into linoleum very
satisfying and she got used to picking up stray pieces of lino and carving long lines on them. She progressed to parallel lines and then a per-
pendicular set of parallel lines that crossed the original lines. Before
she could play tic-tac-toe on the linoleum, she found herself rummag-
ing around for a sharper instrument, a penknife, which she then used
to cut her abdomen, her leg or her arm. She would go into what she
described as a concentrated state as she worked away setting up her
game of tic-tac-toe.

As a teenager Joanna cut herself in this way a couple of times a week. She was not really sure why, it was just part of her routine, a private activity that she did not much reflect on. After graduation it had tapered off but when she left home at twenty-two, the first girl to do so without having married first, it had come back into her life. For the past thirteen years it had been an intermittent activity and a dissociated one. From time to time, when taking a bath at the end of the day, she entered a mental space quite at odds with the world of a Joanna who functioned with such effortless competence at work. Unless the phone or doorbell rang, and she was startled out of what she would later regard as her trances, she would find sometime later in the evening that she had dug into herself, engraving the four lines needed for tic-tac-toe on the skin of her abdomen.

This secret life of Joanna's was almost a secret from her conscious self.

What had started off as a soothing activity—the attempt to place some order within the nine squares—became driven. Not only did Joanna feel she had no choice or will about cutting or not cutting, she was also not fully conscious when she was doing it. The activity seemed to just take her over and until she had brought the knife to therapy and shown me her arm, she was not much aware of what she was doing until after the event. Once we knew about it, she had no difficulty invoking the activity in her mind and talking us through, frame by frame, how it went. We worked to get a hold of what was enshrined in it, her thoughts and actions and how they connected one with another. We went through it in her imagination so that she could slow down and stop to take account of the feelings that accompanied what had now become a ritualized event. If we could find a way to explore the thoughts that drove her feelings, and then the feelings that drove her thoughts and actions, she might find an alternative way of processing what, up until this point, had been managed by the game of tic-tac-toe.

Slowing herself down in this way meant that Joanna came directly in touch with a great deal of terror. She was afraid that she would be overwhelmed by the fear surging through her. Without access to an instrument that would help divert this fear into wounding her body, she wanted to kick and scream. I could see that she was in terrible physical distress, beset by sensations she did not know how to escape from. Prickly and sick, she wanted to scratch away at the irritant, to relieve the physical, psychic allergen that was overtaking her. Watching her, it was as though she had been effaced to become only a vexatious body.

It was easy to see how hard it was for her to suffer this agony, how as she took the knife and cut herself her mind would try to trick the terror. By seeming to create her own pain through cutting, she had a fantasy of being in control of it. By inflicting it on herself, she temporarily reduced her feeling of vulnerability. [11]

When this could be spoken about between us, it became less frightening. Being with someone who was not invested in her making things pleasant for others, who could sit with her while she tried the words that might go some way to describing her experience, I could see her distress gradually subside. It was not an easy ride. She was not sure that she could trust either of us to manage what she was feeling and much questioning, fretting and checking accompanied her attempts to hold on to the feelings within herself.

Over the weeks her terror began to abate, lapping at her rather than overwhelming her. There was a part of Joanna that was now neither so immersed in her pain that it took her over and out of herself, nor so distant that she dissociated from it. Instead, a gap opened up where she could observe herself while she was in the midst of it. This allowed her to accept that she was fearful, that she might cry a lot and that she felt drawn either to hit out at me physically or to calm herself down by cutting. She began to have an inkling that by having and then partially observing her feelings and impulses, she might be able to survive them and process them. If she could slow down what was occurring and tolerate what she was feeling, her thinking processes could also be prolonged so that she might be able to feel less taken over or driven.

There was much to discuss about the cutting and the paradoxes it encapsulated. Any symptom that is entrenched, becomes a way of being with oneself and the original impulse for it soon gathers into itself all manner of other meanings, becoming a vector through which much that touches the person becomes processed. [12] If, as in Joanna's experience, the trauma of the fever hospital and the transformation of home life following her and Daniella's return home became too much to bear even to be repressed, then her symptom—cutting nine squares into her body—worked as a way to manage the unmanageable.

We might be scared by the cutting—as indeed it is hard not to be—and stop there or we could take Freud's advice and see what rich and multiple meanings inhabit such acts. Psychotherapy allows one to take the latter route, to reveal the drama of the individual mind and life, the routes it takes and the solutions it seeks, the deeply personal ways of an individual psychological life, by intercepting a symptom and opening up a wider canvas on which to draw out and examine the themes embedded within the symptom.

For Joanna, the cutting was a window into her mental processes. It told the emotional story of her hospitalization. The tic-tac-toe showed the way she had distracted herself while in the hospital. The nine squares depicted the nine large windowpanes through which she had so often stared and which had cruelly separated her and her sister from contact with those on the other side. Joanna's use of a tool which cut these shapes on her body showed the physical side of her scarlet fever medical experience where cold metal depressors were routinely placed on her tongue. At another level, the repetitive making of a pattern into which X's and O's were to fit revealed Joanna's attempts to bring shape to what felt like disintegration and to place herself (the O's) and her sister (the X's) within an orderly structure. Her crosses actually looked more like sideways Y's, giving the impression of stick figures lying prone.

Central to Joanna's experience of cutting herself was the drawing of blood. When we were able to talk about these things, Joanna initially connected the blood to medical scenes—doctors, needles, vaccinations and injections. This was one set of meanings but more salient was her search for a physical release from the excruciating feelings in her body which demanded discharge by a kind of bloodletting. The awfulness she experienced was under her skin and through her veins, as she described it, and impelled her to seek a physical purge.[13]

Joanna, in common with other women who cut themselves, was caught in a curious paradox. She had an intense psychological life. But this psychological life, with its messy emotions and feelings which did not quite fit, could be boarded up and hidden away. Then Joanna would experience extreme irritability and frustration that she could not master. She did not know what to do with herself. It was as though she was trapped in a mind-made hell that was at once diaphanous yet physical. Her resolution was to cut herself. The blood she made run forced her to see her pain. At the same time, her blood demonstrated that she was real flesh and blood and not only a mind.

When Joanna came to her session with the knife—embodying the emotional state of being tied to her hospital experience and severed from her conscious experience—that state of mind, and the trance-like state into which she entered while cutting out her patterns, took her outside or away from herself. Although this protective mechanism of the psyche enabled her to get away from herself, it had a downside. It temporarily denuded her of her physicality.

The psyche seeks an equilibrium between its mental (psychic) and physical (somatic) elements. Joanna's urge toward bloodletting could be understood as an attempt to rebalance what had become for her a mental torture, albeit one that was split off and dissociated. It was as if she needed to *feel* something physical and *see* something tangibly physical to reassure herself that she did indeed exist physically. Seeing her blood gave her the evidence that she was a body self, not exclusively a mental self. Through her cutting, then, Joanna confirmed the sense that she was real, that her pain was a body pain as well as a mental one and was not imagined, not something that she had "invented" or which could be contained or explained away in the mind.

Insofar as the carving on her body became the means by which

Joanna assimilated intense experiences, the cutting invoked and at the same moment was her attempt to master her feelings about her father's violence. Although Joanna's childhood memories of her father hitting her mother had remained conscious and had not had to be repressed or dissociated, some aspect of her feeling and the fear this violence aroused in her had become split off and divided up into the before and after experience of her father, pre- and post-scarlet fever. Now we could see that she had been much more terrified than she had been able to let herself know. To have surrendered then, as a child, to her fears when she heard her mother's distress and her father's violence felt dangerously close to the mental place she had inhabited in the fever hospital. But it was more than that. Her father's violence *had* appeared after the hospital. That event *was* life-changing for her. And because she had not been able to talk about the before or the during, a present fear such as the one provoked by her father's violence became unendurable. So when she heard a fight she had held herself tight in the moment, had snuggled up to her sisters and waited for time to pass. The next day she would find herself cutting, as though in slashing herself she was making the violence hers and thus exerting some kind of control over it. Her father's violence became more tolerable as she remade it hers.

It is in this sense that a symptom becomes a vector, sucking in new experience to known channels, so that the new is not so much experienced as coped with and managed by being transposed into a familiar form. There is a psychic power struggle when new experience occurs in already threatening circumstances. Is the new going to challenge the known or the known going to transform the new? If the new can be rendered into a familiar form, it is not a challenge. It does not need to be confronted, felt or thought about. It becomes psychic fodder for a system that has entrenched ways of regarding outer reality. The inner reality, the pictures that can be created in one's mind about how relationships are, how the world out there is, become far more compelling than any new reality. If the world is of one's own making, it may be dismal but there is a certain safety to it. What had shattered in Joanna's world on her way to the isolation unit was her safety. When she returned home, this safety could not be restored to her because her parents too had been traumatized by the events of the preceding six weeks.

Earlier on in our work together, Joanna and I had wondered whether her violence toward her boyfriend captured something—although we did not quite know what—of what she thought occurred between women and men. In taking on her father's behavior, we had surmised, she had made it her own. We now began to augment our understanding of her father's violence and of her own when she punched and kicked Jeremy. In the tradition of an autobiographical endeavor we began to rewrite Joanna's violence not only as an account of her response to feelings of abandonment but as an account of her helplessness too. For embedded within what she took on of her father's violence was the expression of his collapse, his shame at his inability to protect his girls and his wife from scarlet fever and from the death of his mother-in-law.

Leo, Joanna's father, was a proud man. He was modest in his worldly desires but very determined where his family was concerned. He expected himself as head of the family to keep it steady and strong. While the illness of his daughters and their removal to the hospital might not have struck him as so damning had he remained in the small village he grew up in in Greece, here in London, displaced from his family of origin, from his cultural references, from a ready community with which to commiserate about his fate, and feeling desperately guilty and sad about not being able to visit Daniella and Joanna in the hospital, he felt helpless. Unable to summon his wife out of her depression, he lost his girls, his wife, his mother-in-law and a sense of the possible. This helpless feeling, one he was unaccustomed to, overwhelmed him. When he was confronted by a situation which he could not sort out, and with no psychic space to process his own considerable losses, his confidence left him and was replaced by an uneasy helplessness. He overcame this helplessness by a rage whose force seemed to gather him up into one potent piece again which he would then fling at his wife or girls when things became too difficult.

A helplessness nestled next to Joanna's feelings of abandonment after she had driven Jeremy crazy through not believing in his love for her and he had become withdrawn. Threaded through Joanna's violence was a psychological inheritance of helplessness. As we came to rethink her experience after the hospital, and came to know the changes in her during and post-hospital, Joanna felt able to engage with her feelings of helplessness. Dissociating had helped her through the terrible hospital time. In the hospital and subsequently this dissociated part came to embody the sad and haunted parts of Joanna that she could not find room for. As Joanna grew up this cut-off part of her slipped out of her life and had not, to Joanna's conscious recollection, appeared until its recent surfacing with us.

TWO YEARS AFTER the menace first came to our time together, Joanna left therapy. She was no longer frightened or distrustful of herself. After a period of deep depression, which lasted about six months, she had ended with Jeremy, who had ceased to be the longed-for partner. She had cracked up what she had known about herself and although, as it all came together again, she was greatly strengthened, some of the pieces now fitted together differently and she expanded and changed in ways that meant that the relationship with Jeremy and some of her friendships were no longer right.

Although she had never physically been much distanced from her parents, she found a new relationship with them, less as the dutiful, successful daughter and more as the compassionate and also vulnerable adult who sensed the suffering that her family had experienced each in their private ways. She became involved with a man whose love she did not think she had created and which she was pretty close to believing in—close enough that she wanted to start a family together. The cutting had ceased fairly abruptly as Joanna accustomed herself to managing pain, fury, fear and helplessness when she felt it in her body through the more conventional expressions of crying, being angry, feeling scared or by experiencing the profundity of her direct helplessness.

She was still an incredibly vivacious and lively woman but now she had an added timbre to her voice and her body. I marveled at her, thinking of what she had locked away from herself for thirty years in order to get on with her life, and at her courage in going through and reconnecting with an episode that had been sliced off. I felt a tremendous joy that through the basic plodding work of her first eighteen months of therapy she arrived at a psychological place safe enough to be able to challenge the vector through which, unknown to her or myself, most of her experience had been channeled.

And what of my story? What had I encountered, where had I been, how had I been changed by my time with Joanna?

An experienced therapist approaches each clinical situation with a reasonable confidence in her knowledge. This confidence, which is not about the particulars of how any specific case may unfold or be understood, has to do with the possibility of understanding and becomes the ground on which uncertainty and surprise can be thought about and managed. Psychotherapy and psychoanalysis are not about what is known and predictable so much as about what needs understanding, what needs accounting for, what the therapist needs to stay open for, what it might be possible to understand and how curiosity can be fruitfully pursued.

This I was forcefully reminded of during my time with Joanna. This was not a therapy to relax into. This was a therapy in which confidence about my capacity to understand was severely tested. At times during the period I describe as the menace, I was in a fog of unknowing. I would veer between utter confusion and reminding myself that such confusion can be a rendering of the patient's emotional experience, as well as a vital communication from her about her mental state.

My tentative footsteps in the dark, which is very much what my words to Joanna felt like at the time, were my attempt to articulate those feelings in the hope that, once they were spoken of, they would lighten. As it turned out, they did—but not without plunges into further confusion, darkness and terror.

Confronted with the knife, I had wondered whether I was losing my mind, whether there was a knife at all, whether I was caught up in a paranoid state. Whatever it was, while I was sorting through what it might be, I learned to hold steady in the face of fear. Although I knew I was not in physical danger from Joanna, she was in psychologically difficult territory, and it is not unknown for one deeply disturbed person to loop another into her panic. Joanna's panic, however, taught me to be still. The absorption the situation offered me was an alertness and a steadiness—the kind of hypersensitivity that is the other side of panic, perhaps akin to the state of giving birth or to feeding a baby. This image surprises me, for there was little about my time with Joanna, even during the menace, that called forth the maternal in me. What I felt more was a deep compassion for her, a wish to reach her and relieve her sense of bleak isolation. I wanted all along to help, to be able to reach Joanna, but this impulse was too superficial. And that is the beauty of psychoanalysis: it forces both patient and therapist beyond the superficial. It was not possible to relieve her of her terror, of her fright, without first being in some approximation of it with her. Joanna showed me how I had to be outside her, in my own isolation box, to be able to bear her pain and really take it on without being able to do much for her in the first instance, in order for her to be able to digest the pain herself. As a consequence I came to develop a capacity for deep stillness.

Above all, though, I believe I tasted her fear. Encounters of meaning inevitably stretch the confines of our own limited experiences and with Joanna I felt my emotional range extending so that I knew, smelled and touched something of what fear meant to her. It was as though where previously one or two notes for fear had existed in me, now there was a chord or two. The play of the notes with their discordance and resonance made fear thus both heavier and lighter.

The final way Joanna changed me was through permitting me to see the satisfaction she experienced in cutting herself. Because she brought it right into our relationship, inviting me to partake in a—to me—unthinkable activity, I could be neither a bewildered spectator nor a psychoanalytic theorizer. Even while I refused what she was offering, I was forced to travel some distance into what she was experiencing. In that journey I had more of a sense from the inside, rather than theoretically, of the control she felt she could exert through cutting and of the tremendous pain she was in.

As with almost every therapy experience, Joanna's taught me humility. She had arrived, as others do, in need. To the therapist is given authority, knowledge and the belief that she can help. All this is an inescapable aspect of the therapeutic endeavor. And it is true that through our experience and our craft we can sometimes be of great help. But we are always capable of being wrong, of getting it wrong, of not understanding and even of misjudgment about how much pain an individual can bear because we have seen, heard and witnessed such pain countless times before. Joanna taught me, as have many of the people I have worked with, about what for her was so unbearable that it was out of reach. This confrontation with the reality of another reminds me of the very modest limits of my understanding, of my need neither to lead nor to abdicate but to strive to participate with humility.

Fat Is a . . . Issue

H E CAME reluctantly, approaching the therapy like a political campaign. A proud man, a fifty-year-old trade union leader who was losing his grip on his food and his family, Edgar was tired and complained of endless work. He was a borderline diabetic who realized that he had been eating without regard to hunger for years.

The idea that the world was potentially perfectible had been his moral stance, no matter that his pragmatic political experience as a negotiator told him something quite different about the lumpy nature of backroom deals and coalitions. He was a man who divided experience up into good and bad and forgot as much as he could about the things he did not like. To fend off the bad, he turned to blaming, which became a useful orderer of his political and psychological life. If something was difficult, then someone was at fault. Letting the person know was his preferred response and he became feared by his colleagues. Acting powerful, being effective and being seen as purposeful built a self-image that suited him. He was a tough guy on a tough battleground.

"Mine has been an easy enough climb for a black man," he said. "I had a close family. My grandmother Doris lived with us and looked after me and my sister and brother while our parents were at work and studying at night for their qualifications." Edgar had a strict upbringing but with a lot less interference than many first-generation British blacks experienced. His family expected him to fit in; they told him that racism was everywhere but that he could make his mark and they counted on him and his sister and brother to get on with it.

He was not exactly harsh with himself but principles and practicalities were what governed him. Feelings were indulgent. It was going to be an odd marriage, this therapeutic relationship. In my mind's eye I could see myself suggesting something about feelings and him being wary. Our vocabularies, our frames of reference, were poles apart. If I was going to make any kind of alliance that would be of use, I guessed I would have to be quite didactic, at least initially.

It helped that he had respect for qualifications and training and believed that he was with "an expert." Otherwise he might reject what I said out of hand. And it helped too that I came from a political background. I had had to work my own head around the fact that emotions might be of some value. I was used to a sensibility that saw economics as central and I was not about to disagree with him. I had simply added to my understanding of its centrality the importance of our emotions and of individual and group psychology. I would have no argument with Edgar if we went down the road of how our psychologies and emotions are constructed in time and place. Those issues had interested me ever since I had decided to become a therapist. I had been intrigued by how the particulars of our family circumstances melded in with our gender, our class and cultural backgrounds to create our sense of who we are. Edgar's therapy might profit by talking about this. On the other hand, it might not.

I felt a lot of sympathy for him. His Caribbean story was one I knew little about. But as a second-generation Jew in England I did know something about the experience of immigration—the displacement, the confusion of trying to fit in with a new culture while trying not to lose your identity brought from the old country. The anti-Semitism my parents' generation had experienced in Britain and in the States sensitized me to the racism individuals and groups faced and to how what can be so damaging about that racism is the partial taking up of the unflattering view of oneself transmitted by the racist elements of the host culture. So I presumed that Edgar's biography, despite his declaration about how easy it had been for him personally, would include lots of instances of racism and I imagined that he had also suffered for his children and for what they might have had to encounter.

I knew too how hard my grandparents' generation had worked to make a home for themselves in a new country, how much they wanted their children to succeed, to put down roots, to thrive. The second generation, of course, has a very different story from the first one born in a new country, but certain threads run through immigrant experiences and I hoped I would be able to pick up on the ones that were salient for Edgar. Already I was wondering whether his sense of losing a grip came from the often driven nature of first- and second-generation immigrants to make it. Despite the verve and determination to celebrate the good that could be wrested from life, these were often contradicted by the newcomer's sense that there was always something more to do, to fix, to aspire to and to conquer which made life a series of hurdles rather than something to be lived.

Our sessions began. Edgar was trying to hold his life together, he said, but it seemed to be unraveling. He was an ambitious man and had managed to bring significant changes to his union. He was always on the way to his next project, breaking new ground in imaginative ways, but his successes brought him more pressure than pleasure and made him wonder about the relentless push to secure advantages for his membership. All the time he was getting fatter and more exhausted. His diabetes was threatening and he could not seem to hold things within his girth. His doctor recommended yet another diet but his wife and daughter knew that he had been down that road so many times before, losing and then regaining the equivalent of enough bodies in the course of his adult life to fill a union executive meeting, and they feared the stress another diet would cause. His daughter had told him to read a well-known book on compulsive eating and not to worry that it was written for women. [1]

Dieting or restricting foods induces a response that leads people to binge on the restricted foods when they are not hungry and to lose a sense of the mechanisms of hunger and satisfaction. Emotional reasons lie behind compulsive eating; emotional problems become turned into food problems, that then seem solvable, or at least postponable, in the way that the emotional issues do not. And those with eating problems also have unconscious ideas about what different body states mean which jar with their conscious ideas about fat and thin. When these discrepancies go unrecognized, they can interfere with an individual's capacity to change their body image and body size.

Unlike many of the women I have seen with problems around eating and body image, Edgar was not looking for a magic cure so much as a set of instructions he could follow. He could see the logic, if not the immediate relevance to him, of the argument that eating for hunger is different from eating to soothe oneself when emotionally distressed. He was quite prepared to accept that he habitually ate more than he was hungry for and he was well aware that the various excuses he had given himself over the years about either not having time to eat properly or just loving food did not hold up. There might well be emotional reasons for his habit, he told me. If it turned out that unconscious reasons for being attached to fat were getting in the way of his eating in a straightforward way, he would be eager to get to them and knock them on the head.

It can be helpful to turn upside down the ideas that people have about fat and thin when working with people who have eating problems. On the surface, thin seems to equate with capability, happiness and sex, and fat seems to equate with

pain, self-destructiveness and discomfort, but if we investigate further we dis-
cover meanings that are far more complex and less congenial, such as thin
equating with fragility, with too much visibility and with an inability to protect
oneself, while fat may symbolize substance, comfort and protection.

Edgar's directness and the clean way he approached this, his latest campaign, endeared him to me. Maybe, I found myself thinking, it could be
so easy. Certainly it had not been for most of the people I had worked
with before but every therapy is an adventure in which individual ingenuity is a prime aspect of the work. I was used to compulsive eaters
whose initial enthusiasm for learning to eat when hungry and stop
when full faltered when they began to lose weight. They had discovered for themselves that the psychological meanings of size were every
bit as consequential as the emotional reasons for eating.

I decided to use Edgar's eating patterns as a focus for the work
since this was why he had come. Although I could sense that it was not
just his body that was growing but the list of things that did not quite fit
in with his life, a focused approach seemed as good as any way to begin.
Exploring an individual's eating with them and discovering the many
personal meanings it has are wonderful ways to learn about someone.
Moreover, the things I imagined might come up for Edgar as he thought
about the role of food and size in his life might find an easier reception
if they were linked with something he was doing every day.

Suggesting that Edgar keep a diary for a few days of what he ate, to
include whether he was hungry or not, how the food tasted and where,
when and why he ate, produced in the second session a book of minutes exquisitely detailing his involvement with food. He was able to be
so attentive to the task, he said, because this week he had not been running from pillar to post. His wife was away visiting her family in
Ghana, there were relatively few union commitments and two of his
three children had taken turns to feed him regular suppers at their
apartments.

Being given an exercise to think about his food, rather than a diet,
had made him aware of all sorts of things. His first and most startling

revelation was that he rarely felt hungry. Edgar's eating had little to do with hunger. It was primarily a sensual, comforting experience in which delicious tastes and textures teased and pleased his palate and made him feel reassuringly solid. His second discovery was that when he did eat—which continued to be often and plentifully—he was satisfied pretty quickly, too quickly for the apparent size of his appetite.

Edgar had not tried to change his eating habits during this time, since he was not trying to do more than observe how he routinely ate. In paying heed to this, he noticed how easily he lost attention. He would notice the first mouthfuls of whatever he was eating or drinking and savor them but that was it. He realized that he continued to eat even when he had stopped tasting. Then there was the dilemma when he wanted one particular taste or food and not another. For example, he had only wanted a piece of fruit for breakfast but this was a problem with his diabetes, so he had eaten cereal and milk. He said that he was not sure how much of his frequent eating was dictated by trying to regulate his diabetes[2] and by the fatigue that plagued him.

From Edgar's observations about his habitual eating I could envisage a way to help him discover how to eat *with* his hunger and also to protect his blood sugar levels. But what struck me, beyond his detailed account, was that Edgar was one of the very few people with an eating problem I had seen in therapy who had actually observed themselves as I had suggested. I was used to patients who became so enthusiastic about the possibility of change that they would steam ahead to try to modify their eating before we had collected enough data to know much about what their eating actually looked and felt like. With so many people who had eating problems I had a tendency to feel I was on a rescue mission. The information could come out only when it was engulfed in a bout of bingeing, so that I rarely had a picture of the background eating. But Edgar had let us see what his eating was like and how it felt.

Edgar liked to eat until he felt full and heavy. It gave him a feeling of contentment, a sense of "it all being right." He recognized at once the emotional nature of this pull to fullness and that really got him going. The idea that he could be mixing up two different kinds of wishes—a wish to be full and a wish to satisfy hunger—and the fact that there were different sorts of satiety were like windows opening for him. He had never stopped before to think about whether he was still hungry or full or what he might be hungry for. Through meticulously following what I had suggested, he had convinced himself that he did indeed eat when he was not hungry; that he did not need anywhere nearly as much food to satisfy his hunger if he could slow down enough to savor every bit of every mouthful; that there was a fusion or a confusion between his wish to be physically full and his wish to be emotionally full.

Rather promising for a second session, I thought, as I gave him a second exercise.

This exercise built on what he had been able to observe about himself. He was to endeavor to eat only when he felt hungry. And he was to try to pay attention to what he was eating so that he could stop when he felt physically content. Simple as this might sound to someone without an eating problem, it was anything but simple for Edgar, whose impulses to eat rarely originated in his digestive tract. Stopping when he was physically satisfied would be especially difficult as the delicate mechanisms which signal satiety are often disturbed in those for whom eating is divorced from physical appetite. Nevertheless I suggested that Edgar try this, even though it might mean eating little and often and at inconvenient moments.

His workload continued to be lighter than usual and he was prepared to take the necessary steps to get food as soon as he felt he required it. I felt encouraged. He was not hitting a lot of resistances in himself. His diabetes meant that he would have to balance what he ate, so we looked at the foods that did the job of placating his pancreas and talked about how he could eat them in combination with the foods he craved and which might be less nutritionally helpful for a diabetic.[3] If he wanted the "nutritionally unsound" food, then by all means have it, I said, but back it up with one of those slower-acting complex carbohydrates that the pancreas accepts. I asked him to use his notebook to record what he felt when he stopped at the moment of physical fullness. What, I wanted us to find out, would he experience if he did not push on to that moment of heaviness?

The third session was not easy for him. He had had a very enlightening time with his food as he followed the instructions but he had also been terribly disturbed. He felt he had disrupted his (albeit chaotic) patterns and was out of sorts. "I can diet with no difficulty. Best dieter I know," he said, smiling at himself as he realized that he must be repeating sentiments expressed by many people with eating problems who had sat in the chair before him. "You've got me all messed up here with your scheme. I'm not hungry for much. I found myself eating little and often—well, not that often—but to tell you the truth, I didn't like it. I felt wobbly and unsure of myself like I'd fall over. Like I was a huge man balanced on a pair of ballet slippers."

He took out a pad from his briefcase and spontaneously drew this image.

It was an image sharply at odds with the bulky but graceful man sitting opposite me who seemed well rooted in his body. I waited before I made a comment because I was wondering what might emerge. Before long he took a deep sigh.

"I've been watching my body fall away from me. I have the uncanny feeling that the substance of me has keeled over and I'm left with a skinny, sunken frame." He drew this second figure, paused and then seemed deep in thought.

"It's my dad," he said, breaking the reverie after several minutes. "That's who it is. It's not me at all." He did not look at me as he spoke and I remembered from the brief history I had taken in our first session that his father had died when he was ten. If it had been from cancer then he might well have been a slight man at the end whose mass, to a small boy's eyes, had been sloughed off.

Edgar was silent and reflective. A couple of times he pulled himself out of his pensiveness with cracks about himself as a ballerina but these were sniffles against a much quieter background. His body relaxed and he seemed to be in a private meditative place it did not feel right to intrude upon. After ten minutes had passed in this way, he shook his head as though to shake off where he had been, looked at his watch, noticed that we were at the end of his time and asked what the homework for the week was.

I tried to look him in the eye. I did not want to respond as though nothing had passed in the session. He seemed surprised to find me looking at him, as though my attention was unwelcome. And yet I persisted. I was not ready to hand out an assignment. Grudgingly, he held my gaze. It was a long twenty seconds in which we both seemed uneasy. The conventions of social intercourse had been disrupted and my brain tingled. It was like being super-alert; anything could happen. I could not be on automatic because there was no automatic to respond to. In therapy it is often the unexpected that needs marking but in my attempt to mark it I seemed to be bouncing us into one of those off-key moments when unsureness is the only known.

The silence was beginning to feel like a power struggle yet I felt very far from being at odds with Edgar. While he had been deep in his reverie, I was pondering the two powerful images of his line drawing: Edgar as the fat man wobbling on ballerina toes and Edgar/Edgar's father with the fat melting away from him, revealing a gaunt collapsed body. My aim in looking at Edgar had been to underline and under-stand the significance of the previous ten minutes *for him*. While I was excited by the clarity of his images, I was not sure how he took them. How did he feel? What did he feel? The way he had looked at his watch and asked for homework was some kind of signal. Was this a way of let-ting me know that his feelings were encircled, off limits, a way of telling me to please back off? Clearly they were not for sharing now. The way he had seemed to shake himself free of them made me won-der if, following their brief and unexpected appearance, they had to be cut out and buried.

I was not against giving him homework *per se*. I was bridling at the abruptness of his request. My mind circled round what I could offer, what might bring us to a meeting point and give him something useful to reflect on. I rejected my first thought of asking him to go about his week imagining himself at his ideal size. It felt as though it might be too close to what had happened inside him during the session and which, as yet, he was not eager to disclose.

The imagining exercise has many uses. It can help an individual recognize what might be difficult for them at their ideal size, an invigorating idea because it is usually thought of as problem-free. ("If only," the patient says, "if only I were thin, I would have a man, a good job, I'd feel good, I'd be happy, my mother would accept me . . .") It can help an individual prepare for whatever fantasies she carries about what will emerge if she is her ideal size; the world doesn't change, things don't necessarily get better, the same conflicts can remain. It can help her "accept" or at least have curiosity about the parts of her that are afraid or wary of being their ideal size; size doesn't solve the issue. Imagining oneself at one's ideal size and staying with what it engenders long enough to dispel the fantasy of its magical healing powers can bring to the surface the conflicts and issues that have kept the person from attaining her ideal size. Knowing what fears or problems are accentuated and what disappointments lurk in reaching one's ideal size, one has the opportunity to engage and reflect upon them. One discovers how emotional problems have become translated into problems of size and what emotional states are unconsciously coded within the ideal or smaller body. An examination of these emotional issues can be a prelude to an individ-ual's inhabiting a smaller body.

So while there was a logic and considerable value to this exercise, since Edgar was unwilling, reluctant or determined not to make known what had so absorbed him, I felt to ask would be to pry. It is one thing to convey to an analysand one's willingness and confidence to confront what he may find difficult or terrifying or to tolerate a menacing confusion, or to bear witness to dreadful pain, but to crudely jump in when the individual is in a private place is unhelpful. After what felt like an age, I chose the simplest and least alarming thing I could say. "Edgar," I started, "I'm loath to suggest a specific homework without quite knowing what you've been pondering, but perhaps thinking about the time in your life when you first started to eat when you weren't hungry might be useful."

The tension between us was broken. Edgar looked relieved to be given a concrete task. I felt relieved that he felt relieved. I hoped this idea could link up something about his desire to eat and the need for bulk with whatever he had been so deeply considering.

Once a pattern of eating compulsively has been established, all manner of situations will incline the person to eat and all sorts of ideas will attach themselves to the significance of different body sizes, but it is interesting to discover the original impulses that might have led someone to eat compulsively. It may be that the child's cues for soothing had always been inappropriately responded to, so that when she cried she was thought to be hungry or offered treats. It might be that a baby was fed by the clock on a schedule rather than as a response to her hunger. It might be that there was insufficient food offered when a child needed it. Reasons such as these can make it hard for someone to have confidence in knowing what physiological hunger is and how to satisfy it.

Besides the specific miscoding of emotional distress as hunger or the misreading of hunger signals, there can be other equally complex reasons to do with closeness and identity which can instigate compulsive eating. For example, it may be that one parent loved food and communicated her love of everything to do with food to her child and that their time together was permeated by the sensuality of food. The preparation of food and the anticipation of its delights, the eating of it together, established and signified a particular bond between them. Or it may have been that food was always a battleground. As a youngster the individual had been put on a diet 'and rebelled, eventually developing a full-blown diet—binge syndrome. In Edgar's case, knowing that he had started to gain weight in adolescence, I wanted to give him an opportunity to pursue what had come up about his father.

Edgar's reverie and the way it ended stayed with me after the session. I turned over what I knew about him from what he had told me, from what I read in the papers and from what I was finding out. He had been the hope of his parents; his elder brother had gone temporarily off track when he was a teenager, although he straightened out in his thirties. Edgar had been brought up mainly by his grandmother in west London in a small house rather fenced off from the world. I wondered where she fitted in, when she had died and what his relationships with his mother and sister were like. He had been a good student, showed early promise in the debating society, trained as an engineer and worked at Plessey's, where he had become a popular shop steward for his relaxed but forceful defense of his co-workers' rights. A large man, emanating dignity and graciousness, and with a beautiful melodic voice, he defied the stereotype of a union man and he was soon recruited by his union leadership to join the head office. After a few years he became a middle-ranking official and the union sent him to study at Ruskin College. While at Oxford, he found himself drawn to a group of Ghanaian upper-middle-class graduate students, among them the woman who would become his wife. He wooed her while she was getting her doctorate. They married, returned to London and started a family. For the last fifteen years his wife had worked for a UN agency. The notes from Edgar's doctor stated that he had become diabetic at thirty-eight, although he had been bulky since adolescence. Those were the bare bones of his story as I knew it. The only other information I had about him was what I could gather from my own senses.

I had seen a reflective Edgar that afternoon. It rounded out the boyishly studious part of him which had listened attentively and applied itself with a resolve I recognized from his toughness as a union leader. He was in the news from time to time, so I had heard his public pronouncements, and long before he had come to see me, I had been impressed by his ability to communicate clearly the issues in an industrial dispute so that there was little difficulty in seeing his members' perspective.

I was drawn to him and felt great warmth and admiration for him. I appreciated his seriousness of purpose and was charmed by the rather twinkly side of him that appeared every so often and must, I presumed, be evident in his work, where charisma and hard analysis combine with the gritty reality of deal-making in first-class organizers. But I also got a very strong sense of Edgar as a loner, although he was nearly always surrounded by people. He could direct and lead. He had warmth. But he was alone, maybe even isolated, in his thoughts, his feelings and in his political strategizing.

Over the next week he seeped into the nooks and crannies of my mind. I wondered about his life at work, whether he was a good manager or whether it was understanding and flair that were his gifts. I imagined what his wife was like, how they managed the three very different cultures they lived in, the Ghanaian, Afro-Caribbean and the black British. I wondered about the class tensions that might exist between them and the work worlds they inhabited. I was curious to know how they had brought up their children. How much had Edgar been involved? What kind of marriage did he have? I thought about what it must be like to live with a medical condition that needed watching every day.

It is not unusual for me to be caught up in a new patient as this is very much the way the work went for me. I am used to finding my mind floating toward someone recently taken on in any spare moments, particularly before falling asleep or on waking. I suppose it is a way of absorbing this new person into my (professional) life and allowing her to get under my skin and find a home inside me.[4]

Edgar aroused my warmth and interest. I emphatically liked him, his fighting spirit, his ideals. I liked his formality. We shook hands when he arrived for a session and shook again when he left. Even his no-nonsense attitude toward himself—which I imagined we would be dismantling if we were to get anywhere—appealed to me. I knew this kind of man from my own political work and I was interested in how the public and private sides of him hung (or did not hang) together.

The nature of the particular warmth he aroused in me was, of course, as important to discover as anything else. At this juncture it was a collegial warmth. The word respect formed on my tongue and I wondered whether it was particular to what had passed between us or whether it reflected the feel of his familial relationships. Respect was what he had aroused in me when he had moved into a deeply thought-ful and private place after the line drawings and his revelations about his father's slightness. I wondered about his emotional temperature. For a man who experienced himself bursting at the seams, he was no drama queen. He might be unaccustomed to recognizing his feelings and he might not know how to integrate what he felt but he was well able to handle his feelings without their spilling out. What he was showing me did not fit with his picture of himself bursting at the seams. A lot of questions hung around my head and I was eager to see what would happen next. Above all there was the contrast between his toughness in the world and the almost bashful way in which he presented himself to me.

For the moment I felt that I was holding on to Edgar's insight into his father and into his own fat. He did not want to or he could not take it forward and I was not able to find an immediate way to help him do so. I guessed he had felt some fear and grief when the image of stepping out of his fat came to him. I could not know because he could not say and I felt I would be trespassing to bring it up at this point. The therapy continued. We moved away from being quite so task-oriented. Edgar was actively applying himself to identifying the times when he was hungry, to eat then and to stop when he was full. He was terribly pleased to be able to do (and feel) this, even though it opened up a Pandora's box of problems as to what he was to do instead of eat. His clothes started to hang more easily on his frame.

Gradually, several months later, Edgar spoke of the fear he had suffered when his father died. This had never come up for him since that time. Partly there had been no right place to talk about his fear, partly there had been no way even to conceptualize it when he was a youngster. As for the illness that preceded his father's death, he could hardly recollect it. He remembered a great quiet in the house, with whispering voices. Edgar's image of stepping out of his own fat, precariously wobbling on ballerina toes, stayed with him, punctuating the talk about his father.

Following the highly emotional wake and funeral, he tried to emulate his mother and grandmother by doing his best to move on. He was stunned, outraged at the unfairness of losing his dad but he consciously shelved thoughts about it. No one wanted to talk or listen. It was off limits. The hush stayed in the house. His fear and grief and upset dogged him until his mother told him he was lucky to have her and his gran and to pull himself together. He was jolted into reality. He became a very conscientious and obliging boy. Helpful around the house and good in the classroom, he soon developed a reputation for being very responsible. When he left school at sixteen, he began engineering training. He became a determined young man, efficient and personable.

Edgar's present grief about his father's death lessened his need to feel quite so heavy. His sadness seemed to fill him up, as though some of what he had been empty of were his feelings of loss and sorrow. This grief brought a weight and gravity to our therapy sessions at the same time as it provided relief. But it was not only here. He had found a remedy in talking about his feelings and he now sought out his brother and sister to talk with them. The conversations, reminiscences and emotions of which he now spoke engrossed him and filled him out in a new way. It seemed to me as though there was less of a divide between the tough, sometimes genial, sometimes controlling, in-charge, know-ing-what-to-do-and-doing-it-forcefully man and the shy, almost diffi-dent man seeking his feelings. No doubt there was more of him inside himself, but paradoxically that sharpened his sense of a certain persist-ing emptiness.

His size was decreasing. It was slow and steady and he was pleased and he felt healthier. He updated his wardrobe. He looked less formi-dable but no less dignified. He reported having lost his sexual appetite. He could make love with his wife and he enjoyed it when they did so, but he had no urge now. Inside himself he was enveloped by loss, not just the loss of his father he felt now so acutely, but the loss of certainty about who he was and who he had been for the past thirty to forty years. He felt he was questioning the ways of being that had held him together for so long and that under all the fat there was an Edgar who was undeveloped, unsure and nervous. Physically and emotionally he experienced a certain precariousness, which in his intimate life pre-vented him from carrying on as though nothing had changed. It was a touching period of the therapy. I saw the courage that he had brought to his union work now turned toward his personal struggles. He was tiptoeing around the more tender and unsure aspects of himself that were so undeveloped, while holding himself somewhat at arm's length from the noisy, aggressive union leader he was adept at being. It was a bit as though he was testing everything around him. He felt very delicate. He could not trust that there was new ground underneath him (for it was not yet firm), while the old ground was pretty depleted. He could go to stand on the new ground, but it was not very solid. He was teetering between two mental landscapes, the one he knew, which was pretty used up for him, and the one which was as yet unexplored.

Meanwhile something rather peculiar was happening for me in the sessions. It was something that I caught sight of stage left, just out of the frame. After a few weeks of not quite wanting to or knowing what to acknowledge, I realized what it was. As Edgar would come into the consulting room, I would feel myself expand. My body seemed to grow so that I felt myself to be several inches taller, to have broad shoulders, a large lap, substantial thighs and arms, and a very ample bosom. Surprisingly, given how hated fat is in our culture, I did not find this enlarged body disagreeable. Rather, I found it quite calming and comforting, although there was a tinge of stolidity about it which perplexed me.

In truth I was perplexed by more than the stolidity. It is always strange to have the sense of being physically transformed during a session. I had had the experience with Joanna of feeling pain in my arm and certainly took physical resonance as an important feature of the therapeutic encounter. Now, it seemed that as Edgar slimmed down, I was filling out and feeling something of the same emotional satisfaction that his bulk had given him. I could not be sure. I did not know why it was happening.

Clearly I was imagining these bodily changes. I had not literally grown in the session and then shrunk when Edgar left. If ever there was evidence for the power of the imagination to influence our experience and sense of self, this was it. But in a way that was beside the point. As a psychotherapist I had certainly observed how moods, feelings and body states of patients find echoes in my states of being. I could not completely explain it and I was unconvinced by any of the explanations my profession had been able to come up with about *how exactly* the transmission of such states, particularly the transmission of *unconscious* states of being, occurred.[5] But that did not stop me thinking that there was something extremely valuable and useful in taking what was happening as valid and that it had significance for the therapy being conducted.

For many years I have been interested in the phenomenon I call body counter-transference: the physical feelings that arise in the therapist's body when work-ing with an individual. Historically, psychoanalysis has focused on two kinds of bodily feelings—the erotic feelings and the somnolent. Stimulated by my work with anorectic patients (whose body image and sense of physical stability are precarious) but gradually extending its awareness to my work in general, I have found it extremely productive to regard the physical sensations that might arise in me as valuable as the more generally noticed thoughts and feelings that can be evoked when working with a patient. In noticing this wider kind of body countertransference we have a window into understanding aspects of the physi-cal development of the individual, which is as important as the more commonly regarded emotional development.

My first thoughts were that I was taking on Edgar's fat. Perhaps he was not quite ready to get rid of it altogether and so he had deposited it on me while he experimented with being without it. Could it be that its significance was such that he needed to *concretize* it in me as a way to further understand what it represented? Of course his fat was not con-cretized in me; this was only an idea, a way of looking at my experience with Edgar, and to those unfamiliar with a psychoanalytic way of think-ing perhaps a rather odd one. But it is with such "odd" ideas that psy-choanalysis works to allow us to enter into realms of the unconscious, the highly imaginative processes outside the known or the logical.

If my expansion was Edgar's fat then I was surprised at the big breasts, thighs and lap that I experienced. It did not feel manly, it did not feel like Edgar's fat and it did not feel like Edgar's father's fat. It felt distinctly womanly. Perhaps while Edgar's way of invoking the feelings he felt about his father was to stimulate my enlargement, my imagina-tion could not extend to experiencing myself as a large man so I had feminized my growth. I was keeping an open mind.

• • •

Despite the strong images we all hold of the maternal and of laps, I have encountered a paradox in my work. For many, especially women, it is the still lap of the father that is recalled as a place of refuge and refueling within the family.While the image and feel of the mother's holding might relate to babyhood and a time before language, it is often the father's still holding that is remembered as a precious part of childhood. Mothers, by contrast, are often too busy doing—preparing food, cleaning, cooking, sorting, fussing and so on—to provide the calm that a child might find on a father's lap as he reads the paper or sips his drink after work.

Edgar's bulk, we had worked out, had been protecting him from the horror he felt at the physically diminished image of his father at the end of his life. His solidity had, in fantasy, bolstered him against his father's sudden frailty. I wondered whether this was the whole story. Psychoanalysis is accustomed to believing that symbolic acts carry many meanings and that a symbol also contains within itself its contradictions. Edgar's fat, and now mine, could represent the strength he had wanted for and from his father *as well as* the distance he felt from him. There was also a sense that Edgar's upset, fear and anger about his father's death could have been locked behind the fat, creating a barrier between Edgar's private feelings and what he could let himself know. But from where had Edgar's idea come that physical substance and bulk were a comfort? Had he started to eat in adolescence to be more robust, more manly? Certainly he was of a generation where substance and strength could be accompanied by girth in men. Had it comforted him that he could switch off his pain by eating? Had his bulk given him a manliness of which he felt denuded? Had his fat been a way to safeguard himself?

As I reflected on these questions and felt myself grow large, I wondered whether my "expanded" body was a fleeting phenomenon or whether it would persist and join up with something Edgar might say. Edgar had been able to discuss and feel his sorrow and pain but the fear that had emerged around the loss of his father had not been much talked about. Was this a key to aspects of Edgar's personality, was it a key to his feelings of emptiness and to the "fat" that now seemed to have gravitated toward me?

Before I could pursue this fear and how his fat might have been a way to surround and gird him, Edgar's mother-in-law died. Edgar had been very fond of her and was deeply saddened. Uncharacteristically, he let himself feel his distress instead of turning himself into the reliable husband, getting everyone on the plane to Accra and making all the arrangements as if it were just another efficient campaign. He did not bypass his own feelings. It was not that he failed to make the arrangements—that would have been unthinkable—but that his grief had a direct and immediate expression. The manhood he developed after his father died had depended upon sealing off his raw and tender feelings, his fear, his uncertainty and his sadness. Out of his own pain and difficulties, he had learned to galvanize others into action. Now something else was developing. He could be sorrowful without compromising his efficiency.

The death of his mother-in-law led Edgar to reminisce about his father's mother, his grandmother Doris, who had lived with them until he was twelve, two years after her son's death, when she had returned to the Caribbean. Edgar described her as a warm, no-nonsense powerhouse who had pushed his father to come to Britain and then had made it possible for both him and Edgar's mother to get qualifications and good jobs. She was enormously important to Edgar and her return to the Caribbean had seemed almost incomprehensible. Rationally he had been able to explain to himself why she had left but emotionally he was devastated. For years he told himself she was coming back, that she had just gone for a long trip. Since his mother thought the same and there had never been a farewell party, it was easy enough for him to cloak the reality of her departure.

Now his shame poured out. Doris had left. He had been unable to write to her. He had felt guilty, he supposed, about not writing which made it even harder to write. Then, when he turned eighteen, she died. He had never forgiven himself for not keeping closer in touch during his teenage years. Guilt and remorse weighed him down. Might he also have felt angry with Doris for leaving, I posed, so that along with his guilt, or perhaps overriding it, was the problem of tangled feelings with no words to write what he really wanted to say? Could he no more forgive himself for being an undutiful grandson, I continued, than he could forgive Doris for leaving him?

Edgar sobbed. Then he talked and he talked and he talked. He had loved his grandmother's shortness, her grace, her large arms and breasts, her firmness and surety. She was a great mixture of qualities. Straightforward and sensitive, strict and generous, sturdy, sure and vigorous. With her leaving, his world fell apart for a second time. He was scared. And he was bruised. Of course Edgar understood why she had left, of course he was not judging her, of course she had suffered her own loss and of course she had given her best and had then deservedly gone home.

As he talked his words revealed a phenomenon we all experience, knowing when something absolutely crushing is occurring while simultaneously trying to explain, forgive and accept it. Yet even as one is doing this, one knows that despite one's best efforts it does not work. The unacceptability of the blow remains and the feelings are indigestible.

Edgar had lived for all these years with a split. There was the grandmother who had comforted him, whose large, reassuring presence had been the bedrock of his childhood, and there was the grandmother whose departure had so devastated him that he had not been able to "let her go" or come to terms with her departure. Instead he had, as so many of us do when loss builds on loss, found magical ways to restore her to himself.

Now my "fat" began to make more sense to me. Edgar had unconsciously summoned up Doris's presence in our relationship. There were many parallels between how he saw his grandmother and how I might appear to him. Firm boundaries surrounded our relationship, I was *there* in that I paid attention to him, I controlled the leaving, I was short (and now had become "fat" as well). Although it was the death of his mother-in-law that brought Doris's importance to the fore, he had been trying to communicate something about her through this corporeal invocation of her in me. I needed to think about how to use what had been physically elicited in me.

Analysis, for the therapist, always involves decisions about what to say and when to say it. Whereas the starting analysand is encouraged to say whatever comes into her head without hesitation or forethought, to speak freely, so that what has been curtailed or repressed might become visible and comprehensible, the analyst's job, by contrast, is to absorb think, reflect, ponder. This does not preclude the analyst's mental free associations. Alertness to one's mental process is crucial but this is essentially a silent process, one in which only fragments are shared with the analysand. Nor does this imply that an analyst's responses necessarily lack spontaneity, for anyone skilled at her job can perform certain operations at great speed and almost without conscious effort. However, the choice exists, more so than in ordinary social intercourse, to take time about what one wishes to say and to select, quite purposefully, what feels right, what keeps the conversation alive and meaningful, what touches the emotions sometimes hidden by words.

Inevitably over the course of several sessions I had considered what I might say about this growing body of mine, wondering if sharing something I was not even at the edge of understanding would prove useful to Edgar.

And even now I was not sure if there was anything I wanted to say. I was interested in seeing whether the conversation and reflections about Doris's importance would modify my sense of the large body I seemed to have when I was with Edgar. I had a hunch that if Edgar could find a way psychologically to incorporate the feelings that he still had about his grandmother's departure my fictive weight could shift. It would mean that he had taken into himself what he had been unable to give up but had, up until that time, been unable to recognize.

His therapy was almost textbook in feel, a kind of "old-fashioned" therapy in which one trauma, screening another, unfolded neatly. Slowly and steadily psychic oxygen was being pumped into unaired psychic spaces, allowing them to be aired in all the ways they required.

While Edgar's emotions remained a very private matter in sessions and I could not easily surmise what he was feeling from his posture or facial expressions, except for the time when he openly sobbed over Doris, he reported what he had been feeling outside the sessions and appeared relieved to be able to do so.

With regard to his size, Edgar had been able to understand something about his fears of living in a slimmer body. He had some grasp of the symbolic meanings of his fat. He was struggling quite hard with the altered space that now existed between him and other people. In losing his fat he had become aware of how he kept people away from himself. His conviviality and warmth and his ability to look after others so well had, up until the present, been unproblematic. But now he wondered how much they had covered up a difficulty in being close, how much his endless availability and talent for fixing things for others gave him one kind of contact—contact with a tremendous amount of control— while leaving him deprived of mutuality or connection. His clearer physical self-definition underlined the gap in his life. The loss of his food, so long a close and private companion, exposed what was not there. He now felt acutely both his discomfort with and his desire for deeper connection with others. I welcomed this shift as I sensed that in some way he was retrieving some of the warmth and hope his relationship with his grandmother had once given him.

Edgar now began to realize that his will and control were a consequence of his need to conquer his childhood fear and vulnerability and what he perceived as others' fears. He felt that the inside and the outside of his life were starting to hook up, as his actions and what motivated them became clearer to him. His work with people who needed representation had been a wonderfully appropriate outlet for a psychological muscle that had developed out of his own adversity. He had been able to use his identification with those in need to assert over and over again to himself at a private, not even conscious level that what was wrong could be righted. His success at sorting things out meant that more and more people came to depend on him as he had moved through the union hierarchy. He liked to tackle other people's prob-

lems, put their case for them, fight in their corner. If you wanted anything done, you went to Edgar, who could always see his way around a
problem. Although this had been his way of operating for a long time,
during the therapy he felt strong enough to question whether his way
of sorting out things for others showed enough sensitivity to them. He
also questioned his motivation and his own need to sort things out, to
repair, to restore what had been unfairly taken.

There was a new rhythm to our sessions. Homework was a thing of
the past. Edgar trusted himself and was sufficiently interested in his
internal processes to allow himself to discover what might be important. There was none of the physical or psychological puffiness of our
early work together. We were steadily exploring issues below the surface of his daily concerns: how he dealt with conflict, his sexuality, his
passion for collective rights, the role of the individual and, crucially,
how he might allow himself to let people give to him rather than be so
intent and busy giving to others that he did not have to confront his
own dependencies and hesitancies.

It would be easy enough to leave the story here. Edgar had come
in as a compulsive eater, fat and dangerously diabetic. He was now eating when hungry, was at a body weight that was better for him, and he
had expanded the space he gave to feelings and self-reflection. In one
way it is an account of a successful therapy. But as it stands it lacks a
certain soul. It is not so much that there are untied strings, for those
exist in any therapy. Unlike a thriller, to which therapy has been compared many times, the story can be unraveled and then sewn up in
more than one way. The points that at one moment in a therapy feel
dramatically crucial lose salience at another. Therapy starts a process
that continues long after the seeds have been planted in a session. So it
was not the reassembling of an emotional jigsaw that was incomplete.
With Edgar what was left out, and had disquieted me through much of
his therapy, came to the fore only when it looked as if we were coming
to an end.

The matter of my "corpulence," which felt so clearly to be some
part of him—or if not a part then a communication from his uncon-

scious to my unconscious—created an uneasiness in me. I was uneasy too with my feeling that despite the enormous changes Edgar had made—being able to regulate his eating in tune with his bodily rhythm rather than his emotional needs, reducing his size so that he was no longer endangering his life through exacerbating his diabetes, and attuning himself to his various non-eating appetites, desires and conflicts—the issue that had been exposed by his literal loss of size was a dimension that lay untouched between us.

That issue—how he could be close—intersected with another issue he was struggling with, how to get people to be the right distance from him. For me, but not for him, the fact that our relationship existed only in the patient-doctor, pupil-master formulation was a clue to the "soul-less" quality I felt about his therapy. The formal structure of our relationship relieved Edgar of the burden of relating to me. He saw me as a surgeon who could excise his disease or as a consultant who engaged in a particular kind of conversation at one remove. He rejected the idea that as the conversationalists we were making a relationship.

I kept wanting to grab Edgar and insist that we address the nature of our *emotional* connection. From my perspective the way our relationship had developed would give clues to his difficulties and strengths in other relationships. By exploring what passed between us we might get a handle on his difficulties elsewhere. Although I had tried to indicate my respect for him, I felt rebuffed and as if anything *personal* was inappropriate. When I tried to link his descriptions of his feelings for colleagues, or for his wife and grandmother, to the feelings between us he looked at me as though I were from another planet. What could whatever did or did not occur *between us* have to do with his personality, his neurosis, his compulsive eating, his problems? Why, he would say, are you putting yourself into the discussions? My problems have nothing to do with you or with you and me.

Whenever he said this I would feel slapped down. I had got it all wrong. Where *had* such an idea come from? As I reflected on what had transpired, I found myself torn. Because the concept of transference is somewhat arcane, reference to it by the therapist is like introducing something in a foreign language and can seem quite maddening if crudely applied. So, viewing it from Edgar's perspective, I was somewhat in agreement with him. Maybe it was impertinent to insert myself into the therapy. Maybe I was imposing on this man by asking him to accept the fact that observing, reflecting on, commenting on and examining our relationship is an essential part of the healing process. Maybe it would be better for me to refrain rather than attempt to explore with him his objection to it. Maybe this was a cultural difference and my interpreting to him or myself his discomfort as a form of resistance would be seen as an expression of my racism.

As soon as I reached that point I would feel caught. My thinking led me into an alley framed by racism. If I did not pursue what I felt was a useful arena, then was I in danger of succumbing to an implied cultural pressure (coming from me and not from him)? Certainly, many of the objections I could see from Edgar's perspective were ones I would have to encounter in any therapy. If I did pursue what I felt was an essential ingredient of the therapy process, might I then experience myself as bludgeoning him? But if I did not confront him with something I thought useful, then was not *that* a form of racism? If I did not respect his view of my presumptuousness was not that another form of racism?

Perhaps if I had not continued to feel so corpulent when I was with him I could have accepted the thought that it was correct not to pursue what was in our relationship. But the fat sitting between us insisted that something needed addressing.

The subject of race was not absent from our discussions. Edgar would talk about antidiscrimination proposals he was working on in the TUC. He would laugh about his wife's class and ethnic confidence mingled with the "white attitudes" she had absorbed in an anglicized education in Ghana. He talked bitterly about how a black boy could arouse feelings of pleasure and love when he was little but could provoke feelings of fear in others when he turned into an adolescent. He recounted how awful he had felt when his daughter had gone through a phase as a little girl of hating the way she looked and had wanted to be white or at least lighter-skinned. The daily indignities of racism were never far from his consciousness.

But when I raised the issue of racism between us, he was horrified. He was furious and did not want to discuss it. It fell into that same category of my presumptuousness: I was coming from another planet. While I felt on firm ground as a therapist wanting to address our relationship for what it might be able to offer him therapeutically, I wavered and become uneasy at insisting that we explore his thoughts about the racial dimension in therapy.

The subject of race is inflammatory. It is painful for all of us to look at. I sensed it was something Edgar and I were in together, neither of us being able to take greater responsibility than the other for it. There was a sensitivity and care we took with each other when we finally grasped the nettle and confronted what was between us. It finally happened when I brought my "fat" into his session.

"Edgar," I began, "I know you dislike my, references to us and our relationship but I want to tell you about something that has been happening for me when I'm with you that I haven't quite been able to understand. It has intrigued me and I think we might be able to make use of it in some way together."

This was more promising. He did not balk although he looked startled. What could I be bringing up now?

"I've noticed," I continued, "that for months, as your body has been changing, I've had the sense that my body has been changing too, only in the opposite direction. When you come into the room, I seem to expand. It's an odd thing to explain."

I was going to go on but Edgar jumped in and surprised me.

"Yes, I know," he said, laughing mischievously. "When I come in and you greet me, I don't really notice your size but when you get up at the end of the session you're small, a bit too small really. I'm not wanting to seem impolite."

I knew what Edgar was referring to. It did not surprise me. The substance that a therapist seems to take on simply by virtue of being in the therapist's chair can make her seem rather bigger than she is. But I was struggling to get somewhere a bit further along from this.

"Edgar, what I've experienced in particular, which is hard to put into words because it sounds so bizarre, is this. I've been feeling that my body grows. My legs, thighs, arms and lap widen, my bosom expands. I feel quite contented with it and I like it. But this more substantial, more stuck-to-the-ground, more rooted body feels borrowed. It's as though I'm an actor inhabiting a character of a different age and whose movements now reflect her attempt to embody the person." I finished, "I put it this way because I haven't any other way to describe it."

Edgar looked at me, then looked away. He did not answer. I could not read his expression although it might have been sheepish. I had probably said more words to him in one go than I had for months and months. I was reluctant to say any more. He looked down and then he looked up and then, as I was about to reformulate what I had just said, Edgar responded to what had been at the edge of my awareness. "You're describing Doris." He said it as if he had been caught out. "That's why I haven't wanted to discuss it whenever you've brought up the subject of us. It's not that I've thought about it in this way until now but I suppose I haven't wanted to ruin my illusion. I've wanted you to be like her. You are like her." There was a long pause, then he continued. "I worried that if I told you about Doris you'd be angry. I've been nervous about losing weight in case you'd tell me to stop coming."

Edgar cried and tears filled my heart too. Edgar looked at me. He was not in the private sorrowful crying he had experienced before when he remembered his father and his shrunken size. His tears, my tears, our tears, were those of understanding and connection. I could almost feel the scalding of his heart and the pain of his grandmother's leaving. I felt myself move toward him and my own heart melting. Allied to my respect for him were a great tenderness and caring for this very wonderful man. Edgar could see my feelings for him. He did not turn away. He allowed himself to be touched by himself and by what had transpired between us.

When he left the session I felt very peaceful. A profound sense of well-being permeated my spirit. Something I had been hoping for without even knowing how to put it into words had happened. I had been given Edgar's precious soul to carry for months and now it was time for him to take hold too and for us to carry it together for a while.

The next few sessions Edgar came in with that lovely bashfulness I had seen before, mixed in with a new lightness. He would wink at me at the door, say "Hello, Grandma," sit down and smile. He did not say much. He looked. He was pensive in an open way. Sometimes he brought me a dish he had cooked from a recipe of his grandmother's. I accepted these dishes warmly,[6] while pondering on whether I was becoming more his grandmother or less so. Cooking her recipes obviously nourished him. Could I and our *present* relationship do so too? I did not want to be Grandma incarnate. Could he experience that he had *my* love, acceptance and appreciation for who he was today and for the struggles he had been through?

Enjoying this new warmth between us and the less formalized feel to our relationship, I felt that we now had enough safety to pursue something that we had been avoiding.

"Edgar," I said, confident that I would not get told I was from another planet. "Edgar, we've got a slight problem here if I am your grandmother. It's this question of race that we haven't found a way to talk about together. I think, and please don't get me wrong, that this honeymoon of ours is going to flounder if we don't face the fact that I'm white and you're black."

"Yes, yes," he said, "I've thought of that." He paused. "The reason you are Doris is that I don't want to take on the fact that you are white. I know a lot about race and racism. I'm not sure I can love or be loved by any white person." He stopped but I knew that he had not finished what he wanted to say. "Don't get me wrong either," he said when he continued. "It's not that I don't want your love. I do, I really do. But I'm not sure I can trust it, trust you."

I paused. I did not want to rush in. What was Edgar reaching to say? Was it a miscegenation issue? Was it that alongside loving me, he

hated loving me because I was white? Was he worried about the therapeutic boundary and whether this love might threaten it? I was inclined
to consider every psychological barrier, for that felt familiar, but I
sensed that we were really talking about race and what that meant. I
felt sad and full of rage. How could we have created a world in which
racism so damagingly marks our relations with self and others? Inside
myself I railed. I felt like an idealist naïf wishing it could be different.

"If I love *you* and not you as my grandmother," he said again as
though to emphasize the difficulty he was encountering, "then I have to
love you as you and accept that you care for me as me, not beyond our
respective races but including and because of them, and that"—he
paused meaningfully—"isn't easy. It isn't easy to trust the white in
you. I'm not sure where you are in all of this," he continued. "Of
course I'm only saying this because I do trust you. Mostly. But then I
wonder. Do you want me to accept your love and affection because
that rids you of your white guilt?"

I looked straight at him. Racism is such an ubiquitous aspect of
Western life that neither of us had a hope of escaping it. How much
was my caring for him, my *respect* for him, my holding my distance
from him as he had requested, a function of my own racism? How
much had I pussy-footed around the intimacy issue and gone along
with his ridicule of my interest in raising the question of our relationship because of my racism? Had I treated him as special and different
and "made allowances," rather than see him as an equal who could
engage with and challenge my argument? Why, too, had I been prepared to sit so long with "his fat," his grandma's fat me? Was black fat
acceptable in a way that white fat was not? In the abstract I would have
been surprised to find myself having such an easy time experiencing
myself as a fat white woman. And what about my wanting him to
accept my love? What was I trying to do there?

I could not answer these questions. I had to take them, for the
moment, as one of the psychological fallouts of racism, just as his feeling that he could not quite love me in the present was a fallout for him.
But even if we could not advance the situation much further, our artic-

ulation of it brought us closer, it unfroze what had happened within the therapeutic frame, and Edgar felt that the feelings between us began to fill an emotional hole that had haunted him for thirty-five years.

Edgar was not the first black person I had worked with. My practice in the United States and Britain has included people of color from different continents and with the differing histories that British and French colonialism and North American slavery have deposited on later generations. In each one of the long-term therapy relationships, issues of race and how it intersected with class came alive in therapy.[7] I had never been unaware of my own ethnic background (or for that matter my class background) in the therapy room. It was not a neutral issue but an element of the relationship. And of course race and racism are also there between me and a white patient. It is simply not possible for them to be absent when we live in a culture in which race permeates social relations, but with two white participants it is quite easy to avoid looking at what becomes immediately apparent when the therapeutic couple are from different racial backgrounds.

A more startling point that emerged linked the issues of Edgar's lack of sexual desire, race and attachment. When he mentioned his lack of libido several months earlier, I had thought this might have to do with a reworking of the manhood he had been prematurely thrust into when his father died. I had wondered how much the loss of his bulk had precipitated a questioning of his sexuality and his sexual prowess. Was he, underneath his fat, more sexually reticent than he had realized? Or did he think that he was less of a "man" now that he had engaged with his vulnerability more directly? Were sexuality, or sexual activity, and manliness one for him?[8]

I was pretty content to leave the discussion here. But Edgar's curiosity about himself and about our relationship had taken off. Now it was time for me to feel embarrassed. He desired me, he said, but had been too ashamed to bring it up because of his own "prejudiced" view that black men are predators. "I worried that you would hate me. I didn't want you to think I was just another man, a black man, hitting on you. I didn't feel like I wanted to have an easy flirtation with you, the kind of thing that I do all the time that makes the world go round. This felt different," he continued. "I think I felt a great love for you and that's another reason why I think you became my grandmother."

Love, sex, race and loss all muddled up and silencing one another. Edgar was not even convinced when he talked that it was sexual desire he had for me. He simply had no other way to explain what he did feel. He had felt disturbed early on in the therapy about the strength of what he had felt and he had managed it by becoming a very good patient, a very good boy. Since he had some view of the therapist as neutral and the therapeutic environment as antiseptic, he had pushed his affection into a category (a sexual category) that, although uncomfortable, was at least within the range of what he knew about. But it was misshapen there, it did not quite fit, and he had tried to cut off from the feelings he had toward me.

Now that the feelings between us were open, they frightened him less. Neither did they appear particularly sexual and this greatly relieved him. There was something about the elision between his desire and his race that made him desperately uncomfortable. He had the terrible thought that he disliked other black men for the sexual prowess they were deemed to possess.

There was a lot of sorting through to do here. Again, nothing could be taken out, looked at and then put away conclusively. Edgar could easily see how his views on race and sex were a refraction of those within a racist culture. It was almost inevitable. But he felt great dismay at his own thoughts, and the narrowness of the categories in which he could think, even when his own experience so transcended them. With a lot of sadness he realized that he could do little more than observe his thoughts as they occurred within him. They could not be banished. At best they could be handled with curiosity, as artifacts of mind which one might have to encounter. If he could accept the appearance of such thoughts, he could explore a little less apprehensively what they might mean and in this way they could become less toxic.

I had my counterpoint to Edgar's discomfort over black men's sexuality. It was impossible not to. How could the imagery that had saturated the culture not have affected me? I remember moving to New York as a young adult and being thrown by the particularly sexualized way in which white New Yorkers expressed their racism. It disturbed me deeply. I was relieved when some of the political groups I was involved in tried to struggle with the way in which white people had absorbed prejudiced and stereotyped views around black men and sexuality. In my women's group I had heard American women link their racism to black men's mythologized sexual prowess and heard how that myth had, in recent years, come to be extended to a fear of rape. The group had tried to untangle the connections, the interplay of fantasies between white women and black men, and tried to explore the history of these fantasies. The unresolved nature of those discussions came back to me now. I recalled the fear of many of the women and how contaminating it was. I hated it. I hated racism for creating the fear, the imagery, for how it framed black-white male-female relations.

Now Edgar and I together faced another version of this black-white sexualized paradigm. It did not feel good but it felt right. I was being given a chance to think these issues through again with a man, a black man who, contrary to the facts, was himself fearful of carrying the unjustified stereotype of the black man as predator.

My hate was still there but I would have to think about it afresh. Was it a general hatred of racism? Did it come from Edgar? Was he unconsciously forcing me to consider that I might hate him, that I was no different to many people unable to acknowledge their race hatred? Was he trying to find a way to struggle with hatred, both feeling it and feeling on the end of it, so that I would have a psychological taste of what it felt like to be him, to live being hated? Or, even harder to consider, did I hate Edgar in some way that I was loath to contemplate?

I was churned up. I was accustomed to my racism expressing itself in over-respecting a cultural difference. That, of course, could stifle a relationship even though that was not my intention or wish. But hate—that was a hard one. If my feelings of hate were for Edgar then I was surprised. Consciously I could not find any for him. But then maybe I simply hated being confronted by the discomfort of racism, the pain it aroused in me, the guilt I was not aware I carried but was prepared to believe I did. I would have to explore and examine this hate a bit further and I would have to take on board the racism I encountered in myself that was being unwittingly foisted on to Edgar. What sat most readily with me was that by feeling his hatred and having to think about it, I was being given a glimpse into what it felt like both to hate and to be hated for simply existing.

As I was having these thoughts, Edgar continued. "I suppose," he said, "I'm, like Fanon writes, some part white inside and that part doesn't like me. I've grown up half thinking I'm second best. That really takes the cake. I'm a black man with too much of a white man's mind. I've got to have both kinds of minds, black and white, but the black's all mangled by the white."

Now he showed me his anger and his hate: for the racism he had faced and managed so well and for the doubt and self-hatred it aroused in him. He was outraged that he was personally tainted, that despite everything, despite the self-respect his parents had bequeathed to him, despite his personal success at holding an important job fighting for the rights of his membership, despite his successful marriage and his lovely children, he felt a racism toward himself in his bones. He wanted to vomit up that feeling, step aside from it, cut it out of himself. His words came out in a frenzy as he used every image he could draw on to articulate how desperately he wanted this poison of racism torn out from inside him. Did his children carry it too? he worried. And what about his wife, who although Ghanaian was living in a world saturated with subtle and not-so-subtle-race hatred? It was an excruciatingly difficult time staring at this aspect of racism.

Not surprisingly my feelings of hate dissolved in the face of his pain. It would have been too much for both of us to be "in hate"; one of us had to hold the feelings that make human life bearable when we are faced with a pain that is so great and a disgust that is so profound. I felt a kind of honor that Edgar had been safe enough to share his feelings with me. In the midst of all the hate, perhaps there was still hope for us humans, who had hopelessly messed up our relations with one another, especially when it came to difference. Then I checked myself. Was it not patronizing on my part to feel honored? Surely that was my job, for people to share their feelings with me, whatever they were?

My hope was considerably dampened, too, by a strong melancholy that pervaded my whole person. In being allowed into Edgar's grief and rage, I had lost something that needed losing and I hurt all over. That something was my sense of the possibility of human regeneration and change. It was the idealist side of me that thought if we just put in all the energy and thought deeply and complicatedly enough, and changed the structures, a lot of what was wrong with the world could be alleviated. My friends often chided me for my optimism. Maybe they were right. Maybe my hope was a defense against the pain of how awful human social arrangements can be. Melancholy penetrated my bones as self-hatred was penetrating Edgar's. There was a truth to what we were both feeling that no amount of understanding could soothe. We were a white woman and black man living in Britain at the end of a century in which racism, along with class and sex relations, had been center stage. There should have been no surprise that we would feel as we did, that psychology makes the person in the mode of his and her times. Edgar and I were of our time; we were both bound to feel racism within ourselves and toward each other. That we were both in our ways fighters against injustice was one way we had found of managing this terrible blight, but we could not escape from the tragedy of our times, the irrational hatred, mistrust and fear that insinuate themselves into all of us at the end of this century of hatred.

Two Parts Innocent,
Two Parts Wise

THE STORY WAS so extreme. To have read it in a novel would have stretched credibility. Sitting and hearing it, I was not surprised that Jenny had come for a consultation.

It did not come out all in one piece. There was too much pain and confusion for that. In fact when Jenny came for the first of six sessions, I wondered quite how mad she was. Out would tumble two or three compressed paragraphs before her brakes went on and she would stop abruptly as though what she had heard herself say was too horrible to be believed.

With the whole story out, she was visibly relieved. The pace changed. Her words followed one another without difficulty and with a lot of feeling. It was an account of such injury and confusion that it had temporarily deranged her. More than that, it had challenged her view of people. The trauma she had experienced precipitated a shake-up of what she believed and valued. Her loss was not only in the events but in their implicit threat to everything she had taken for granted.

Here is the story. Jenny was adopted at birth, an only child brought up in a middle-class family in Sussex. Her father had been an engineering consultant, her mother had trained as a pianist. Jenny went to Trinity College of Music, became a violin teacher and then married Robert, a highly paid lawyer, who was interested in music and drama. They had two children, Sophie, seven, and Jake, nine.

When Jenny was thirty-five, her parents died quite suddenly, first her mother and then six months later her father. Her wish to meet her biological parents became insistent and she embarked on the process of finding them, especially her mother. She discovered that they were no longer together; they had split up shortly after her birth, when her father had disappeared from her mother's life. Her mother, Lily, had then emigrated to Vancouver, Canada, where she married Mike, a truck driver, and had a family, Jenny's half-brothers, Steve, now twenty-seven, and Tony, twenty-four.

Jenny made contact with her biological mother and went to Vancouver to meet her. Lily was delighted to be found. She had longed for a reunion and a chance to get to know the baby she had given up. Jenny extended her weekend visit and stayed with Lily and Mike in their house in East Vancouver, an area of modest two- or three-story wood frame structures lived in mainly by white immigrants. They spent their few days together shopping, having coffees, chatting, visiting Steve and Tony and going to see the Vancouver Canucks play hockey. Although Lily was not prosperous—Mike's job and the area they lived in attested to that—Jenny noticed that she lived comfortably. Lily was well dressed in a flashy sort of way, and her house was crammed with food. This might have been done in honor of her visit, of course, but Jenny also noticed that the house was full of ornaments and clothes, and had a television set in every room. Indeed, the room Jenny slept in was literally a storeroom, full of several piles of unopened boxes and packages for which Lily apologized. Jenny had been so captivated by meeting her mother that she absorbed all the details and the differences in their lives as if in a dream.

Six months later it was arranged that Lily and her husband and sons would come to London for their summer vacation. Jenny's husband sent them the tickets. Once in England they met the members of Jenny's family, went to Robert and Jenny's country cottage, took a brief tour of England, and then were resting up in London for a few days before returning to Canada. Jenny, Robert and their children stayed on at the cottage and planned to return home to London a few days after Lily and her family had left for Canada.

Their time in England had gone well. Jenny felt whole and happy and in the aftermath of her grief over the loss of her parents, she had welcomed her newfound mother and half-brothers. Despite their hugely disparate experiences and expectations of life—Jenny had been brought up in English gentility while her biological mother came from a rough background with criminality around the edges—they had bridged these differences to meet each other and to fill up the holes they each carried. Lily's emptiness was that of a mother who had lost the child she carried too young for her to know how long and how much it would hurt. While Jenny's loss of the mother who had brought her up could be temporarily assuaged by discovering the mother who had birthed her, for Lily their reunion had a particular poignancy: she herself had been adopted before it was really possible to trace one's birth mother.

When Jenny and Robert returned home from their country cottage they were shocked to discover that their home had been burglarized. It was stripped of obvious valuables and some photo albums were missing. There was a note from Lily saying that Jenny was not to get in touch again. The implication, and several other details, led to the unavoidable conclusion that Lily and her men had ransacked the house.

Jenny and Robert tried to contact them in Canada but the family had moved. They went to the agency that had helped locate Lily, they wrote and phoned and pursued her as far as they felt they could. Getting nowhere, Jenny and Robert decided to put the whole episode behind them. Jenny tried but it did not work for her. It was a year following the incident that Jenny, now thirty-eight, came for a consultation.

I met a women in great distress, almost frozen by the pain of what had occurred. She looked as if an icy, violent wind had caught her and pinned her down. Her posture was stiff, her gait gawky and her skin was stretched tightly over her delicate features, rendering her face a mask. It was hard to imagine a body so taut playing the violin. She did not know what she was doing consulting a complete stranger, she said, but she had heard I was a kind lady in Hampstead.

The story out, she wept and wept. When the hour came to an end there was nothing for me to say beyond how very heartbreaking her plight was.

Consultation is the least heralded part of psychotherapeutic practice and yet it is not only the starting place for all therapies, it has a unique role of its own. During and after a first meeting, the psychotherapist is assessing whether sessions will be useful and, if so, at what kind of frequency. Is individual open-ended therapy the right offering? Would a brief therapy make more sense? A group? Is medication indicated? Was the time spent together useful? Did it help clarify what is so troubling and difficult and whether therapy is the right kind of help?

Choices are rarely as free or open as we might wish because the day-to-day constraints of practice mean that at times one can offer a wider variety of options personally, or through referral, than at other times. With Jenny I had a clear sense of wanting to meet with her for a few sessions. I reserved the idea that this might be a prelude to therapy but my strongest inclination was toward consultation.[1] In the course of my practice I see many people for just one or two sessions, either to talk with them about what kind of therapeutic help makes sense or, as with Jenny, to help assimilate a recent event. Consultation is not second best to therapy. It may be precisely what is required. Often a few focused sessions can be extremely valuable.

. . .

Listening to what had happened to Jenny, I felt as though I had been punched in the heart and that my mouth might be hanging open. I had heard many cruel stories in therapy—children tied by step-parents to radiators, pubescent girls sent out whoring by their mothers, boys beaten at boarding school after being caught crying for missing home—but somehow I have never become hardened to the horror of the ways in which people can hurt and be hurt. This case stunned me because what I usually hear is of the daily cruelties between couples or the pain parents unwittingly inflict upon their children—the hurt we do not intend. When I encounter sadism, or systematic abuse, or conscious manipulation of a wife who is living in emotional terror, I may absolutely hate it but I have a handle on some of the dynamics that might have caused it. I calm myself by always trying to see how the individual involved may be able to lever herself out of feeling victimized by her distress by understanding how she has responded or contributed to events and what she might now be able to do inside herself or by taking some action.

Looking at the events as Jenny told them, I could not see what Jenny could have done differently. It was hard to get my head around the behavior of Lily and her family. I wanted to reject it as unbelievable. I toyed with the idea that the Jenny who was sitting before me was deeply disturbed and not quite who she had represented herself to be. For several moments I wondered whether I was hearing a story, a confabulation whose authenticity lay more in its emotional than its narrative truth. Perhaps something terrible had been stolen from Jenny. Perhaps Jenny had been tricked early on in life and had been the victim of some terrible fraud—given something she wanted, only to have it and her desire for it sadistically rubbed in her face. Perhaps the burglary had not been by Lily and her men after all. Perhaps meeting her biological mother so soon after the death of her parents was in itself more problematic than she realized and had sent her into a paranoid delusion.

As these ideas ran around my head—some ran to ground as I realized the fallacies within them—I was struggling with two thoughts. The first was that I was trying to fend off the horror of what Jenny had told me. Perhaps my paranoid thoughts were my attempt to discount what I was hearing and feeling. Although I was not frozen in the way that Jenny clearly was, I was more than shocked. I felt as though someone had thrown me up against a wall. It was one of those moments when my values and my own innocence confront the reality of what people can do to one another. I felt sickened.

My second thought was that I might not be able to let go of the "paranoid" thoughts that had crossed my mind. Although I could try to disregard them because I could see that they probably arose out of my discomfort with what Jenny was reporting, I could not fully dismiss them. When such an idea enters the therapeutic space it is hard for it to simply dissipate: it hangs suspended in the background ready for use if necessary. Although I was most inclined to believe what Jenny had told me, I knew that a small question mark might hover a while yet. For me there were two discomforts: the horror of the events and my unease about whether they were as Jenny reported them.

A psychotherapist has to take what a patient talks about as what is. If things seem oddly amiss or possibly misrepresented, the psychotherapist struggles to enable the patient to explain how she comes to see, understand or conceive of things in the way that she does. In the therapeutic conversation fixed ideas can loosen, so that what may seem askew can develop a different coherence.

People outside of therapy often wonder why it is that psychotherapists believe the stories we are told. They wonder whether we are conned by those who see us, who seek some kind of false solace for a problem that they have invented.[2] *Of course such an idea is plausible. But for a psychotherapist this question is of limited interest. For if the patient is an inventor or a liar (which she may be), this does not make the individual's struggle any less legitimate, rather it further opens up the psychoanalytic inquiry. We are interested to understand with the patient why invention or lying*[3] *has importance. What cannot be voiced without fabrication? What wants telling that chooses a particular form for telling it in? A psychotherapist accepts as a proposition that the patient is in difficulty. That*

is, after all, why she has come. A psychotherapist does not so much suspend nor-
mal moral judgments as be interested and curious about the ways in which indi-
viduals construct understandings of their lives and their difficulties, including
whatever mechanisms, such as invention or lying, that they employ.

At the second session Jenny was preoccupied with her response to Lily. She was grateful to me, she said, for showing her my dismay at what had happened. She had thought I was going to think that either she was overreacting to what had happened or she had invented it all. Seeing the concern on my face, coupled with talking about what had happened, had released some pressure. She and Robert had kept rather quiet about the turn of events, partly because they both felt discombobulated, partly because Jenny feared it would reflect badly on her (did the burglary indicate some terrible family trait she had inside her?) and partly because they were not accustomed to talking about very personal matters with their friends. Of course she had been to her doctor and he had prescribed pills, but they did not seem to have helped much, although she was still taking them. Now, she said, the airing of what had happened had brought some relief.

Jenny was still in shock and emotionally bewildered. She was not sure if it had been wise to embark on finding Lily originally. I was not surprised that she was questioning herself. She was hoping to do away with the pain of the trauma by taking the responsibility for causing it. Who would not want to be able to turn the clock back and live rather with the sadness of not knowing one's birth mother if one had experienced the reality of this betrayal? Of course another part of Jenny knew that this was a kind of nonsense. She had had no choice. Finding Lily had been one kind of dream.

Jenny had been adopted into a happy home. She had been cared for and felt valued and had not dealt with every crisis of adolescence by pining for her "real" parents. Finding her biological mother had answered her desire to fill in the pieces of a puzzle. Once she had become a mother herself, she had developed an active curiosity about the woman who birthed her and who had not been able to keep her.

Jenny had wanted to know where she came from, what had happened to her biological mother and father and whether she had siblings. When her parents died she had decided it was time to find out.

All the issues around genetics and environment intrigued her. She wanted to know if her biological parents were musical or shared her temperament. She had always been amused to watch people's faces after they had commented on how much she was like her mother when she told them she was adopted. Indeed there were so many ways in which she was definitely a creature of nurture that Jenny's question had become how much she was also one of nature. Her adoptive mother was a pianist and their interests, style and sentiments were similar. When she told me this, I wondered how much she had taken of her mother's inclinations to make herself more her mother's daughter than a biological child would need to demonstrate. She had known she was adopted for as long as she could remember, she said, longer than she had even understood the meaning of the word. She had accepted it as an unproblematical fact. Now something was catching up with her. She had been compelled to find Lily.

Being rejected by Lily was a nightmare for which she was totally unprepared and for which she had few defenses. No wonder her skin was stretched tightly over her face, stunned and frozen. There had been no indication from Lily that meeting Jenny was difficult for her. Quite the contrary—Lily had said how relieved she had been to find her daughter, especially in light of her own unfound biological mother. "Perhaps if it had gone badly when I went to Vancouver," Jenny said, "I could have anticipated something going wrong, but I was totally unprepared. Meeting Lily was like a dream come true. I felt at peace. I had something more of me."

The trauma of the last few years had fractured Jenny's belief in the way the world is. Outside the situation, and simply listening to her account, I myself was deeply shaken. There are times in all our lives when we hear things that do not accord with the way we think the world is or should be. Depending on the nature of the new information, we have at such moments the options of disregarding the information, of repressing it, of becoming cynical, of becoming a turncoat or of trying to stretch our understanding so that we can find a way to incorporate what we are hearing or experiencing.

The pressure to reject unpalatable or unacceptable experience is very great. People who have lived through the horror of war, of forced emigration, of disasters, often want to put it behind them, to forget it, because there is no proper place for it to fit into. How much greater is the temptation when one's pain is not part of a collectively recognized experience but an individual event?

The psychotherapist who is faced with hearing the detailed stories of human suffering and the cruelties that can be perpetrated between people cannot run away. It is her job to listen. She has to find a way to hear what is being spoken of, to bear witness to the perverse, the sadistic, the barbarous and the unimaginable. In this she is aided both by the skills developed in training to listen, feel and hear without becoming overwhelmed and by the theoretical frameworks available for thinking about the gruesome material that enters the consulting room.

For Jenny there was no mechanism readily available. Such things did not happen. She did not have the intellectual or emotional receptors to process what had happened. She had to come to terms with a terrible sense of loss and of not being wanted by Lily. We had to help her get beyond or behind the feelings of shock to experience the loss. Although, as our six sessions unfolded, we could see that this was a moment when innocence failed Jenny and she had to confront the way the world is, with realities until then unknown to her, the first step was for Jenny to face the tremendous pain and poignancy of losing Lily after the experience of finding and connecting with her.

Creating the ambience within our session for Jenny to focus on the loss rather than on her outrage at the events was my first task. It would have been easy enough to go for explanation or to have pursued the issues raised by the theft, but the issues surrounding loss—the loss of Lily, the loss of belief, the loss of certainty and the loss of expectable decency—were so much more psychologically present. The theft needed thinking about, to be sure, but I had a hunch that pursuing it would only underscore the loss. Besides, the theft was not where Jenny's emotional energy was. Her pain seemed saturated with loss. I wanted to make it possible for Jenny to unfreeze that pain, to feel her sorrow rather than have it held in with the mask that seemed to have stretched across her face.

Rejection is one of the things we find most difficult. Many of us will do almost anything to avoid feeling rejection and its associated loss and hurt. We turn the situation inside out so that we appear to be the cause of it. We get angry so as to fend off our feelings, as if by creating enough ire we can use it as a shield against the hurt while making sure that no one comes close again. We go dead inside in an attempt for it not to matter. In one way or another we try to avoid, separate or hide from feelings of rejection and loss. We are not sure we can bear them.

As Jenny was soon to discover, opening herself up to assimilate the painful feelings allowed her terror to decrease. Her face began to have some movement in it. It seemed less translucent and taut and I could see what very pretty features she had. Her body started to ache terribly as her fear gave way to her pain. Now she felt the physical after-shock of the strained posture she had taken on as her body began to release its rigidity and found its more habitual stance. Despite her physical hesitance, I could see movement and suppleness and the signs that she was a musician whose body worked with her violin to create its beautiful sounds.

She was now not so much in shock as in agony. She was terribly sorrowful and pained and yet a certain aliveness emanated from her. In the second session my thoughts that Jenny was delusional or paranoid all but dissipated. We had both emerged from shock and I could see and feel with her something of her distress.

As she was able to take on more of the pain through crying and sighing, I noticed that my body felt bruised and sore. Privately I wondered whether I was coming down with the flu. After Jenny left, the feeling disappeared and I had to think about what I had experienced physically when I was with her. The sense that I had suffered a blow or had the stuffing punched out of me made me think that I too must have been holding myself tensely after hearing her story. It was as though, in empathy with hers, my body had stiffened to bear what should not be borne.

It was after this session that I called her doctor. I wanted to talk about the medication he had prescribed. I was not sure whether it had dammed up her pain, whether she was in such a depressive shock when he saw her that he feared she would retreat too far into herself, or whether he was simply overwhelmed by her story and grabbed at medication as a way to give her something.

When working with someone on medication, I always like to consult with the prescriber to understand why a particular drug has been selected, what the doctor was responding to in the patient and was therefore hoping for from the medication. I need to know how long the patient is expected to continue with the medication, the alternatives that we might consider and so on.

The recent renewed interest in psychopharmacology, with the hopeful claims of those dispensing or using Prozac and the S R R I-type preparations, has made patients and doctors very much more willing to consider medication as a treatment or as an adjunct to treatment for a whole host of difficulties from eating problems to obsessive behavior, mild depression, anxiety and help in adjustment following a traumatic situation.

While undoubtedly certain people feel helped by medication over the short term (and few psychotherapists withhold it from their patients if they believe such medication is appropriate), in many cases the claims of psychopharmacology are unable to meet expectations. It is hard to create a pharmaceutical preparation that does not have effects other than those intended to lessen mental distress. It is also the case with the newer drugs, as Peter Kramer discusses in Listening to Prozac, *that the success of a drug can reshape the diagnoses that clinicians are making and thus extend its use beyond its original more limited brief.*

With many medications, particularly the antipsychotic preparations and the older antidepressants, patients complained of unwanted physical and psychological side effects. Some people felt muffled or psychologically coshed. Their pain had diminished but at the price of a dulling of their sense of personal will.

The pain of the distress an individual suffers may be sufficient reason to choose such a trade-off. Writers and sufferers as eloquent as Kay Redfield Jamison, detailing her experience of manic-depression in An Unquiet Mind, *and Lauren Slater, discussing her repetitive gestures and manic episodes in* Prozac Diary, *have chosen to do so. But in their accounts of prescribed drug taking, we hear about the considerable losses as well as the gains associated with a quieted-down psyche.*

For many patients there is the fear that once they are on medication they have redefined themselves stigmatically as people who now require drugs to function. This tends to be less true in the United States, where the pharmaceutical companies have been more successful in suggesting that drug therapy is like wearing corrective lenses for short sight—an aid for living not an expression of disability.

My working experience over the last twenty or so years has been with outpatients, most of whom are not on prescription drugs. When they are, they tend to be so for a very short period to help them over a particularly difficult time. Patients who have come to me on medication or who require it during the course of therapy are generally inclined to want to come off it as rapidly as possible. They fear their dependence on medication and are uneasy with what they consider the slight distance they have from themselves.

In Jenny's case her doctor had first prescribed Prozac but when that had not seemed to relieve her chose a Benzodiazepine, a class of drugs that can help mobilize people who feel paralyzed by anxiety. I could see the logic of his choice but even though I was seeing Jenny for only a few sessions, I was not convinced that the medication would make continued sense for her. Whatever edge it had taken off her pain had enabled her to avoid a breakdown but I wanted to discuss with her doctor how useful it still was and what his thinking was about its continuation. I wondered whether it might inadvertently be suppressing what needed to come out.

Like almost every doctor, Jenny's physician was pleased to have another clinician's view and to know that she had sought out therapeutic help. He himself had been frustrated. It was a horribly heartbreaking story and he for one had not really known how to help. When her husband first brought Jenny in to see him, he had prescribed because he had had no other thoughts. Knowing her to be a very private person, he had cautiously encouraged her to speak to her vicar. The medication had not done what he had hoped for and so he was relived that she was in my hands. We agreed to speak again before Jenny's and my last session to see where things stood then.

In between our second meeting and our third, Jenny reported feeling tender all over. Her heart ached and her limbs felt wretched. She wept, ate very little, went about her daily life, looked after her children, taught her pupils and ran her household but she did not attempt much else. She felt fragile. It was a very different state for her from one of shock. She had moved from being dazed to looking after herself with some gentleness. She had restored some important feelings to herself. She had more awareness of the world and she was acting as if she wanted to protect herself from it.

When she came to her third session she had the kind of fragility that goes with an about-to-be-found strength. Her hair, which had been held back by a headband, now fell about her face, giving her a softness that echoed her delicacy. I was relieved and delighted for her because although I knew this was a terribly painful place to be, it was a long way from the frozen terror that had held her together for the previous year. She again expressed relief that she could come and talk. Then, speaking tentatively, she said that she had been able to face what for her was the most horrible aspect of the whole business. It took her some moments to speak. Her eyes welled with tears and her face and body seemed full of hurt and sadness. She looked at me as though to speak before turning away several times. I could see she had the kind of fear that can arise when something of enormous significance wants saying. After several minutes she stared at me again, gripped the chair and spoke.

"I've realized," she started, "that Lily has left me. Lily has left me."

Repeating her words seemed to emphasize what she was trying to come to terms with. It was so upsetting and horrid that she had not been able to believe it. "That's the nub of what's happened," she said, getting to what seemed to encapsulate it best. "She left me not once, but twice."

It was a fiercely painful moment. There was no way to ameliorate the starkness of her words. We sat quietly together, feeling the truth of what she had said. It hurt so much I felt my insides ache. I knew that I had tears in my eyes.

"Robert wrapped himself in a rage about the ingratitude and deceitfulness of Lily and her family," she said when she went on. "Although I knew he was right to feel that, it wasn't my response and it's only now that I'm beginning to find mine."

She sat quietly again but she seemed in less pain. When she resumed talking it was focused on the incomprehensibility of the burglary after the important time she had spent with Lily in Vancouver and in London. The bizarre nature of the loss of Lily had made her feel acutely the loss of the mother who had brought her up.

The pace of the session was very slow and purposeful. She wondered whether her search for Lily, which in one way was a search for the missing piece of who she was and where she came from, was in essence a wish to replace her beloved mother who had died.

Now a deeply felt gratitude toward her mother and father for having been such able parents and for giving her so much permeated her. Her grief at their loss was something she thought she had mourned. Now she was feeling it again, doubting whether she had grieved deeply enough at the time. She had not yet realized that grief is something that gets reworked throughout life. We do not just feel it once in an appropriate way and then have it over with. It comes upon us at anniversaries or birthdays or when a smell, a taste, a piece of music, the quality of light or a phrase evokes the loss and we feel its sharp pain. Jenny was likely to feel her parents' loss again and again, as well as the double loss that Lily had wrought.

As we talked and sat together in her sadness, two losses in my own life repeated themselves on me. Along with feeling empathy for Jenny, I knew I needed to reflect later on those griefs of mine, to allow them to be felt again and so resettle. I registered my own thoughts and returned my attention to Jenny.

The consultation was giving her a space to explore her feelings to recognize the complexity of her responses. She now knew, she added, that there was no way she could make everything all right. Something deep had been ruptured. She would not be the same Jenny again. Her life would not return to normal. Before these wretched happenings, she had never been confronted with anything horrible or challenging enough to question her view of who she was or where she belonged or what the world was about. She had never been so deeply disappointed that she had not been able to understand something, or so confused that she was unable to explain it to herself. With her certainties now shaken up, the best she could do for herself was to know what she felt. Up until now she had been holding herself tight, hoping that by not moving an inch, by almost pretending she did not exist, she could stand apart from what had happened or make sure that she would not incur anything else untoward.

Once she was able to feel beyond the shock and began to accept the loss and rejection, Jenny started to speculate on the theft, on what might have led Lily to act as she did. With the feelings of loss now with her rather than attempting to stave them off, she felt much less scared of thinking about the meaning of Lily's actions. Although many psychotherapists might see such speculation as a retreat from feelings or as a way to blot out pain, that was not my view, particularly in the context of consultation.

The balance between feeling and thinking is the cause of much disagreement between various schools of therapy. The argument as to whether therapy works because repressed feelings are allowed to come to the surface or because faulty cognitive ideas are addressed is an alive one. Some schools see the release of feelings as primary and vital. They hold that repressed feelings block thinking and self-questioning and must be released. Other schools believe that it is the individual's stance toward situations that causes the problems. They stress that the

way a situation is construed creates either emotional harmony or distress, and
that the naming of feelings rather than experiencing them is sufficient. In my
view, thoughts and feelings are partners; they inform each other.

As Jenny began to absorb her feelings of rejection and loss, she was
able to think again and in so doing make the recent events in some way
palatable. Ideas had always been important to her, as they had formed
the backbone support against the normal chaos of everyday life. Ideas
were as important to her as her music and both came back into play to
help her through a convalescence from the traumatic events she had
experienced.

Jenny wondered about Lily's guilt and shame at giving her up originally. In her quest for Lily she had read numerous accounts of the
remorse biological mothers suffered day in day out. Perhaps, she
thought, the reconnecting had been too much for Lily in the face of the
differences in their lives. While some women had wholeheartedly
embraced their newly found children, it could be that Lily was a
mother who could not make the shift from being guilty and ashamed to
forgiving herself. Perhaps the barrier she had constructed to survive
giving Jenny up at birth was too fixed to dismantle.

Jenny had read that unmarried women who became pregnant in the
1940s, '50s and early '60s were considered immoral and bad, and that
adoption of the child was often forced on the mother, almost as an act of
revenge. Underlying the practice of adoption was a notion that in time
the wayward woman would find giving up her child a redemptive act.
When Jenny tried to put herself into her mother's head, that of a young
working-class woman of nineteen living in London in the 1950s, she
thought it possible that this "immoral" identity had stuck with Lily, the
more so because she herself had been adopted. Lily's withdrawal, Jenny
now tried to consider, might be a way for Lily to protect Jenny. Perhaps
Lily had worried that somehow she might soil Jenny's family and bring
disgrace upon them. Or there again, thought Jenny, now that she felt
free to explore this, perhaps Lily *did* believe she was immoral and bad,

and that her stealing would serve as a concrete expression of her bad-ness, an unmissable sign that Jenny and her goodness should stay away.

Speculating at a different level, Jenny recognized the great divide between their families, economically and by class. Jenny supposed that Lily had found her and Robert's relatively wealthy life hard to bear. They must have appeared squeaky clean compared with how Lily's family made ends meet.

The ransacking remained a mystery. There was no adequate expla-nation that Jenny could come up with. It was such a violation that she preferred to see it as the work of her half-brothers and of Mike, the missing photo albums notwithstanding. It was, Jenny posed, an expres-sion of some envy or rage they had toward her and Lily and the unique-ness of their connection. She fantasized that Lily was being silenced, defenseless against the rage of the three men. It was all too much to fathom. Jenny wished she were a novelist so that she could come up with a better ending.

But she was not and there was no better ending. She was destined to struggle with these questions until something changed or she found a further clue. For now, she had to sit with the realization that none of the ways she had used to try to understand the situation seemed satis-factory. The motivation seemed too thin, the explanations too simplis-tic, to do much more than put a band around her continuing questions.

I could see that it was hard for her, for a part of her wanted to be able to settle what had happened in her mind and in her heart. I could feel that impulse tug at me too, to find an explanation that would mit-igate the continuing shock and helplessness.

A set of rather more fanciful ideas came to my mind. I wondered whether Lily was indeed Jenny's biological mother or whether she and her men had serendipitously seized upon the letter from the adoption agency, concocted a plausible story and had "adopted" Jenny only to perpetrate the heist. It seemed unlikely yet it was not too hard to imagine Lily putting herself on a register for children looking for their biological mothers. Her surname was common enough, the years coin-cided with the adoption and the distance was useful for a fudging of details—such a proposition might appeal to a con artist. I concluded that my paranoia was probably just that: the legacy of doubts I had had during our first session when I had wondered whether Jenny might be so disturbed that she made the whole thing up, as well as my own near disbelief at what had happened. While there was no longer any question about the veracity of Jenny's story, I could not find an explanation within myself. I balked at what had happened. Naively I could not believe that Lily, given the chance to repair whatever bad feelings she might have had about herself, had been unable to choose heroism rather than villainy.

Of course I had "non-paranoid" and less naive thoughts too. The idea of Lily as a thief led me to speculate on what stealing can sometimes mean. It was possible that Lily had felt that Jenny was stolen from her at the home for unwed mothers and that now, nearly forty years on, it was all too late. She might have found that having restored what was once stolen was too much for her. She could not find a way to treasure Jenny, so she had found herself stealing from Jenny's home as though to negate the turn of events. I knew my speculations were wild but what Jenny had mentioned about Lily's Vancouver house being so crowded with goods, including unpacked ones,[4] had stayed with me. I wondered whether Lily was a compulsive shoplifter. Perhaps years of living with the theft of her baby, the lack of knowledge about her own biological parents and her possible helplessness in the face of it all had found emotional expression in taking goods that were not hers. Unopened packages can be the hallmark of a woman searching for what has been stolen from her and unable to use what she had appropriated in its place.

I realized that, like Jenny, I was searching for an explanation. A lack of comprehension can increase emotional distress of this kind, whereas understanding can hold the waves of hurt at an almost manageable level so that one is not entirely swamped. Jenny had already been submerged but was now climbing out of it. I felt great empathy for her wish that an understanding—a satisfactory understanding—could materialize.

Positioned next to my empathy was a sense that if I could let our impulses for explanation simply be, rather than rush to respond to them, we could find a way to help Jenny through this period. She had been able to unfreeze some of her feelings. She was not devoid of emotional resources. The awful discomfort she was now in could just about be tolerated.

As I shifted from wanting to find a plausible explanation to knowing that we could not and would not find one, I wanted to tell Jenny that not being able to find an account that could quiet what had been disturbed was part of what might help, but I could not find a way to do this that did not strike me as patronizing. It is one thing to experience the satisfaction that can come from recognizing that certain issues have to be kept alive as questions for a long time, that life means revising what we understand so that while certain things become clearer others become demonstrably less so, and it is quite another thing to talk in platitudes. Therapists have to watch what they say because it is not what they know that is so valuable, it is their capacity to enable others to find ways through to what might be useful for them. I knew I would be wrapping things up too neatly if I just said that Jenny might in time welcome the continuing questions. I hoped that through the way we had conducted our conversations she would be able to feel how it was possible to add, subtract and rework—even in mid-sentence—our reflections and that it was their mutability that made us alive.

But the inexplicability of the burglary was something Jenny would have to find a way to accept. Even though, for the moment, it sat there refusing to be digested. Mystery was now something to be recast rather than necessarily solved. Unlike the conventional detective story whose loose ends are orchestrated to come together, a therapy, an analysis, offers a different kind of resolution: one in which certainty gives way to tolerating the unanswerable, the unknowable or the mysterious. The questions continue to be asked but the answers may become less clear. The ability to hold on to the questions and to the mystery without foreclosure becomes a psychological achievement, a psychological development.

Jenny's traumatic loss marked the end of innocence. She was brought up with the moral values of the Sussex middle class: politeness, honesty, modesty, hard work and loyalty. Since childhood, her life had been a progression in which privilege increased as she got older. Her rites of passage from school to college, to partnership and mothering, had passed smoothly enough, confirming to her that good things happen to good people. Through her music she had found an expression of her passion and deep feelings.

Jenny had handled the loss of her parents with equanimity despite her grief, and nothing much had come along to disturb or disillusion her sense that her certainties were solid. The meeting with Lily in Vancouver confirmed her view that life was progress, that things that were troublesome could be resolved and that life had a certain fairness to it. All this was shattered in the aftermath of the ransacking. So contrary was it to Jenny's perception of the world that she had held herself frozen in shock against the horror and incomprehensibility of it. Now that Jenny had been able to approach the pain of her loss and rejection, we could go back to the task of confronting that shock.

To accept the shock Jenny had to come up against what remained unarticulated and unthought of since they had never been contested—her beliefs. In confronting the simplicity of her unquestioned beliefs about how the world operated, how people treated one another and how life was essentially just, she suffered a terrible loss of confidence. She felt adrift, uncertain how to categorize things, dislocated both in her life and in her mind because she could not make events fit into her existing categories of experience. Jenny's efforts to improve her community, to volunteer where she was required, rested on a belief system that drew a straight line from cause to effect. Now, in the latter part of our third session, moving from a state of innocence to one of disillusionment, she was distraught.

I, by contrast, felt hopeful for Jenny. Painful as disillusionment is, it is part of the process that forces maturity on us. It allows us to come out of our cocoons, to learn something new and find responses that augment us. True, the particular agony that had been visited on Jenny had never been mine, so it was easy for me to feel that in the end Jenny would be able to develop in ways she might never have dreamed of without this terrible thing happening to her. But in my work with people over the years, I had seen, beyond the aphorism, that disillusionment need not be only a disaster. I had witnessed individuals, forced out of their normal channels of responding and thinking, spurred on to develop in ways that offered more complexity and richness. If Jenny could find a way to accept what was incomprehensible, to hold on to the tension between wanting to understand and knowing that it was not possible to cleanly categorize what she had experienced, her emotional repertoire and her life might be profoundly enhanced.

It is one of the characteristics of development that the clarity we are encouraged to search for, and the skills we are taught when we are young to help us with life, our studies and our work, are the very things we need to surrender from time to time to allow another kind of development. Certain ways of knowing can imprison us. In offering channels for certainties, for modes of explanation involving rights and wrongs, they curtail a different kind of thought.

"I'm not sure how I'm supposed to go on now," Jenny said, looking at me expectantly. I took her words more as a summary of where she was in her life than as a question.

"I'm really not sure," she said a minute later.

"Yes, that's difficult," I said, making a comment that would give her the contact it seemed she was reaching for, while stopping myself before I said more. She needed to sit with what she was groping toward and feel supported in doing so, rather than have the homilies that were running through my head foisted on her. Of course I felt tempted to tell her that there was no blueprint, that for now it was a matter of recognizing that she was grappling with the limits of her explanatory powers in this her first personal encounter with the cruelty in human relationships, with life's harshness and the human struggle to come to terms with the limits of our power. But I knew that whatever I said would sound banal. Words would not offer much relief.

Jenny was too distressed and the moment of her acknowledging not knowing was too important. If she was to come through this experience with something from inside her, she needed to go through it and not be abandoned or spoken to in that moment. What felt potentially more useful was to hold on *with her* to her sense of "not sureness," underscoring in our quiet her loss of innocence. She did not know quite how to place herself. She felt vulnerable and somewhat helpless.

In the next two months we had met twice more and I had once again spoken with her doctor. Jenny had been to him because she wanted to wean herself off her pills. The three of us conferred; and it seemed the right decision. Jenny felt strengthened and robust enough now not to need medication. I looked forward to seeing her again.

Jenny was rather different from many of the people with whom I've sat in consultation whose angst has plagued them for years. Although she sounded quite crazy at the beginning of the first session, it was a situational craziness born of the pain of confusion of the recent events. The present trauma was not bouncing us back into a history of hidden distress. In fact her early family life had been good. She had been adopted at a week old, an unusually early time in the 1950s when babies frequently remained with their biological mothers for six weeks. However, in the case of private adoptions, enlightened doctors arranged for a speedier transfer of the baby to its adoptive parents and Jenny had been a wanted and much loved child who had grown up secure. What she was struggling with now was a fit subject for consultation.

Of course whatever she might have discovered about her birth mother would have disturbed the unconscious thoughts and fantasies that she, like other adopted children, had about her biological parentage. Most adopted children imagine or invent stories about their origins which have to be revised on meeting their actual parents or finding out something about them. But that apart, because Jenny had never suffered much beyond the "normal" range of self-doubt and because none of her certainties had evaporated, there was a way in which she was psychologically quite an innocent.

. . .

Theory told me that disillusionment is the price of entry into adulthood and a means to sustain psychological growth. In each psychological stage disillusionment propels or prepares the ground for the further development of the self. Looked at from the outside, progression seems to flow from the mastery of developmental milestones. From the inside, our experience is much more tortured and involves the struggle to find the capacity to absorb loss and disillusionment.

As babies we must give up the notion that we are the center of the universe. Then we move out of what analysts call the narcissistic phase of development and begin to recognize the presence of others. As toddlers we are again disillusioned as we begin to perceive that we are separate people, that those on whom we depend are not part of us but distinct others with their own intentions. We can ask or want but we cannot command what we think we need; we realize that not all our wishes can be met. Out of that disillusionment we experiment with our power. This is not only a moment of defeat but one of joy as we begin to inhabit our own will and a sense of being able to make things happen. From this derives our sense of agency, our ability to transform and act on and in situations.

The Freudian story of the oedipal phase brings us to our next great developmental disillusionment as we come to terms with the realization we cannot have our mother or our father—our first love objects—as our exclusive possession. We register, sometimes grudgingly, that she and he have other loves, interests, activities and loyalties. We feel the loss of our imagined union, adjust ourselves to the idea that we may not be at the center of our parents' preoccupations and are once again propelled outward, now beyond the family circle, to make new attachments.

As adolescents we grapple with disillusionment as the limits of our power are continually and humiliatingly enforced. We become determined that the world we create as adults will be less arbitrary and more of our making. When we are adults, broken hearts, disappointments at work, political events and illnesses disturb our illusions about our capacities to determine our lives. But with luck these shattered illusions do not limit our world but open it up for us, forcing us to be braver and bolder than we knew we could be. As parents, we suffer the disillusionment of not being able to make our children's lives the way we hope. We struggle continually with the conjunction between who our children are, the world they are facing and the limited ways we can have any influence. We are caught short by the realization that when we imagined ourselves as parents we saw ourselves with all the power we vested in our own parents. And so we finally come to understand that they were and were not as powerful as we thought.

These disillusionments are not the stuff of compromise or of deadening allegiance to conformism. Despite the conservatism a reading of Freud and many psychoanalytic writings can give rise to, the experience of disillusion is far from constraining. It is a way of developing in directions that were never before apparent.

Although I knew Jenny was suffering now as her worldview took more than a blow, I could sense in her the kind of vivacity that comes from being able to tolerate ambiguity, confusion and a not knowing quite what to make of a situation. She could now allow something to be unfinished. I smiled inwardly about the pleasures she would come to know as this experience matured her. Bob Dylan's words about being so much older then and so much younger than that now sang through my mind. Through her disillusionment Jenny was acquiring a flexible openness toward life that come from the experience of engaging with its contradictoriness.

When I opened the door to Jenny for our sixth and last session, I encountered a woman with dignity. She said it had been a sobering and important two months. Lily continued to elude her and she continued to hope that she might succeed in contacting her. But her focus had switched. She was now fascinated by her responses to things.

"I feel as if I've slept through my life until now. Well, that's not quite right because I've enjoyed it, especially the children and Robert and my music, but there's a way in which it was just there . . . I feel I was such a naive, protected person. . . It wasn't a purposeful, aware, alive life." She paused.

"I could never understand what those words meant before; I always tended to sneer a bit when people talked about enlightenment and awareness. I think that I just didn't have a clue that I was living in such a limited way.

"After the last meeting," she went on, "I was terribly worried about my marriage. I wasn't sure whether it would survive. No, that's too dramatic. It's more that I hadn't even realized that there were things in it that I couldn't stand and that I'm changing and Robert isn't. I had a real crisis."

This did not sound quite like a summing up but more like the prelude to a whole new consultation or at least another few sessions. Jenny seemed to have so much to say and the words to say it with. "Robert's one-note response to the Lily situation frustrated me. I didn't want to just hear his anger. It was wrong. For me, that is. I felt I knew more than he knew, that there are lots of different feelings—hurt, bewilderment, rejection—and that by accepting them all you don't cancel out a part of yourself. And I wanted to convince him."

She paused before going on, as though she were ordering her process rather than ordering the narrative. "Well, that was hopeless. He didn't want to know. There was a great rift between us. We'd always been very close and this whole crisis with Lily threatened our happiness. Anyway, then I realized that I was trying to change *Robert,* just as I was trying to make the ending with Lily different. I wasn't accepting the fact that we were having different responses. It probably doesn't sound significant to you—or perhaps it does. I think I was trying to make Robert more the way I wanted him to be because I couldn't make Lily the way I wanted her to be. I was transferring my unfinished feelings for Lily onto my marriage."

Jenny talked almost nonstop and I very much liked what she had been able to do with her insight. She told me how she had felt up against a brick wall for two weeks in terrible despair. Then she had woken up, probably after a prescient dream, she said, and realized she would have to let go of an illusion she had always had that if she could see something, or if what she judged was a better way, then that was what would or should prevail.

Now she was struggling with the idea that her insight into herself might not be of use to Robert, helpful as it was to her.

"I'm not a pushy person," she continued, "but I've always felt that life progresses and what is better always comes to the top. I suppose this whole experience has been one in which I'm beginning to realize that right is often irrelevant. It's a small thing and maybe nobody but me would notice the difference. God knows I've often gone along with Robert's wishes. But I know that this is very different. I wasn't going along with him or what he wanted, I was seeing him as different to me. I had to struggle to see my opinions and feelings as being just as valid as his opinions and feelings, rather than trying to convince him because mine were so strong. Somehow that tiny change has been enormous.'

She looked at me to see whether I understood the significance of the shift for her. I was thinking that she was talking about the process of separation, of seeing herself and her thoughts and desires as having an integrity of their own whether or not they were confirmed by others. She did not need to have them validated by Robert. She did not need to persuade him. She did not need things to be as she wanted them to be, convenient and satisfying though that might be. She accepted the idea that she was a little part of life and that her surrender of what therapists like to call her omnipotence allowed her to resituate herself and her responses. Meeting Lily and suffering and surviving that terrible disillusionment had allowed her to develop.

"If I've understood you right, you've been pleased to notice that even though you wanted one kind of outcome you've found a way to accept the fact that the world isn't quite the way you've construed it," I responded.

"Yes, that's right," Jenny continued. "I think when the Lily business happened, I couldn't accept it at all. It was easier for Robert because he could be rational and furious. He was in his aggressive lawyer mode. It was something different, deeper for me. Everything I relied on had evaporated. I was so scared. Terrified, actually." She cried a bit, then smiled.

"I've been through a revolution, you know. A quiet one that my neighbors wouldn't detect from the outside but I'm not the same me anymore. Or rather I am me but with something added. I'm beginning to taste something new. I don't know how to say what I want to say. I'm even hearing more in the music. Do you understand?"

I thought I might. If I made a bridge into my very different experience, I did understand how enriching her subtle shift was. I reflected on my youth when life was more clear-cut. I loved the decisiveness and certainty and the sense that we could remake everything the way we knew it should be. It was exhilarating and, as I see now, a necessary part of coming of age. But it was age specific. It did not hold its charms indefinitely and as I had aged I had come upon the pleasures of complexity and the relief one experiences when certainty is given up about those things which it is not possible to be certain about.

Jenny had held tight because she was frightened. She was able to relinquish her grip when she could allow her feelings to flow. Her husband found relief in dismissing Lily and her brood as beyond the pale. With the forcefulness of his response, Jenny had become further isolated until she was able to feel a confidence in naming her own very complex responses. The violent polarities of thought that affect so many people when they are young had never captured Jenny. She had not needed them. Until recently her life had been unquestioned and content. Nevertheless her encounter with Lily had pushed her into a frozen position for a time. When she was able to unfreeze processes that had never been activated in her before, she got going. If that was the kind of thing that Jenny was getting at, then I felt I did know.

The Impossibility of Sex

I T STARTED OFF pretty alarmingly. No sooner were they through the door than Maria started shouting. It was the shrieking of someone in terrible anguish putting her case before me, for that moment the judge and jury of emotional life. Carol, the accused, emanating stillness, sat on the sofa next to Maria. One white, one black; one calm, one wild—mirror images of each other. I could not tell whether Carol's stillness would continue or whether she would be drawn into an escalating fury and the whole room would take off. I would have to wait and see.

Some couples invite you into the center of their relationship by having their arguments in front of you. Some show the sourness between them. With others there is contempt that often conceals deep disappointment. The first session can be like a tableau, capturing the essential elements of the couple's relationship.

Maria's shouting was extreme and compelling. Such fierce rage could signify some terrible sense of injustice, some hurt too heavy to be quieted. Was she coming to therapy to make sure it was heard and addressed? It took more than a few minutes to make out the context of her rage. Deception, betrayal and abuse were the condemnatory words that Maria threw at her lover, her ire increasing with each word.

I am not a therapist who is inclined to see the expression of anger as necessarily positive in itself so, although I was looking for a place to intervene, I needed to wait, to take the measure of what was occurring. As the anger reverberated across the room I looked at the two women facing me. They were both elegant. Carol was tall and sat with a very straight back. She had fine features, a peachy white skin and softly curling shoulder-length hair held with a couple of ebony- and ivory-colored combs. She was dressed in a stylish black suit. Her nails were manicured. A luxuriously supple deep brown wallet-type briefcase leaned against her left leg. She had the style of an architect or a designer whose clothing and looks radiated an unworked-at confidence. I guessed that she was in her late thirties. Maria was also very stylish and beautiful. She had tiny features, short-cropped curly black hair, chocolate-colored skin. The casual but elegant bohemian flavor to her dusty-green cotton jacket, beige boots and brown linen pants went along with her free expressiveness in the room. Maria was an African-American, first-generation educated. Her clothes made me think she was a poet, artist, publisher or writer. I could not quite peg her age but I had the sense that she was younger than Carol, in her early thirties.

They were a striking couple. I could have kept my eyes on them for a long time without losing interest. While Maria continued to shriek, Carol remained silent. I was taken by her stillness. Where did such sphinx-like calm come from? Was there a division of emotions in this couple—Maria angry and Carol still? Were Maria's expressiveness and Carol's quiet a part of what drew them to each other? How was Carol able to accept the rage that was directed at her? Was this how they usually were or had the therapy session skewed their stances and pushed them to opposite poles?[1]

After several minutes it looked as if Maria's frustration would propel her to shake Carol violently. Interceding at that moment, lest it was the stillness that increased Maria's rage and my silence was now adding to it, I simply said, "I can see how terribly upset and angry you are, Maria. But I wonder if the two of you could back up a bit to tell me what's brought you here."

Earlier in the week Carol had outlined to me on the telephone some of what was bringing them to seek couple therapy at this point. They had been together three and a half years. Four months earlier a friendship Carol had with Sonya, a university lecturer some ten years older, had developed into an affair. Maria felt threatened and upset. She thought she was about to lose Carol, although Carol insisted she did not want their relationship to end. Carol was trying to work her way out of her sexual relationship with Sonya but it was still causing both Carol and Maria tremendous pain. They had decided on couple therapy because they needed a place to talk through what was happening.

When I open the door to a new couple I never know what I shall encounter. Is this a couple who have come to try to stay together? Is this a couple who have come to break up? Is this a couple who are no longer able to feel love for one another but are entwined in ways that make separation impossible to contemplate?

What kind of challenges and dilemmas will this couple present me with? How can I be sure to take sufficient account of each of them individually, along with seeing them as a couple? Can I be even-handed, sufficiently empathic to each one, not hearing their relationship through the filter of my own relationship and the relationships of my friends? How can I ensure that an unconscious moral filter does not distort how I listen and what I hear when our values are dissimilar?

Carol and Maria began to talk about the crisis that had precipitated the great anger and distress I had witnessed. There were a number of appeals from Maria for me to affirm how wronged she had been but as Carol talked and showed her pain the dominant feeling shifted to one of confusion and bruising. Although they were in difficulty as a couple, there was a vibrancy and aliveness between them. It was clear that this was a relationship that neither was about to relinquish. The energy that passed between them was charged. It was passionate, argumentative, insistent and urgent. I began to think of Carol's affair not as an attempt to leave Maria but as her way of trying to address something that was not right in their relationship. I wondered what it was.

For a year prior to Carol's affair with Sonya, sex between Carol and Maria had been sporadic. For the first two years of their relationship, their sexual life had been blissful, imaginative and highly erotic. Then it had tapered off. Life—going to work, shopping, cooking, dealing with relatives, making social plans, arranging for the plumber or who would be home for Chloe, Carol's seven-year-old—funneled their daily contact into the pedestrian. Dissatisfactions—the normal kind that come up when ecstasy gives way to the business of ordinary life—began to surface. Differences and pressures arose. The demise of their sexual passion had a certain logic.

Many couples experience a similar change. Sexual intimacy, once irresistible and exciting—*the* way to connect and communicate—turns humdrum. Sex becomes less frequent, less urgent, and moves from being an opening up and exploration by two people of one another to becoming a block between them, an act surrounded by expectations, disappointment, worry or routine. Sex is now a hurdle to get over rather than an exquisite exchange. It is almost impossible to imagine that the person in bed next to you was once sexually irresistible. Impossible to remember the time when the way her face looked in repose, or when she smiled or walked into a room was an erotically loaded moment. And so it was for Carol and Maria. They were partners but rarely lovers. By day each hoped for an erotic nighttime tryst with the other but, engulfed as they were by the business of living, the contact failed to materialize. Despite the story they told themselves about it, both of them felt a sense of loss, anxiety and some despair. It was not surprising that Maria became very upset when Carol got involved with Sonya. The affair had all the hallmarks of how

Carol and Maria had come together. It challenged the idea that it was okay that sex had disappeared between them.

Perplexingly and dramatically, exciting, lustful and irresistible sex had come back into their lives with Carol's affair. It had prompted (as these things can) the kind of crisis in their relationship which meant that making love was suddenly very compelling, very exciting and very significant. There was renewed dynamism between Carol and Maria. Their love, desire and commitment to one another took center stage. Gone was the dismaying near-celibacy of the previous year in which a cozy, warm and supportive ambiance seemed to have banished passion. Drama and danger appeared and with it sexual passion.

It was Maria, whose more open, sexual and sexy manner seemed to go along with her rage and her demand for justice, who articulated the confusions from her side. During the period of relative celibacy, she felt as if her femininity and attractiveness had been consigned to the reject pile. Carol's affair had ignited the passion between them but it had still made Maria feel that she was unwanted. She had been wobbly and angry and had veered between thinking she could understand it and a feeling of being used.

For Carol, her affair had, paradoxically, highlighted how much she valued and wanted Maria. Since she had taken up with Sonya, Carol had found Maria fantastically sexually attractive in a way that she had not during the previous year. Maybe it was inevitable, Carol ruminated. By threatening the relationship she saw Maria as a separate and highly desirable person, and no longer part of her. Their closeness had made them too much of a unit, absorbing their strong personalities and eclipsing their individuality.

Carol was puzzled by why this should be and although I had some thoughts that might illuminate this problem which can beset couples, I stayed quiet while I listened to Maria to see what she made of all this.

Maria was less measured. Her rage was still rampant as she accused Carol of always "looking for the exotic because that's what makes her feel alive." Sonya, she complained, was "Carol's latest quest to charge herself up by getting close to 'ethnics.'"

Sonya was Asian, Maria African-American and Carol was upper-middle-class English with a twist. She was a Jew from an anglicized and assimilated family, educated at a private school. She was confused, Maria suggested, about where she belonged. Something about cleaned-up and educated "otherness"—Maria was Harvard-educated and Sonya went to Oxford—charmed and attracted Carol. It was part slumming, part trying to find her place. She found other misfits with whom she could brave and shock the British class system.

Although on the face of it, Maria and Carol's views could have been interpreted as antagonistic positions, they seemed rather similar. Both pointed to the importance of separateness as an important feature of an alive sexual life for them. Both linked difference with the erotic. Both equated excitement with otherness. I did not rush to explore the similarities because I was not quite clear where the therapy was headed or what they wanted from it. In individual therapy one has the luxury of following whatever makes sense in the moment. Stumbling over whatever is at hand and straying wherever one might be led are features of therapeutic inquiry, so that conversations in therapy have different parameters from those of ordinary conversations. Working with a couple demands that the therapist be more aware of what is wanted by both of them and this can force a kind of definition. Beyond the report of Carol's infidelity, I was not sure whether they were in therapy ostensibly to help Carol give up her lover, to help Maria accept Sonya or to discuss the weaknesses in their sexual relationship or their relationship in general.

The session had started with Maria expressing her hurt and rage at Carol, while Carol took her punishment. Now I needed them to clarify what hopes they had about what might emerge from the sessions. In a quiet but authoritative voice Carol stated clearly that she wanted to try to stop seeing Sonya and that the therapy was part of her mission to do so. She was committed to Maria, wanted to stay with her, and she wanted to repair the hurt. Maria said that she wanted to stay together too but she did not feel she could go on unless Carol guaranteed that she would not see Sonya at all and would accept that she had wronged her. Maria wanted to be able to trust Carol again.

Trust is one of the most widely used and yet ill-defined words in discussions of relationships. It has great weight attached to it but it is also most delicate. The hurt of broken trust often propels an individual to seek therapy when a relationship ends or is endangered. By contrast, a frequently expressed sentiment at the beginning of a therapy is that the person feels safe in therapy because she feels she can trust the therapist. Although there is a way in which, of course, I understand what this means—therapy is confidential, it is dedicated to understanding and making comprehensible, and so on—at another level the use of trust as an idea is ironic, for the process of therapy reveals how very difficult it can be to trust. We may trust at one level but often when trust has been eroded what we see is its fragility.

Not uncommonly a central aspect of the therapy relationship is the investigation of how great the impediments to trust are on an unconscious level. Individuals find themselves encountering their own resistances and hindrances to trust even when they believe they are trusting and when they most need to be so for their own development. They then discover that they do not easily surrender or trust another to care or to hold something precious and meaningful for them. Early disappointment which has gone unrecognized and unacknowledged means that most people have a store of repeated hurtful experiences bowing their notion of trust in ways that they are often unaware of. People crave trust and believe that they enter new relationships with their capacity to trust intact. It is more often the case that they consciously suspend their distrust, for when their trust is threatened it soon collapses, revealing how tangential or fallible it is.

So Maria's aim to trust Carol again, and her wish for Carol to take responsibility for having "wronged" her, meant that we would have to clarify what trust signified to her to see whether what she wanted was viable. How might she be able to trust Carol again? What could Carol do? What did Carol need to guarantee? What would trusting Carol require of Maria? Who had responsibility for that? Was Maria's continuing distrust of Carol a way of staying in the hurt and in feelings of betrayal?

Although psychoanalysis can seem excessively laborious in its examination of the commonplace, its questioning of everyday ideas, such as trust, allows us to understand the subtlety of our desires, conflicts, feelings and concerns. The kind of reflective conversation that marks out psychoanalytic conversation depends upon questioning the habitual and the understood to clarify, extend and make sure that we portray more accurately what we long for. This is not so much navel-gazing—the mendacious term used to dismiss the study of the subjective—as it is a different kind of discourse on human experience and intersubjectivity. Through examining in depth the issues that arise when individuals, couples or families are in difficulty, we extend our understanding of what human relationships are about for all of us.

Maria complained about the fracture in their relationship: she had lost an unqualified belief in its trustworthiness and in Carol. She worried that she would never again be able to fully relax with Carol or quell her need to be alert to every nuance of Carol's interest beyond her. An examination of trust led us to hear how much distrust she evinced, how dismayed she was about feeling unsure of Carol, and how fearful she was that what had happened between Sonya and Carol had irrevocably altered the shape of their future relationship. Of course the latter was true. There was no way to press the delete key on the affair as if it—and the accompanying betrayal and hurt—had never happened.

Both Carol and Maria experienced some relief in having this stated. It is often an unarticulated wish of the couple visiting a therapist that she will be able to achieve what the couple has been unable to do: to restore the relationship to what it was, as though it had just fallen off the shelf, broken into pieces and now required simple gluing. My naming the obvious—that is, exposing the fantasy in Carol and Maria's minds, and dispelling the myth of an easy repair—made it possible to go forward. Not pretending was important. They both knew very well that the events had changed both them and their relationship.

But then we had to avoid being ensnared by the attitude that the affair had changed everything. We needed to avoid encouraging Maria to become wedded to being a victim and Carol to carry endless guilt. It would be better to see whether understanding the affair—why it had happened and what it meant—could allow both Carol and Maria to get out of the grip of an emotional policing so that they could come together again. Carol's declaration that she would not do it again could assuage one part of their joint distress but it could not make right what had gone wrong. It was that tension and the short-term insolubility of that predicament that needed to be accepted.

An enormous amount of ground had been covered in this first meeting. We now had a basis for couple therapy. What had started with a shriek had turned into an agenda: how to trust and how to understand the psychological factors that had led to the demise and then to the resuscitation of their sexual life and what might evolve from that. We agreed to meet weekly.

SOME MONTHS later I noticed a change in the character of the sessions. There was an excitement and an intensity about them akin to the atmosphere that a new love affair can bring. Thinking about seeing Carol and Maria brought a smile to my face. I looked forward to them as though with their entry into the room something vibrant was about to happen.

Their lives together were a triumph over their upbringing. Carol, essentially unparented, raised by a nanny in London and sent to boarding school at an early age, as though to efface everything Jewish about her, had connected with Maria, brought up with her four siblings on the North Shore of New York's Long Island, where her father worked as a carpenter and her mother as a schoolteacher. Neither woman would have predicted that she could have crossed the class, ethnic and national divides as strikingly as both did. Ten years earlier Maria would never have dreamed of living in London. But a combination of the lesbian culture in which they circulated and Carol's work in environmental design had opened up the transatlantic world for them. They were women of their time, free to work, to enter social territories that had previously been off limits, to be more or less open about their sexuality, to map their own lives. They inhabited their lives rather than merely adapted to the roles assigned to them.

Sonya by now had begun to disappear as *the* issue. She had become absorbed into their extended circle of friends and this made her less threatening to Maria. The topic of trust was being addressed. I now had a fuller sense of the personalities I had been introduced to in the first session and it was very easy to be taken with them both. They were extremely attractive, articulate women with appetites for their interesting work—Carol in environmental design and Maria in landscape architecture. Much of what they were struggling with in their lives went to the heart of the preoccupations of women today. They loved their work and found it very meaningful but they did not want it to overtake them. Because they were women brought up in the shadow of a time when being supported economically within marriage was still an option, they battled internally with the conflicting choices still available for women of their age—that they should be taken care of and have a level of economic reliance on another, that they should take care of the emotional and domestic needs of others, that they should be independent and not need another or, conversely, that they wanted to relinquish the independence that they had achieved.

Conflicts such as these threaded through their lives and were mediated by the flexibility in their relationship. They struggled with the issues of dependency and independence, with nurturing one another and being nurtured, with an awareness of women breaking new ground for themselves. That they both made a very reasonable income helped them escape from relying on roles that were predictable and fixed. They both parented and were thinking about raising another child along with Carol's seven-year-old daughter, Chloe. They were domestic and could more or less do the household repair work that came up.

Carol remained the calmer of the two and Maria the more volatile but they had a deep sensitivity to one another and could, in the therapy room, listen to the other talk about her experience of the difficulties between them. I was impressed by their awareness of each other's point of view. Their upbringing as girls, which, despite the huge difference in backgrounds, had laid stress on their caring for, tuning into and attending to the needs of others, had made them, as women, acutely aware of one other's desires. Often that aspect of a woman's psychology can be crippling, expressed at the expense of a certain self-development, but in this instance it was deeply enabling.[2] It helped them to hear one another, to be empathic and thoughtful, and if neither was feeling threatened at that moment it made the complexity of each of their feelings able to be accepted.

One might have thought that in this happy state of affairs things were going so well between them (and had moved so far on from their initial agenda) that we could well stop the therapy. But I had the sense, not yet put into words, that there was something in our threesome that was energizing to them and their relationship. I had a hunch or, I should say rather, a whiff of a feeling that if the therapy were to stop the aliveness between them might evaporate or the energy that had been generated between the three of us might implode negatively on the two of them. My presence *as a third party both inside and yet apart from their relationship* seemed important and it was as though this third axis had remagnetized the relationship for them erotically and emotionally.

The process was not unfamiliar to me. Colleagues working on women's psychology had drawn a picture of the particular issues which can beset women when they are involved in intimate relationships which plunge them into conflicts and difficulties around sameness and difference, regardless of the sex of the other. An intimacy that is blissfully satisfying, which starts from openness, understanding and recognition, can become derailed by a fear of the very charms, opinions, thoughts and sensibilities that drew the two people together initially. What was once charming, intriguing and different is by the nature of its contrast potentially threatening. What was once invigorating induces a fear: *if this person is so different from me how will they accept and love me?* And the sharp edges of difference can rub down, creating a relationship which is now sustained by those aspects of the two individuals that meld together; the former pleasure of surprise sacrificed for an ambience which can be cloying and suffocating. Indeed there is now also an irritation with the different habits or pace of the other. Continuity and seamlessness are sought so that that which was the other's is now one's own. That which was individual now stretches to accommodate the other. That which does not fit now annoys.

When two women are together the sense of being understood and the sense of similarity are emphasized. For Carol and Maria this sameness created a psychological merger, sufficiently acute to need an other to break through it. Unlike male-female couples who can unconsciously use their gender to symbolize the difference between them, Carol and Maria needed an other, someone outside the relationship but within its emotional field, to demarcate the two of them.

Such theoretical underpinnings which structured my thoughts made me question whether I might now be being "used" by Carol and Maria to break through whatever had deadened their sexual life together during that celibate year. I do not mean "used" in a pornographic, erotic sense; I mean rather I felt I had been assigned a role in their relationship.

I felt I had been designated the *other* and in doing so in a professional sense I had also done so in a psychological sense. By being interested in both of them as individuals and as a couple, I had temporarily interrupted the merged nature of their attachment to one another, prying them apart and separating them out from the indivisible couple they had become before rendering them back to one another as exciting individuals. It was in this way that I wondered whether Carol's affair had played an important role in saving their relationship. Now, it seemed, I was playing a role like Sonya's, although my being there for both of them and their relationship rather than as Carol's special friend had changed the equation.

I was reluctant to share these thoughts with Carol and Maria at this point because I had a lot of sifting through to do for myself. Were my thoughts simply an easy theoretical construct based on working with many women? Was I really an other for them or had I fallen into their romance, joining the now revived vibrant relationship that they had created? Was I longing to be part of the closeness that emanated from them? Certainly I had very close female friends and treasured my friendships. But the idea that I wished to join their relationship did not really resonate for me because my own female friendships were deeply sustaining and an important enriching part of my daily life.

Was I being asked to be the third party, customarily understood in psychoanalytic theory to represent the more distant parent, the oedipal father who breaks up the entwined relationship between mother and daughter and who, through his masculinity, enables the daughter to make her transition to heterosexual genital love? To be sure, I was the third party, but this seemed too hackneyed and predictable an interpretation. If I were the other, the oedipal figure, then I needed to ask for whom? Was I the outsider to the couple or the outsider to the individuals?

Was I the exciting other? As a therapist available only fifty minutes once a week, encouraging them to open up and discuss their difficulties, while conveying a sense of being able to manage them, my stance did share something with the slightly distant but potentially tantalizing, oedipally wooing father. But then again this interpretation failed to reflect women's psychology as I had come to know it over more than twenty years of practice. For what many girls and women seek, whatever their sexual orientation, is a relationship with a woman who can be involved with and close to them without being merged. That women seek this in men and are often sorely disappointed is no secret. That women seek it from one another but then falter on encountering each other's pull to merge is one of the hidden aspects of women's psychology that a gender-conscious ear within psychotherapy has been able to ascertain. [3]

From whence came this need? What was it about the constraints and pressures, the unmet psychological needs that mothers brought to their relationships with

their daughters—which were themselves a development of the mothers' relation-
ships with their own mothers—that left this particular shape to girls' psychol-
ogy? Why was it that daughters (like their mothers before them) were often
stranded, longing for, but not able to create for themselves, clean, uncomplicated
attachments? How could daughters free themselves from the emotional fastening
which had bound mothers to daughters and daughters to mothers through the
generations in a crippling merged attachment? How could women avoid repro-
ducing similar merged dynamics in other intimate relationships?

We want love free of impingement. When we fall in love we imagine that we
are creating a relationship on a virgin canvas. But the pigment of our early rela-
tionships (with our mother in particular) traces its way through our adult love
affairs and stains the present. We find ourselves merged with our partner so that
our individuality now encompasses them. We deeply affect one another so that
the other's anxieties, hopes and desires are experienced not as those of a separate
person but as part of us. We cannot help but react. Our emotional responses
become entwined and there is a blurring of boundaries. We might not quite
know where we begin and end, whose emotions belong to whom. We have incor-
porated the other into our sense of self.

While women in heterosexual relationships are often able to "use" the differ-
ent gender of their male partners to create a sense of difference, for women with
women partners the need to differentiate has to be faced more squarely and it is
sometimes through the introduction of an other that the need for a sense of dif-
ference is addressed.

Considering myself as the exciting or self-contained other, I chuckled
to myself. God knows, no one is less exciting than the diligent analytic
worker in the consulting room. But by the processes of transfer and
transference to the therapist, perhaps I was having visited on me the
sense that I could fulfill this role as the outsider for Carol and Maria
and in so doing break apart the merged aspects of their attachment to
enable them to enjoy each other's individuality once again. Simply by
accepting them as individuals but also as a couple rather than trying to
cleave them apart, their sense of themselves as individuals with their
own uniqueness was restored.

I was easier with this idea of what might be creating the warm feelings between us than I was with the reductive oedipal interpretation.

Carol and Maria's closeness had brought about the unexpected hazard that intimacy poses. In becoming intimate and drawing on each other's love, support and acceptance, they had *found and strengthened* themselves as individuals. Their talents, wants and desires were reflected and appreciated by one another, and their concerns and wishes respected. They had healed some of their childhood hurts. They had grown well beyond the constraints that had faced them. But that very medium of growth, the love, acceptance and closeness within the couple, had produced the contradictory sense that they had also *lost* themselves as individuals. They had become a couple rather than two distinct people connected in a relationship. I was beginning to think that they avoided sex because, paradoxically, it brought them closer together than they could psychologically handle now that they knew each other so well. Could it be that they felt their individual identities would disappear altogether if they were so sexually and psychologically open to one another? For women sexuality, with its powerful metaphors of melting and melding, is often a way of dissolving barriers. But what if you were too close already? Would it then become psychologically dangerous?

Here too there is a gender difference, at least insofar as it is expressed in my therapy practice. While women find their identity and sense of self initially confirmed through recognition and similarity, men often find their identity through the confirmation of difference or separateness. In sexual intimacy, connection is primary for women. Many of the men who have talked with me about what sex means for them, say, on the other hand, that while connection is part of what occurs in intimate sexual contact, another equally powerful aspect of the sexual encounter is a reassuring confirmation of a sense of feeling their 'me-ness,' their potency and their separateness.[4]

When Carol and Maria first were lovers, not yet creators of a shared orbit but individuals who had to stretch across the space between them to create a shared intimacy, sex was their way of being close. The sexual imprint that Carol and Maria left on one another's bodies transformed each of them physically, often leaving them aching for reconnection. With their bodies opened up in this way, each one felt herself to be both less *and* more herself without the other. This curious dynamic often accompanies love. One feels enriched and expanded by love and its erotic expression and yet somewhat bereft when apart because one has now become dependent on the other physically and emotionally for a sense of completeness. Carol and Maria's erotic bond and the way it marked each of their bodies filled the space between time spent together. It spoke of their need for one another. Before they had committed themselves to each other and lived together, the play of their bodies took the weight of their intimacy.

In time their lives braided together in a close weave of intimate activity. Sex was no longer *the* intimate moment. Carol and Maria were intimate when they cooked, they were intimate when they looked at a picture together, they were intimate when they invited friends over. They were so close that squabbling or disagreeing became a way of asserting their individuality. And there was something else too. So much was known about one by the other, and so much was created together, that sex between them became almost too much. To make love with each another, to stand emotionally and physically naked, full of desire and love for each other, was overwhelming.

Perfunctory sex could occur, the easy coupling of two people familiar with one another's bodies and preferences. But if they added to their daily contact the kind of sexual intimacy they had had at the beginning of their relationship—where they had looked at and seen each other, exchanged their hungers for self-revelation and contact, for pleasing and knowing—then they had, if not an explosive situation, a situation they were not sure they could contain.

Why this should be for Carol and Maria and for so many other couples in committed relationships is something of a conundrum.

• • •

*While we tend to take for granted the idea that sexual intimacy fades because of
the familiarity of the known, this explanation falls short. It may make superficial sense but it is not convincing. For while some activities pale after being
repeated because they depend for their charge on pure risk (such as parachuting
or bungee jumping), intimate sexual exchange is initially enhanced through
repetition as people feel more comfortable exposing their most private feelings
and desires as a way of getting to know one another better. Bodily desires unfold
together and it is the revealing and authentic nature of the encounter that
makes it exciting and deeply fulfilling. Of course there is a risk involved and
undoubtedly that is part of the gestalt. But what goes hand in hand with the
emotional risk of opening oneself up, discovering the other and rediscovering
oneself with the other, is the repeated sexual encounter.*

*In many activities, whether solo or with others, such as hearing or playing
music, eating new foods or playing sports, their repetition increases the pleasure.
Familiarity is satisfying and the activity is sought after rather than avoided. So
it is worth pondering a bit more deeply about why sex, once a stunning jewel in
a relationship, might be avoided after a time. What are the factors in the individual and in the couple that lead to a period of ennui in their sexual life?*

The downturn in Carol and Maria's sexual life occurred eighteen
months to two years into their relationship. Although there is no evidence to confirm that this is anything but a chance occurrence, the reg-
ularity with which this time frame has popped up anecdotally in my
clinical practice has been striking. It has led me to wonder whether the
"life cycle" of erotic intimacy in a committed couple mirrors something almost pre-verbal, pre-cognitive as we know it, about our memory of and relationship to intimacy itself. When two people begin to
get close, they withdraw into a private space, create themselves as a
couple and then reintegrate themselves as a couple into the ordinary
things of life.

*We know intimacy first with our mother or with whoever first assumes that com-
mitted responsibility for us. Before we had language, our ways of communicat-*

ing were physical and gestural. Held and suckled in an intensely physical relationship, sensual exchange and attention to bodily needs were the ways in which we expressed and received love. Our mother, or the mothering person, was our whole world, the beacon around which we revolved. Everything—the words we learned, the movements we understood, the sights that were interpreted to us and the responses to our initiatives—was expressed within this ambit. By about eighteen months, we had the ability to toddle and some words to communicate with others. We could briefly leave our caregiver's side without distress and taste things on the edge of her orbit. Our world was now separating itself from the physical intimacy of infancy in which every nuance, every desire (whether heeded or not), was expressed in the physical ambience of mother and child.

Between eighteen months and two years, the child is coming to know herself as a subject, an "I," with a beginning and an end and a relationship to other subjects, what Margaret Mahler has called "the psychological birth of the human infant."5 Of course, this is not an entirely discrete process. As the analyst and infant researcher Daniel Stern has shown so beautifully, very young babies are well able to perceive others, to register the intricacies of their comings and goings and the emotional nuance of their relationships. But this knowing is in essence visceral, sensual and self-referring. The infant is unable to see the others who tend and relate to her as subjects in their own right, with their own needs and desires which lie beyond the baby's. Rather, the others are seen as consorts to the baby's needs, in this sense as the baby's objects.

In the baby's mind the link between her needs and those of others is not thought to be differentiated before eighteen months. Indeed, the magic of babyhood lies in the baby's illusion that what the baby requires is what the other, the caregiver, wishes to meet. Desire itself may not be distinguished from the act of receiving for the baby. For what the baby wants is what is responded to.

The disillusion of this idea is a crucial developmental step we all take in our journey toward personhood. As we recognize the fallibility of those on whom we depend, so we recognize the individual nature of our desire and with it our limits and the limits of our power. That recognition spurs the post-nursing baby to find other sources to amplify her emotional nourishment. She turns beyond the infant-caregiver couple to others—adults, peers, siblings—and this development now draws in other and varied relationships which are less intense and less private, more mutual and less asymmetrical.

In adult romance leading to deep intimacy and erotic love, a process with some parallels seems to occur. Touched in highly personal ways, we retreat with the loved one, become cocooned with the other and find ourselves anew. We imagine that we are "reborn."

When we have been sumptuously bathed in that wash of giving and receiving love, we feel filled up enough and sufficiently secure to reach outside—like the toddler—to see how the wider world engages. With this endeavor, sex is inevitably reformulated. The sexual relationship of the couple can continue to be their private language designating the place of intimacy, or emotional refueling. It can be the exclusive activity that demarcates the couple's relationship from other relationships. It can be the act which implies ownership of or attachment to the other person. But, equally, the sexual relationship can be reversed from its former position and become a withdrawal from intimacy, an activity in which we are not so much reaching toward and revealing ourselves to the other as hiding and retreating.

Why should this be? Why should what has been so precious now become problematic, pedestrian or disappointing? If sexual intimacy has, as one of its elements, invoked for the individuals a re-creation of the emotional and physical intimacy of early life, does the survival of an erotic sexual relationship require a particular personal history? Does it require an early intimate relationship in which adventure outside the nursing couple was encouraged by the mother so that attachment and interest elsewhere does not diminish or threaten the eroticism or the intimacy of the couple?

While we might not be able to explain adequately how sexual intimacy becomes so dangerous between people who know each other well, we can use this parallel of separation-individuation—the toddler's emotional development— to reflect on. It might, if we hold the question in mind, help us move some way forward to understand why the one-to-one intimacy is spurned.

This was what Carol had alluded to when she wondered whether a deepening of their love had evicted the passion. It was not that they were less in love. If anything, Carol said to a reassured Maria, she was more in love with her and more committed to her. Lack of love was not the issue.

I thought that what Carol might be getting at had something to do with the dissolving of personal boundaries that sexual intimacy can create. Maria and Carol's sexual and emotional intimacy created a sense of psychological fluidity between them. It had bounced both women, I thought, into a state of merger simulating an aspect of their early childhood experiences. Or, to put it another way, it had created intimacy in the way in which they had both first experienced it.

While sexual intimacy was gratifying in the early part of their relationship as an intimacy between two adult people, with the advent of aspects of a psychological merger between Carol and Maria, it was as though they had lost something. The merger psychically regressed them, effacing the other. There was then, in a sense, no other to make love with or to. Sex, in the state of merger (which it paradoxically creates), is masturbatory rather than communicative and connective.

I thought of ways of trying to explain this rather curious phenomenon to them. The theoretical clarity it gave me would not necessarily be meaningful for them. I was sure they could see how two had become one and how they then needed an other, an outsider, to become two again, but I was not sure whether this was an adequate enough explanation. It worked for me because it was underpinned by the psychological theories of separation-individuation, but pared down it seemed oversimplistic and as reductive as the oedipal theories I was rejecting. I was not convinced that understanding the dynamic would shift the problem for them.

Carol and Maria both referred to me as their good mother and although it was a joke it seemed a possible way in. If we could talk about what kind of qualities they attributed to me and what function I served as good mother, we might be able to extricate me from their relationship without interfering with their restored erotic life. Perhaps what they were seeing in me was a woman who supported and encouraged their separateness as well as their togetherness. Perhaps they were attributing to me the sense that what lay outside the couple need not threaten them but could be an enriching adventure. Perhaps they sensed that I was offering them an attachment based not on merger but on separateness and that a new form of intimacy was possible.

Before I could talk through what I was thinking, Carol and Maria left therapy. They were so happy, they said. The therapy had worked. They felt confident and sexually alive and, much as they enjoyed seeing me, they wanted to leave. I could understand their wish but it worried me. While they had indeed reinvigorated their erotic life together, I was less sure that they had done much more than switch Carol's external other—Sonya—to me. Yes, I had been both of theirs, which I suppose was some development, but the consideration of the need for an other to break their sexual ennui, or to gain even an understanding of that dynamic, had been too scant to consolidate the changes. I asked them to stay for enough sessions until we could understand the reinvigoration rather than take it for granted. They teased me about not wanting to be left and stopped therapy anyway.

Perhaps, I thought, I had underestimated them. Perhaps they had managed to achieve a greater degree of psychological separation than I had estimated. Perhaps their well-being had not been quite as contingent on my being the third person breaking through the murkiness.

But these were thoughts I was forcing into my mind, trying to right a situation that had not resolved itself as I might have wished. I felt torn. Torn between the therapist's goal and the goal of the couple. For my own satisfaction I had hoped for and wanted a technically aesthetic resolution, one which I felt might have some permanence, one in which Carol and Maria could manage more psychological space between one another. Then I scolded myself that they had not come to therapy to be psychologically better educated and sophisticated. They had sought therapy to continue their relationship and to deal with the Sonya problem. From their perspective, they had accomplished their goals.

Of course I missed them. They had been an interesting couple to work with and I had enjoyed getting to know them both. I loved their opinions, their take on the world, hearing about the issues that galvanized or paralyzed them. I felt, as I often did, that my job was a wonderful one, allowing me into worlds I could not have known so intimately in the normal course of things. In this instance it was the world of two women, one an English Jew, one an African-American, with a sexuality different from mine, who were bringing up a daughter together, facing the challenges of their generation. I took that gift, made my notes, closed the file and tried not to worry about what still felt unresolved.

Ten months later Carol called. They were in a mess. Could they see me urgently? It was too complicated to explain on the telephone. Tuesday. Thank you.

They came in breathless. This time it was Carol who started the session. Maria had been trying to get pregnant and Carol had found the whole process unbearable. They wanted a father of sorts for the baby, not just sperm. They wanted someone they knew who could reliably be in their lives for the baby's future. An old boyfriend, Charles, whom Maria had dated at Harvard, who was now a friend of both of theirs and was doing research in England for six months, seemed the ideal choice. He was bisexual, would want to have some kind of relationship with the child, loved Maria and was happy to oblige.

The three of them had decided that the best way to conceive the child was for Maria to sleep with Charles. She had done so before and did not want her baby conceived via masturbation and syringes. Of course, she did not want the act of sexual intercourse to be an act of lovemaking either, but she did want the making of her baby to involve a penis and a vagina. Of that she was sure. But while Carol thought it was a fine idea in the abstract—her own child, Chloe, had in fact been conceived through intercourse with an ex-boyfriend—she found she could not handle the thought of Maria sleeping with Charles. She felt unbearably jealous, terribly frightened, and convinced that she would lose her. Before the Charles crisis, their sex life had flagged again. She had wanted to come back to talk about it but hubris had prevented her. Now she feared that Charles and Maria would really hit it off; they would fall in love again, want to keep the baby, shut her out. They were from the same background, had faced similar issues in their move out of the suburban black lower middle class. One day Maria would want to return to the States despite what she said now and Charles could offer that and also provide what Carol never could. Carol was frantic in her quiet, anglicized way.

There was a great deal to sort out. Carol's panic encompassed the particulars of her life choices as well as it encapsulated the larger themes of class, heterosexuality, race, belonging, similarity and differ-ence. Carol felt that she had nothing to offer. She could not make a baby for Maria, she was not enough to hold her, she was inadequate. Heterosexuality was clearly superior to homosexuality, black superior to white, the United States superior to England.

I was saddened to see such a collapse in Carol. The equanimity she had demonstrated during our many sessions had given no hint of how she might show deep distress. I turned to Maria. From Carol's descrip-tion I might have thought that there was some foundation to her panic. Was Maria considering leaving her? Had she fallen in love with Charles? Was a lesbian life still too hard—one stigma too many for her to bear? Was living in a foreign country with a white woman, albeit a Jew, too far out? Or maybe, I pondered, had the confidence and love she had received from Carol let her develop a confidence to pursue a new path?

But I saw no evidence of Maria's desire to pull away from Carol. Yes, she was pleased that Charles had agreed to be the father; yes, she wanted a black baby; yes, she had some regrets that life had fetched her up on a shore a long way way from home. But no, she was not about to desert Carol and their relationship.

The issues Carol worried about were not in the least bit trivial. In her shoes I could imagine my own fear. She was seeing Maria as having a way out of the undoubted difficulties that a gay, cross-race relation-ship posed. Carol imagined that Maria had reconnected with one of her own and that she, who had never been able to find a soulmate from her own background and who seemed to choose partners who were terribly different, would be abandoned with the fallacy of her choices revealed. She felt frightened and humiliated, as though Maria's decision to make a baby with Charles was a rejection of her.

There was lots of material to discuss in terms of Carol's feelings that she could not give Maria a baby. The limitations of her biology and her powerlessness to change it would have been an angle ripe for a psychoanalytic conversation. But here I was more interested in understanding how the themes that had emerged earlier between Carol and Maria around sameness and difference, about how to find the right distance from each other, were now emerging in another context. The issues of black and white, of their sexuality, of their commitment to one another, were shaded with the themes from our earlier conversations about merger and separation and were being forced to the surface within this new situation. I was interested too in Carol's deep distress.

I was excited with them about their decision to try to bring another child into their relationship. I empathized with them over the difficulties that actually having a baby posed for them. But, at another level, I detected a certain impatience in myself which surprised me. I wondered where it came from and who or what it was with. Was it my eagerness for Maria to get pregnant so that we could move beyond the threat that Charles posed and into the issues the pregnancy represented? Did I want to distance myself from their drama, to stand outside, to reject the murkiness of their merger? Could I maintain my separateness from them only at the cost of an impatience, an impatience that had an implied smugness coming from my position of not having to personally face the issues affecting them? Were my feelings of any use in understanding their dilemma? I ran through various options, hoping to alight on something that felt right, something that might make sense of my impatience and, of course, shift things for them. No help. Nothing made much emotional sense. I could certainly apply theory to almost any of it but I would have to take my impatience and examine it to see what it meant for me. Through understanding what *I needed to resolve* I might find a way to help Carol and Maria through this difficult transition.

The session ended. An image of wanting to swim between them, of my hands forming a breaststroke to part them, of wanting Carol to move out of Maria's business with Charles, came to mind. I wanted to pick Carol up and put her off to one side so that Maria could get on with her own struggles concerning sleeping with an ex-boyfriend, of her continuing closeness with an African-American, of her own issues about her roots and her future. While I was sympathetic to Carol's fears and could easily see how afraid she was, my impatience stood in the way of real empathy, of an emotional being with her in her fears. I could not get inside her experience because to do so would feel like entering into the merger.

I wondered about my intolerance for their merger. Why? Was I less able to handle my own conflicts around merger and separation than I thought? Did their difficulty threaten a personal equilibrium that was less sturdy than I knew? Was my relationship with my partner just as merged? If it was and I was identified with the two of them, then what would I need to sort out in order to help them?

For several sessions nothing much came to me. The work with them was routine and rather technical. I tried to help Carol rein in her projections onto Maria so that she could hear Maria's *actual* experience of what she was going through with Charles. I encouraged Carol to express what she felt and supported Maria in listening to Carol's feelings without thinking that they had to serve as a brake on her pursuing the pregnancy. Their sensitivity to one another meant that strong emotions in either woman could act to immobilize the other. In picking up a feeling and restoring it to its owner, I was part of a disentangling operation. It had a feeling similar to sitting on the floor with my daughter and her friend, sorting out their belongings into separate piles. As with my daughter, I could sense that Carol and Maria's piles would get jumbled up again but the assertion of ownership seemed important. I was doing the rather pedantic but necessary work of couple therapy while waiting to see whether I might understand my own responses better. What could I learn from my impatience and lack of empathy?

As in any therapy there were several concurrent stories. There was their narrative, their feelings and what went unspoken, and there was my account to myself of what was going on. There was what passed between the couple. There was each individual's experience. There was our experience of the relationship in the room. Everything they talked of seemed to fit in with my original hypothesis. The two of them had sunk into a swampy merger in which fantasized or actual betrayal was the only way they could effect psychical separation. The first time Sonya was the problem. Now it was that Maria would desert Carol for Charles. My job was to find ways of effecting a psychological separation that allowed them to be attached to one another but on a different basis.

We knew already that sex was vibrant between them only when there was a degree of separation. This was demonstrated by Charles's entrance into their lives which had, once again, revived their appetite for one another. His position outside the relationship, drawing one of them to him, had rekindled their erotic life, which had once again died down to a mere smolder a few months after they stopped therapy with me. In the time I had known them, three people—Sonya, their therapist, Charles—had functioned in this erotic way for them.

Since there were no rational grounds for my impatience, I had to ask myself whether it was a defense against my discovering or knowing something that would make *me* uncomfortable. Were there uncomfortable points of similarity between their sexual story and my own? Was I investing in their making it, in being a couple, a lesbian couple, who had been able to revive their sexual life? Did I now feel disappointed in them and inadequate as a therapist?

My frustration grew. Then I got it. At one level it was not much to get and yet it was the thing on which so much of love gets impaled. What I realized was that in significant ways both Carol and Maria were wedded to the idea of betrayal, of not trusting, of true love representing an ache and an impossibility. They seemed to insist on seeing rejection everywhere despite their love for one another.

My impatience now made sense to me. I wished they could clear away the hurt and mistrust each brought to the relationship. I wished they could sink, if not sumptuously, then at least comfortably, into the love they had created together without making such a drama of it. With this understanding of my hopes for them, my impatience dissolved. I now felt I could open up a conversation about how the abundance of their giving—lovely and generous as it was—curiously covered up their difficulties in receiving from one another and about how this dynamic amounted to a form of not trusting which could feel like a rejection.

Thus Carol and Maria could each experience herself as a giver, eager and open to the relationship, without reflecting on the ways in which she was at the same time rejecting the love coming from the other. I felt if they could grasp this now, they might learn to trust that what was being offered was real, and might begin to recognize the ways in which they unconsciously batted away the very love they craved.

It was a painful thought. I sensed that a conversation along these lines could be productive, and yet I found it painful to contemplate because this tendency to reject, to doubt what is being offered, is ubiquitous and deeply damaging. So many relationships are ravaged by mistrust and insecurity. I had known this issue and had had to grapple with it in myself. I could feel some echoes in my own rejecting part, my personal attempts to create the right distance between myself and my loved one.

I was also relieved, though I could now understand my impatience and reaction to their need to create drama and also saw that their intermittent rejection of one another resonated with the oscillations in my own attachments. I was forced to remember various attempts I had made to pull myself out of merged relationships. For more than a moment I sighed inside about how lengthy the struggles to reverse our early psychological patterning can be and how, while some troublesome things are easy to change, other problems are reworked throughout our life at every change in our circumstances or in our consciousness. I wondered about how I might best enable Carol and Maria to progress on this one, the Achilles heel of so many relationships. How could they draw back from their rejection of each other and move forward to an embrace without sacrificing a sense of difference?

Knowing how to be at the right distance was not going to be something that came easily to them. What did come all too easily was the dissolving of distance. The right space needed to be found and maintained in less provocative ways. It was also a question of being able to be mindful of the ambiguity. Both separateness and merger had their dangers. The question Carol and Maria faced was how to maintain the desired degree of psychological separation from each other without the sacrificing intimacy. Or to put the question upside down, it was *how to trust that intimacy flows out of a degree of separation*. Whereas, I tried to explain to them, their tendency to merge initially enabled them to get close, that same tendency was hopeless for sustaining intimacy.

Rejection, I went on to suggest, was their mechanism for regulating the distance between them to achieve and maintain the intimacy they could manage. How might they avoid using rejection through attachments to a third person—Carol to Sonya, both of them to me, Maria to Charles—as a way to place themselves at a comfortable distance?

We now had four interconnecting reasons why rejection or mistrusting one another was so psychologically powerful. First, their doubts about one another's love protected them against fully opening up and receiving. Second, the consequence of their doubt meant that their relationship would be intermittently on the brink. The potential for loss put them in a psychologically safe position from which they could fight and show their love for each other. Third, their rejection of one another kept them at a manageable distance so that they could avoid the sense of being merged with each other. Fourth, this distance then made it possible for each of them to see the other as separate and therefore sexually desirable.

We discussed these issues together as they affected their present crisis. What would Carol have to feel inside, what would she have to relinquish, if she accepted the idea that Maria wanted to continue their life together and that having a baby was a way of confirming and extending their relationship, not undermining it? What kind of leap would it be for her to trust that she was loved?

These were the very same issues that Maria had had to grapple with in trying to open herself up to Carol after Carol's affair with Sonya. The two of them had to give up being attracted to a love which involved betrayal and pain on the one hand and over-identification and loss of individuality on the other. They needed to dare to experience a love that was present and available.

Carol and Maria liked having challenges for each of them to work on. Seeing the merry-go-round they had been on, they were energized by having a way forward. They welcomed the idea of examining their individual reactions to see when they were rejecting or doubting. They thought it would be useful to question themselves and each other about what they were frightened of. They felt challenged to see when doubt, fear, the desire to distance through rejecting, or the urge to merge occurred; to feel themselves into what lay behind such feelings so that they could develop new patterns of relating. Children whose parents were able to give them the right amount of attention and contact without being either invasive or withdrawn might be candidates for partnerships without the propensity to merge or to reject. They are the lucky ones and Carol and Maria knew that they were not in that category. With one daughter, Chloe, and with the hope of another child in the family, they were determined to sort out their problems. They did not want to keep on destabilizing their relationship.

For three months Maria slept with Charles when she was ovulating. On the third attempt, she became pregnant. Carol was jubilant. Charles was jubilant. Maria was scared. The pregnancy threw her into a tizzy. She worried about whether the baby was all right, whether she could endure labor, whether her relationship would accommodate the new life growing in her womb, how Chloe would feel about it, how she would tell her parents she was having a black baby with a white woman. Carol understood most of her fears. Having had a baby herself, she was sympathetic to Maria's worries. Charles moved to the sidelines. Carol tried to ignore any continuing jealousy she felt toward him as she and Maria started to prepare their home for the new baby. Their sex life, which had dipped around the monthly encounters with Charles, was once again vigorous.

Of course I noticed that Charles had been evicted from their relationship. They had never meant him to be involved in it in a big way but I wondered about parallels with the role Sonya and I had played and the continuing need Carol and Maria had to create triangles which they then dismembered. My thoughts might have stayed there but a new crisis came up.

As they began to look into the legal aspects of becoming guardians to one another's children, and to set their financial affairs in order, Carol's considerable inheritance (which they had not needed to use to live on) came up as an issue between them. Carol had disregarded this money until Chloe was born and then had put most of it in a trust for her. The remaining amount, which eight years before had seemed reasonable enough for a pension, had swelled. Carol now had a lot more money than she felt easy with. She arranged to put a large portion of it into a trust for the new baby.

Carol and Maria did not share money but the house they lived in had been inherited from Carol's family. They each earned enough for Carol's inheritance not to be much of an issue on a daily basis. But they had never discussed the financial aspects of Maria's pregnancy and although Maria earned a good living, she had not built up enough savings to cut back on her hours or give up work entirely for a year or two. She hoped that she and Carol would take some time off from their jobs so that they could bring up this new baby together. She wanted Carol to use some of her money to make this possible.

Carol could not go along with the money part of Maria's wishes. Although it was a rational thing to do, she felt uneasy. She had no objection to Maria's being dependent on her while she was pregnant, when the baby was little and while Maria would be on leave from her job, but she was not prepared to put money in Maria's account or to set up a joint account. Carol could not bear seeing herself in the role of benefactor. Her parents had lived for many years in a peculiarly dependent way on their parents despite the abundance of money in the family. Begrudgingly they had handed over to Carol and her brother money earmarked for them when they each had a child. Money had been used in Carol's family as a means of control and it made her wary. She had always felt guilty about having so much and for years had let herself be ignorant about how much there was and how it was invested. She tried not to think about it. Her stance toward her money stood in contrast to her calm and confident approach to other matters.

It was only with Maria that Carol had begun to open up about money, to face just how much she had and to take responsibility for it. Carol's embarrassment about her wealth stemmed from many different sources. Although Jewish she had absorbed the British upper-class idea that money was somehow vulgar. She was also embarrassed because she was politically committed to a more equitable society. Being born with a silver spoon, albeit an emotionally tarnished one, seemed to be both a stigma and an invitation to others to take advantage of her. Although she gave generously to causes she supported, she found that she was getting on more and more lists of potential donors. She squirmed at the idea of herself as a money machine and began to resent expectations that she would bale out organizations. And when it came to Maria and the impending baby, she just could not give money to her or open an account for her. It made her feel as though Maria was a charity, a cause, rather than her lover and her equal.

Maria felt hurt and insulted. She could not understand why Carol would not share in this way. She could not see why they could not have a joint account, why Carol was insisting that she would provide for Maria but would not open her account to her. Maria felt infantilized. She worked hard to make it, she earned a good living and she was not trying to exploit Carol. She would expect a shared account and financial support if she were with a man. Anyway, money was there to do good with; she could not understand Carol's attitude. She thought Carol was controlling her in the same ways her family had always controlled people, through money. But this was worse. Because she and

Carol had sorted through some of Carol's difficulties over her inheritance, Maria now felt as if she was being put into another camp, cast out and abandoned.

I myself was curious about the degree of distress the financial arrangement between the two of them was stirring up. Money, like sex, is a channel for the expression of many emotions and how it is handled by individuals and in couples becomes a way in which issues around giving and receiving, control, separation, commitment, sameness and difference are played out. I could see Maria's distress about having to ask for money from Carol. I could see that it felt demeaning and made her insecure. At the same time I could hear how difficult Carol found it to give Maria money directly. I was pretty sure that this hiccup could be worked out and that the issue was taking on the anxiety generated by Maria's pregnancy, anxiety about what it would mean for the relationship and for Chloe.

But in the event the hiccup turned into a convulsion lasting several months which none of us was sure their relationship would recover from. Maria's feelings that she was abandoned and betrayed increased. No amount of talking could alleviate them. She talked of looking for an apartment and moving out. She felt that Carol was showing her that she was not really committed, that she was not bothering to understand how insecure and diminished the proposed arrangement made Maria feel. Unlike previous crises when sex between them became insistent, this time sex between them stopped. It amplified the hole in their relationship. The lack of sex was now not about being too close and merged but about being too far apart. Maria distrusted Carol. She felt Carol had abandoned her now that she was pregnant. Carol disagreed. She accused Maria of being histrionic and of overreacting because of her hormones. She could not back down because she did not think she was in the wrong. She was prepared to support Maria, so what was the problem? Maria could not accept what Carol was offering as it made her feel too dependent and too out of control. There was a stalemate. They seemed to be pulling apart as a couple at the same time as this baby was growing in Maria's tummy, consolidating their coupleness. It was a paradox. But it was not an unusual one to see in couple therapy where, as a couple becomes closer, there is frequently a mini-crisis as the two people adjust. But it was unusual for it to be played out so explicitly through money and sex.

Despite the stalemate, our sessions were permeated by an under-current of desperation, an urgent wish to find a way to patch things up before the baby arrived. I felt stuck. A thriller writer with a plot prob-lem. We had nearly reached the climax but there was no exit point. Maria was offering one by threatening to go. But that would leave too many loose ends. Besides, Carol was not taking the situation seriously because she thought Maria was overdramatizing. I worked hard in my corner to see if there was something I might understand in a new way to alleviate their distress and bring them closer together, or at least to help them respect their differences sufficiently for them to break through this impasse.

I went back to what they each had said. Carol could not have a joint account with Maria because she could not stand seeing Maria as a char-ity case, as beholden to her, as less than. Maria could not bear to be in the position of asking for money. It made her the poor relation. They both seemed to be saying the same thing. They were both searching for a way to express their desire for equality but in their very different idioms.

My sympathies were drawn first to Maria and I followed those in my mind. On the face of it the vulnerable one, she felt less powerful, more needy. Seen from her perspective, Carol's relationship to wealth meant she was going to give to Maria only on her terms. It was a trian-gular situation again, with the money as the other and with Carol in control. Hence Maria's feelings of being turfed out, abandoned. I could see why Maria felt that her only power lay in walking away from the relationship. If she demonstrated that she did not need, she gained back some self-respect.

I turned my mind to Carol's dilemma. She felt caught. She was happy to give but she did not want to be told how. She had been so controlled by her parents through money she had not even wanted and

I could see how bludgeoning she found Maria's request to be given to in a particular way. She thought Maria was ungracious, inflexible and untrusting.

As I saw the parallels in their feelings, I felt hopeful. I sensed we had a way out of the stuckness. If they could recognize that they shared feelings of distrust and misunderstanding, they might be able to connect again.

With the focus on money, the profound meaning of bringing a new life into the world and into their relationship had receded. The focus in the sessions was on disappointment, on the grievances between them, on dashed expectations. It was as though they had united on what was wrong rather than on what was right. The good, the love and the creativity once again posed a problem for them. They did not know how to hold on to it, to treasure their excitement, and so they had fallen into disruption and disappointment.

We did not have a new problem around money so much as a known tension around closeness which bounced them into a merger they violently tried to disrupt. Relieved by my understanding, I turned toward them to explain how things looked from my perspective. They both sighed in assent. There were relief and lightness in the room. A pause while we all enjoyed them. My silent sigh joined theirs as we experienced a calmness after such painful antagonism.

Moments later I felt strong sexual feelings pass between the two of them and suffuse the room. They connected again, laughed and talked about how they had been engaged in a crazy boxing match about the money. Their focus switched. Now they realized that while they had been observing and thinking about their individual responses to rejection, to doubting, they had not considered what they did as a unit, a relationship, to undermine the happiness that was between them. It was in thinking of the relationship as their creation, of them but bigger than them, that they finally seemed able to break the pattern that kept deadening their sexual life. As they thought of the relationship as a kind of other they had brought into existence, they felt less threatened by their closeness. The relationship was a place they both went to for comfort, security and being sexual. It did not engulf them or overwhelm their individuality but was redefined as the expression of their intimacy.

Carol and Maria found a solution. They managed to revive and maintain a sexual life together before and then after Claude, their son, was born. If they had not fully worked through the difficulties that beset them, at least they had enough of a grasp of them. They understood how intense closeness frightened them and how they then used rejection or an outsider or distrust in one another as a way of regulating their intimacy. They understood that an alternative might be to acknowledge together the scariness of their intimacy and how vulnerable it made them feel. Holding on to that formulation seemed more durable than explosions, finding other lovers or turning to rejection. It would be hard but at least it situated the problem where it needed to be, not in sex or money or lovers.

I was pleased and hopeful for them. Christmas cards in subsequent years let me know that they still used what we had worked on together. At times it had been a laborious therapy and at others an exciting one. I had enjoyed working with them. But despite being able to help them understand how rejection worked in multiple ways for them in their relationship, and despite their success at bringing sex back into their lives without resorting to an other, I was left with the conundrum of sex in long-term relationships. I had been intrigued for years about how or why quasi-celibacy was often a feature of many couples (and of individuals in couple relationships) I saw. I was fascinated by the process through which sex becomes dispensable.

The more I thought about it the less I seemed to fully understand the erotic. Certainly, I could add to my earlier explanations other plausible arguments about the impediments to a sexual relationship that a merged attachment brings. Some people, for example, find the closeness of daily living together emotionally reminiscent of early childhood. The flavor of incest is a formidable taboo and if one's lover is represented in one's unconscious as one's mother, father, sister or brother, an erotic relationship may seem impossible: an unthinkable transgression.

A hundred years ago Freud disabused us of the notion of the asexuality of children. For most psychoanalytic theorists, the adult sexual relationship is a grown-up rescripted version of child sexuality. As Freud's account of heterosexuality goes,[6] girls—out of disappointment with their mothers, who are unable to give them a penis—turn to their fathers to provide them with the next best thing, a baby. Maturity then involves the girl's recognizing that she can have neither her mother nor her father and so in adult life she transfers her erotic interest to a man of her own. For boys, the transfer is seen to be more straightforward. The mother has habitually been the parent with whom physical and emotional intimacy in infancy and childhood has been shared, so the oedipal transfer in Freudian terms is about the boy's wishing to take the father's place and, realizing that he cannot, renouncing his desire for his mother and then finding in adult life a woman of his own.

The Freudian account asks us to imagine a situation in which the erotic is both present in the mother-child relationship but somehow (in most cases) successfully managed and sufficiently sublimated so as not to create an incestuous relationship. The Freudian story also tells us that as practicing analysts and psychoanalytic therapists we are likely to have projected on to us in the analytic setting the erotic desires of our patients which we must not take personally but must understand as an aspect of the transference—what necessarily gets foisted or transferred onto the clinician in the therapy.[7] Working through the patient's erotic agenda with us is part of therapy.[8]

The beauty of psychoanalysis is that in trying to understand what is embedded for an individual within the erotic, we have a window into understanding aspects of the erotic for all of us. The in-depth analysis of what is represented in the conscious and unconscious in individuals, in the subjective experience of individuals and between the patient and the psychotherapist, provides ways of thinking and theorizing about the erotic. My clinical experience of working with many women, heterosexual, bisexual and homosexual, for over twenty years has provided interesting and provocative evidence for a different way of conceptualizing sexuality and the erotic for women today.

And So

THERE ARE NO dramatic endings to the stories of Adam, Joanna, Edgar, Jenny and Carol and Maria, no straightforward triumphs over difficulties which will never again darken their lives. In the case of Belle, of course, there is no satisfying resolution. Psychotherapy, as I have tried to show, is not like that. It has bumpy beginnings, unexpected middles and ragged endings. Its aim is not to unwrap and rewrap an individual's life, fix the past traumas and freeze what it has understood in time, but rather to open up ways of thinking that may have enduring value for the people involved long after the therapy is finished.

Psychoanalysis, for me, is not so much a way of interpreting or even of finding out what went wrong—although those aspects of the analytic encounter are central to it—as it is an attempt to reach the other, the patient, and offer her a relationship within which she is enabled to be less perplexed about her difficulties. The psychotherapist sets in train a process. She is not there to discover something about the patient that the patient is unaware of, as much as she is there to enable the conditions for discovery, understanding and connection to occur. My hope is to leave the individual (or couple or group) with the ability to face their troublesome emotions or conflicts. When emotional conflicts, conscious and unconscious, can be held on to without needing to be expelled or instantaneously solved, they can be experienced in some of their complexity. My wish is that the psychotherapeutic endeavour will provide patients with a framework for understanding the relevance of certain issues for them. I hope that it gives them ready access to a kind of reflective process that allows the immediate response to join up with quieter, less obvious reactions happening on another level and in another dimension of experience. In this way relief can be found from seeking solutions to the dilemmas of life which have relied on painful repetitions.

Psychoanalysis is an endeavor of the heart and the mind. The therapist cannot help but be profoundly affected by her patients. Although a patient often feels that the asymmetrical nature of the relationship means that she is merely of clinical interest and has little personal or emotional impact on the therapist, I hope these stories have shown some of the ways in which the analytic encounter is much more than this for the therapist. Every therapy offers something fresh for the therapist, no matter how many patients with apparently similar difficulties she has met. Every therapy makes demands on the clinician to experience new things and think new thoughts.

Adam, Belle, Joanna, Edgar, Jenny and Carol and Maria were not actual patients of mine or of other therapists I know. To convey the challenges that a therapist faces, a sense of the risks of the consulting room and of the excitement and emotional truths told and discovered there, I decided to create a set of stories describing the therapeutic relationships between imagined patients and a fictionalized therapist. As though they were real patients, the patients I invented presented me with unexpected challenges. When I started to write about Joanna, I had in mind to tell the story of doing therapy with a woman with some violence in her psychological make-up and an uncertainty about her ability to sustain a loving, intimate relationship. I had no idea when I conceived of her that she had had scarlet fever as a little girl and had ended up in the isolation ward of a hospital far away from home. Nor had I been meaning to tell a story which involved self-inflicted violence or in which a regressed Joanna would come to a session in a dissociated state. That she did so was as much a surprise to me as the events in an actual therapy.

I was equally surprised when Adam provoked such extreme sexual feelings in my therapist. These feelings are unfamiliar to me personally in the consulting room. The fantasies I wrote about in relation to Adam are far more developed and elaborated than any I have personally encountered in my practice. However, I have certainly heard colleagues discuss the clinical difficulties that arise when they are on the receiving end of an erotic transference or subject to the feelings associated with an erotic countertransference. These are disturbing and disruptive and yet there is something clinically relevant for the patient if the feelings within them can be examined via the kind of inner surrender to the fantasy that I describe. In clinical practice such a surrender would be an aspect of the therapist's ruminations. The complexity of the individual is so much richer than I could portray, so that even when there are strong sexual feelings they would be both mediated and modulated by other experiences and by other emotional expressions that a real Adam and I would have between us—humor, exasperation and seductions of all kinds turning not only around the sexual.

Surprise was a key element in my account of the therapist and Belle. Although I had drawn a character who was a con artist, I was astonished to encounter the lie she told in the first session. I had not expected the immediacy of it. For much of the time that I was writing the story, thinking about what Belle might engender in a therapist, I noticed how much she stayed with me outside the writing time. Her fragility appeared so insistent that it seemed as though she needed to nestle in with the therapist character beyond the sessions. As the writer of her story, I wanted her to pull through and make it, to get beyond the lying and conning of herself. Although I invented her character and that of the therapist, I wasn't sure what the outcome of therapy would be. I did not know that it was ultimately to be a "failed" therapy. When the time came, I realized that it was important to have such an outcome in this book. It would be wrong to misrepresent psychoanalysis and psychotherapy. There are therapeutic failures, mismatches and disappointments on both sides of the couch.

Because my characters acted in ways contrary to my conscious imagination, I was forced in the writing, as I am forced during the course of an actual therapy, to revise and reconsider their problems. Sometimes the similarity between my characters' unfolding and the way psychotherapy progresses was astounding. With Edgar, for months nothing much came out on the page. The stuckness I felt in writing about him had its equivalence in an impasse in therapy. I just had to sit it out, considering this and then that to see what might push the therapy story forward in the way I would if the patient were real and the therapist me.

In all the stories I have been presented with events that I had not foreseen, psychic states that I had not anticipated and responses within the therapist character which took me into areas I would not have expected her to disclose. In this process I have tried to hold the tension between shaping a story and my own free associative state. Whereas I might have anticipated that I would consciously be drawing on my practice[1] to provide me with the feelings or a replica of the situation that my therapist character finds herself in, that has not been the case at all. The pull has been from the invented character who takes on his or her life as fully as has any patient I have worked with in making me confront something authentic with them.

I chose to tell Jenny's extraordinary story because I wanted to write about the other side of the psychoanalytic encounter: the short, dynamic contact of brief therapy and the value it can have. Jenny's dramatic story echoes other almost unbelievable events which, recounted outside the consulting room, are of interest because they transgress our society's moral values and force us to reassess an often uncontested belief in a shared morality. In the context of brief therapy it is the psychological dimensions that move to the fore: the individual's struggle to come to terms with a traumatic event, the brutal collapse of innocence, the way in which the forced confrontation with personal values stimulates a certain kind of emotional growth.

I wanted to write about Carol and Maria's struggle over money because if it were told outside of therapy it would seem minor and overblown, and incomprehensible, but in context it demonstrates the way in which a couple's small disagreements can sometimes be more problematic than a large-scale disruption such as Carol's affair. What appear to be little, often incomprehensible misunderstandings often turn out to be part of larger patterns that need to be grasped in order for the couple to feel confident about their relationship.

The stories are essentially an attempt not to theorize about but to indicate what makes change possible for people in therapy. There are many competing views on this (facilitation, engagement, interpretation, interpretation of the transference, historical reconstruction), as well as many different schools of psychoanalysis with theories not just on psychological development but on what is crucial within the analytic relationship, what constitutes an interpretation, the function of defenses and so on. The Freudians are fond of analyzing the defenses and the Kleinians of interpreting the anxiety and aggression they mask. Modern psychoanalysts such as Bollas and Ehrenberg try to go through the defenses, whereas I have been interested in trying to reach behind them. The point of the theory in this book is to show what might go on in the mind of a psychotherapist while she works with a patient. For most working analysts, theory is so well absorbed that it becomes second nature, freeing them to relate to the analysand without an a priori set of ideas about how the therapy should proceed.

Theory is a structure which enables the therapist to be with the patient during the difficult and incomprehensible times. It helps a therapist to think through what she is experiencing and learning during the process of a therapy. The theory holds the therapist so that she is free to relate and attend to the person she is working with, to make a relationship with her. This function of theory makes sense of the finding that nearly all types of therapy are equally effective, for it is the relational aspects of the therapy that are crucial—the endeavor of the therapist to reach the patient. The theory supports the therapist as she enters territories with her patient that might arouse fear or anxiety, allowing her to sustain and explore those feelings inside herself while she stands up, stands by and stands still for the patient in her own struggles.

That is not to say that theory is not important. It is crucial. With no theory or with eclecticism, one's thoughts can have no coherence, cannot be confirmed or tested, extended or modified. Theory is like a skeleton on which the layers and layers of other systems with their own mechanisms create the kind of complexity required when trying to understand the human subject.

In my development as a psychotherapist, I have been affected by many theorists and psychoanalytic writers. The work of Freud, Fairbairn, Balint and Winnicott count as early and enduring influences. Much of my thinking over the years has been developed with Luise Eichenbaum, our work not just on gender but also on the nature and process of the therapy relationship. We both acknowledge the importance of contemporary American analysts: Ogden, Searles, Bollas, Gill, Kernberg, and especially the work of Stephen Mitchell and the relational analysts Ehrenberg, Arons and Spezzano. In Britain I have been much affected by the work of the Independent analysts and by the Contemporary Freudians such as the Sandlers and Malcolm Pines.

My greatest learning has come, of course, from my greatest teachers, the patients who have consulted me and who have provoked me to think ever more deeply and complicatedly about them and about psychoanalysis. In writing about the kind of work that therapy is I have had to condense what I have learned, but I hope that what has been lost is partially compensated for by my rendering of the aliveness that can exist for the two people doing therapy.

Psychoanalysis can also be, as I hope I have conveyed, a deeply satisfying experience for the therapist. It is an extraordinary privilege to share in such a close way the pains, struggles and psychological victories of another. To know that one has had an intimate hand in this development and to see the development are sources of tremendous satisfaction.

The practice of psychotherapy is extremely beautiful and often very moving. Within the therapy relationship there can be tenderness, belligerence, anguish, despair, depression, love, hope, longing, disappointment, anger, passion and grace. The themes of therapy—betrayal, abandonment, trust, fear, envy, rage, rivalry, doubt—and the ways they are thought about place the therapeutic encounter at the heart of our examination of human subjective experience. I hope that these stories have given a taste of the uniqueness of this kind of relationship and of this kind of inquiry.

Reflections and Questions

N WRITING THE stories of Adam, Belle, Joanna, Edgar, Jenny and Carol and Maria, I wanted to describe what therapy is like from the perspective I know best, that of the therapist. I have wanted to show how extremely interesting the work is on many different levels. The dilemmas presented to the psychotherapist on a daily basis—dilemmas which can be ethical, clinical and emotionally challenging—keep the psychotherapist's heart and mind tinglingly alert. In a job that often appears extremely slow-moving, attention to detail is as important as the patient's story. What is said, what is not said, as well as what cannot be said and *how* the said or not said is expressed—and with what tone, nuance, feeling, shading, color and emphasis—are crucial. Therapists are constantly having to question the basis from which they speak and understand. They have to analyze how what they are hearing makes them feel. As much as the patient, maybe more so, the therapist is kept on her toes.

While the patient is encouraged to speak as openly as she can, to say what comes into her mind as she engages in the process, which is at the same time free-associative and reflective, the therapist has a different responsibility. Hers is to be able to respond in ways that take account of what the patient is communicating, what it might mean, how the sequence of utterances, pauses and silences, and the feelings that accompany them, can be made into a different kind of sense than is possible in everyday conversation. For the therapist to be reflective and think about what she is hearing, she has to allow herself to enter into the emotional territory of the patient's world. She has to taste something of the pain, the anguish, the hurt, the depression, the rage, the envy, the hate, the love, the disappointment, the anger, the hopes, the dismay and the passion of her patient's experience. Without a surrender to such feelings by the therapist, she cannot hope to offer an alive relationship to the patient in which the defeats, confusions and hurts of her life can be addressed.

Each patient who comes into my consulting room brings me an account of herself, her family, friends, lovers, spouse and colleagues. I try to absorb and to understand her many and often unconscious motivations and the possible motivations of the people in her life. I work with the patient to understand what kind of picture or story she is making of herself and of the people who inhabit her world. Is it an accurate, albeit a necessarily partial picture? Has the patient misconstrued a situation? If so, in what ways and can we understand why? Has the patient misrepresented herself? If so, in what ways and can we understand why? If not, then what psychic sense can the patient make of her experience?

To discern the patient's emotional processes and to see how they are brought to play in relationships, the therapist also examines the relationship that exists between the two of them. The therapist sets the parameters that surround the therapy relationship through appointment times (and, if appropriate, fees). The therapist commits herself to focus on the patient's interests. The therapist promises continuity and confidentiality. Within this structure, the therapy relationship develops. The therapist becomes, as much as any other important figure in the analysand's life, a person who is significant both for who she is in actuality and for who she comes to represent to the patient.

Every relationship we enter into involves preconceptions about who the other person in the relationship is and can be. Sometimes we are aware of what we desire of the other, often we are not. In therapy, in contrast to other relationships, what is wanted of the other person, what is imagined about them and what is unconsciously foisted on them become—as I hope I have shown—not a taken for granted and undiscussed feature of the relationship but a crucial dimension of what is explored in the therapy. As the therapist and patient examine the relationship developing between them, the therapist discovers that in some ways she has come to embody, in her responses and reactions to the patient, salient aspects of the patient's view of the *essence* of relationships.

We have all been in situations in which we find ourselves behaving in a way that we might not have "chosen." This happens for the therapist in the therapy too. Patients bring selective aspects of themselves to the therapy relationship and both consciously and unconsciously stimulate responses in the therapist—responses often at odds with the usual manner of the therapist. So the therapist can find herself, at particular moments within the therapy, inhabiting a role, a stance, a set of responses not quite of her making. In the untangling of these unexpected responses, the therapist finds that she has located herself inside the most personal drama of the patient. By deconstructing and analyzing these personal dramas the therapist finds a route into understanding the difficulties and dilemmas which beset her patient.

In modern psychoanalysis this untangling, this finding of oneself as one of the dramatis personae of the significant people who inhabit the analysand's inner world, involves the analyst observing her own associations—where her mind takes her—and reflecting on them in the privacy of her own mind. This turn to the analyst's mental processes within psychoanalytic work has been the greatest clinical advance of the last fifty years. Therapists today see where their patients' dramas take them personally and what is evoked in them emotionally as part of what needs to be thought about to see if it can help them in their work. If we were to eavesdrop in clinics and consulting rooms all over the world while therapists discuss their patients in clinical meetings, we would notice that part of the discussion involves a candid engagement with the subjective experience of the therapist. We would witness therapists talking about the feelings—negative, positive and confused—that are stirred up in them by their patients. We might hear about the therapist's *personal* associations to those feelings. We might be surprised to discover the kind of weight that a therapist gives to the feelings stimulated in her by a patient as an aspect of the diagnosis.

In writing about the therapist's feelings and thoughts about patients for a general readership, I am aware that I may create an unease among professional colleagues who, while familiar with the kinds of feelings and scenarios I am writing about—what we call the countertransference—would be happier if such discussions were confined to the learned journals. Some professionals may well feel exposed, may worry that their patients will be alarmed by what I have written and will ask them pointed questions in sessions about their own ruminations. Depending on their theoretical orientation, either they will welcome such questions and view what has been stimulated as part of what can now come to therapy and the therapy relationship, or they will feel dismayed. They may argue that the mental reflections of the therapist about a patient can appropriately be brought only to clinical seminars or supervision. These therapists will wish that I had not written so openly.

For years psychoanalysis has been shrouded in a kind secrecy and while I understand the concern that analytic practice should not be misconstrued, the old taboos no longer serve the greater interest in society at large about psychotherapy, with the Tavistock Clinic opening its doors to television cameras and with the more widespread availability of therapy. We cannot write honestly about the therapists' experience without showing what goes through our minds at many different levels. Much of what therapists reflect on as we do our work is not revealed to a patient because it may not make sense at a particular moment to do so. But we may have to interpret silently to ourselves what we understand to be occurring in the therapy relationship for the therapy to progress. I have tried to show something about the private ruminations and the psychic states that a therapist can experience when working with her patients.

The analyst-analysand relationship, often thought of as one in which the analyst interprets to the patient what her dreams, associations, unconscious slips and apparently irrational actions and reactions mean, is in reality a partnership. It is a partnership in many senses. The patient influences the therapist and the therapist influences the patient. The therapist learns much about herself in conducting therapy. The therapist develops her skills through clinical practice. The therapist enhances her understanding of how the psyche works through observation of her participation in the therapy. And the therapist learns in depth about experiences outside the realms of her own particular life through entering into the emotional world of the patient.

This intimate access to the thoughts and feelings of another life as it develops and changes is part of what I have tried to convey about the experience of practicing therapy. The purposefulness of therapy makes this access particularly moving. We bear witness to the struggles of individuals, families, couples and groups as they wrestle to change and accept what they have found difficult in themselves. This process challenges and broadens the therapist's conception not just of the other person but of herself and her own limitations. Therapy provides a situation for growth for all those involved in it.

Above all, the therapeutic relationship is private. Because it is bound by confidentiality on the therapist's side, therapists who have wanted to write about therapy have been constrained by a multitude of contradictions. In wanting to share what we have learned—which is based on a superabundant wealth of minute detail about an individual patient's life, history, feelings and therapy process—we have had to select certain details and disguise and therefore necessarily distort who that individual is. In the acts of selection and concealment we make a fiction out of who the patient is. As we change the identifying details which might identify her, not only do we distort who the individual is but what we have learned and wish to illustrate becomes less plausible and less convincing.

Even in the professional literature we present our case material with artifice. We may select so small a vignette to illustrate our point that, out of the best of motives, we unwittingly distort the individual beyond all recognition or, alternatively, we reduce her to a silhouette. This process is unsatisfactory and yet it is inevitable. What we choose to write, and how we transform the particulars of the individual to preserve her privacy, cannot escape being an anemic sketch or a caricature, lacking the richness and integrity of that person. In *My Life As a Man,* Philip Roth's fictional character Peter Tarnapol, a writer in analysis with Dr. Otto Spielvogel, launches a devastating attack on his analyst when he discovers that in an article about him in a learned journal he has been transposed from an American-Jewish writer into an Italian-American poet.

> And surely it goes without saying that to disguise . . . a nice civilized Jewish boy as something called "an Italian American," well, that is to be somewhat dim-witted about matters of social and cultural background that might well impinge upon a person's psychology and values. And while we're at it, Dr. Spielvogel, *a poet and a novelist have about as much in common as a jockey and a diesel driver* [my emphasis].

I feel for Dr. Spielvogel's problems in wanting to write about his patient. I have faced the problem of how to disguise, without robbing a patient of all that she has so generously taught me. Having learned something extremely valuable and profound from my work with a particular individual, I then experience the peculiar sense that I am taking something from her if I do not attribute my knowledge to her in my writing. But much as this is a source of discomfort, I feel even more deeply for what Roth says through Peter Tarnapol of his need to define for himself who he is, and what he wants changed about his identity for the purposes of someone else's publication, as he rails at Spielvogel, "Why, to substantiate your 'ideas,' do you want to create this fiction about me . . . ?"

The solution for many psychoanalytic writers has been to ask for permission from patients to write about them. There is a rationale here. The therapist has her view which, however partial, is legitimate and needs disseminating and discussing for the internal advancement of the field of psychoanalysis. But I am uneasy with the notion of a patient or ex-patient giving consent. I am not convinced that what we mean by consent in this context is actually viable. I am not sure a patient or ex-patient can know that such permission is in her interest and is not an act of assent to the therapist's needs. And although in normal social life such giving can be relatively problem-free, in the context of analysis, the request, the acceptance, the showing of the written work and so on require the same thoroughgoing analysis of the motives, feelings and influences as does everything else in the therapy. Just as we know that any understanding we reach in therapy at a particular moment is only partial and is always subject to subsequent revision, so too must the granting of consent be partial—even if it is discussed over several sessions, even several months—and therefore subject to revision, rendering it, I believe, a spurious kind of consent.

Having written a regular column in a national newspaper and in a national women's magazine, as well as several books, and because at times I have attracted extremely unwelcome media interest in my practice, I know the extreme care that is required when using vignettes. Readers frequently write to tell me that they are the person in an article or on a page in one of my books. Sometimes individuals in my practice have assumed that I am writing about them even though this is something I would never consider.

The predicament posed by confidentiality and the problems posed by fictionalizing an individual or a couple in order to write about them led me to decide to invent the characters of Adam, Belle, Joanna, Edgar, Jenny, and Carol and Maria. Consequently, the therapist in these pages who responds to and shapes the encounters with the patients is a kind of creation too. She does, however, share many attributes with me and my colleagues. She acts as I imagine I might act were I the therapist of such patients. The imagined patients, on the other hand, are made up. They are not based on people who have consulted me.

WHEN I STARTED this project I had the idea that each story would be a means to illustrate a different phenomenon that can occur during therapy. I imagined that in a story I would be writing about a therapist's relationships with a patient whose character structure embodied one of the clinical entries and diagnostic categories—borderline, narcissistic, schizoid, depressive, bulimic[1]—which psychotherapists, psychiatrists and psychologists use among themselves. I hoped that in this way I would be able to show the range of issues that the therapist faces in the consulting room and within herself as she tries to reach the patient. But the stories I have written are not like that at all. They are simply accounts of what happened between my therapist and her patients. I was not able to make my characters do what I wished them to do. Instead, as in therapy and in life, these characters act according to their own logic, challenging and surprising me. They present the therapist at every turn of the written page with as startling or as unexpected behavior and information as the people who actually visit my consulting room.

There are inevitable emotional truths that transcend the characters I have written about and which are distillations of my actual clinical experience. The situations on the page might not have happened but the relationship between emotional truth, biography and narrative truth is one of current interest to both psychoanalysis and literary studies. What many writers involved in both autobiographical and fictional pursuits are searching to express is an authentic representation of states of feeling rather than a strict adherence to narrative truth. In my attempt to show what psychoanalytic psychotherapy is like from the therapist's perspective, I have used the barometer of emotional rather than narrative truth.

Early on in writing this book I gave a shortened reading of one of the stories, "Footsteps in the Dark," at the Freud Museum under the auspices of the Arbours Association. An intriguing and unexpected result of this reading was that the audience, composed in large part of fellow clinicians, discussed Joanna as though she were an actual clinical case. The dialogue following my reading had many similarities to a clinical seminar. Participants inquired why "I" had followed one route and not another, suggested significances "I" had not seen in her symptoms and talked as though she were a real person, the therapist a real therapist and the case a real case. In many ways this was gratifying and confirmed my view of how a fictional therapeutic account could ring true. It also suggested an additional way in which the book could be used.

The participants' contributions at the Freud Museum illustrate how therapy writing and therapy are always subjective and always reveal the therapist's perceptions, interventions and personal and theoretical biases. Each therapeutic couple is unique and idiosyncratic, expressing the personalities of the two individuals and their influences on one another. Therapy can never be free of the values, ideas and constructs of the individuals involved in it and it is certainly not free of the analyst's proclivities. These shape the therapy so that it becomes an experience equally influenced by what the analyst chooses to pursue or emphasize as by what she ignores, misses or sets aside.

In my work and in these stories I have been led to the edge of where our current theory takes us and to some of the interesting theoretical questions that are being posed today in two areas: the psychesomatic and the erotic. The relationship between body and mind and sexuality (implicitly, if not explicitly, in all the stories) is one in which new theory is evolving. This new thinking is not yet sufficiently well worked out to offer the kind of paradigm shift Thomas Kuhn has noted when a new consensus arises about how to think about problems in physics, but it is on the march. In psychoanalysis, in relation to the body, the old idea that our bodies express the conflicts of our minds is being updated by a view which shows that on the one hand the body's integrity or lack of integrity mirrors that of the mind rather than encapsulates the conflict for it, while on the other hand neuroscientific investigations are confirming that our early experiences shape the biology associated with our psychology as the neural signals choose one pathway and not another.

Although Freud's understandings in relation to the erotic have been revised by many analysts, including Ethel Person, Robert Stoller, Janine Chasseuget-Smirgel, Joyce McDougall, Otto Kernberg and Jacques Lacan, they have not yet answered the question of what the erotic is. Much modern psychoanalysis has been preoccupied with theorizing the therapy relationship and has furthered our understanding in extremely useful ways, but sometimes the larger questions of mind/body and the erotic have been taken as givens rather than explored. I offer a taste of my thinking in this area which I hope will be taken further by my colleagues. This is in no sense a comprehensive review of our current understanding but is a reflection of the issues that were set off in me as I ruminated about the patients in the book.

The erotic

Freud's view that erotic transferences are common in therapy is well borne out in the stories of Adam and Edgar. Adam, who sexualized his need for contact, transformed his dependency needs into becoming a great worshiper of women and sought therapy when his faithful penis let him down, and Edgar, whose sexual feelings could not be examined in the therapy for fear that they would be misconstrued, represent two arcs of male sexuality. In a sense the ordinariness of what occurred in their therapy around sexuality means that there is little to explore theoretically or to understand. Ethel Person's view of sexuality as a mainstay of a masculine identity describes Adam well enough. His sexual activity becomes the means by which he makes connection with others and underpins a shaky sense of self. The sex act crystallizes who he is: separate and apart and yet simultaneously in search of another who can confirm him emotionally and physically. It is through his conception of himself as a Casanova that he identifies himself and owns or disavows his needs. From his perspective his penis is the best of him; it can bring him and others pleasure. He can, until his body lets him down, feel a measure of self-confidence that he has things to give. His rather compulsive sexual activity, we discover, covers a multitude of anxieties about his place in the world, his relationship to his mother, to his father and to himself. Sex, while experienced as a soothing activity, contains within it deep hostility, self-hatred and a way of managing his conflicts around attachment.

We do not need further general theory to account for the sexualized nature of Adam's preoccupations. Nor do we with Edgar. His sexuality fails to raise theoretical issues about masculinity that need explaining. But if I reflect on my work with women and with couples over the years, there are issues which do demand addressing and, although I do not have answers, I think they pose interesting questions about the origin of the erotic in general and about the erotic in women.

Two phenomena have led me to wonder about these issues. The first arises out of the dearth of erotic countertransferences between my female patients and myself, also noticed by colleagues whose work I supervise. While we explore the possible sexual elements in woman-to-woman therapy, and especially patients' own fears about sexual feelings, fantasies and desires that might be in the therapy room, such feelings rarely present themselves. The second arises out of my work with individuals and couples who complain about the difficulty of maintaining an active sexual life in long-term relationships.

While I encourage all of my supervisees to observe the erotic and not to overlook it, a troublesome sexualized transference-countertransference between women is a rarer phenomenon than one might expect. Indeed what surprises me is how rarely the erotic component

is actively or openly present in woman-to-woman therapy relationships. For all the love or sexualized transferences that my colleagues
and I experience with some of the men we work with, we experience
a general absence of them with our women patients. It is only rarely
with women that these occur and when they do it is most often with
women who are bisexual or lesbian.

I have wondered about this phenomenon and if I put it together
with the celibacy that can be a feature of long-term relationships, and
the reported demise of sex in lesbian relationships after a few years, I
have been keenly aware of not really knowing what we are talking
about when we speak of sex.

Are we speaking of the erotic? And if so what is it? Are we speaking
of the relations between women and men? Are we speaking of the circumstances of reproduction? Are we trying to understand the taking
on of heterosexuality in the majority of women? Are we talking about
sexual excitement: how, when and why it arises? Although for Freud
sexuality was a given in the instinctual sense but had to be psychically
found and constructed, modern psychoanalysis has no such certainties
and few pathways for understanding what sexuality is.

One might have assumed that Freud's discovery of the importance
of childhood sexuality would have taken an even larger place within
the practice of therapy as it has moved to ways of seeing and understanding human psychology through reflecting on very early childhood
(the pre-oedipal period). I find, however, an extraordinary vacuum
around sex and sexuality that corresponds to the vacuum around the
theorizing about sex and sexuality.

I do find deep interest in the meaning of gender—how we psychologically become girls and women, boys and men—and about questions of sexual morality and clinical practice, the psychic meanings of
reproduction, and the psychological routes of sexual preference. I also
find my patients and colleagues occupied with issues of attachment,
jealousy, abandonment, masochism, and loss of desire. But the evidence from my clinical practice in relation to women hints that there is

something deeply forbidden about sex *per se*. There is a lack of material about the erotic lives of my patients. Nancy Friday's polymorphously fantasizing respondents barely enter my consulting room.

And yet Freud's line of thinking—the tortuous route by which a girl gives up her own desire and diverts or represses her active sexual strivings for her mother and becomes receptive to her father and then to her own adult man—would suggest that psychoanalysis between women should encounter the pain of this transfer and something of a legacy around sexual longing for women. Psychoanalysis is, after all, concerned with uncovering what has been repressed. But despite expecting some show of the erotic in woman-to-woman therapy, some evidence of the sexual aspect of the female-to-female bond, it is rarely expressed. There is plenty of desperate longing shown in the consulting room and an intense wish for recognition from a woman, but sexual recognition is strangely absent in heterosexually inclined women.

This has intrigued me. If eroticism, if sexuality, is first experienced in the mother-child relationship, if that relationship organizes our physical responses to become a template for intimate relating, if adult genitality is a recasting of the physical ambience of infancy and childhood into the adult couple relationship, if heterosexuality involves the negotiation of complex intrapsychic pathways, why would sexual feelings not emerge more insistently, more readily and more frequently within the consulting room? How might we understand their absence? What can we say about the nature of sexuality, sexual feelings and erotic feelings in and between women in the analytic relationship?

If one accepts that both heterosexuality and homosexuality are possible outcomes of psychosexual development, we might suppose that in the transference-countertransference aspect of the clinical relationship there would be little significant difference between the erotic nature of transferences from woman to woman. So, one is inclined to ask, has the erotic become so very deeply repressed in women that it fails to emerge in many female-to-female analyses? If it is not repressed, then how sustainable is the idea of infantile sexuality and sexuality in the mother-child, mother-daughter relationship? And how can we account for those woman-to-woman analyses that *are* sexually charged in both the transference and the countertransference?

Why is it that, in an analysis between a homosexual or bisexual female analysand and a heterosexual female analyst, the erotic can be induced, felt and aroused in the countertransference? If it is so easily invoked in such circumstances, how is it so apparently effortlessly absent (or repressed) in female-to-female heterosexual therapy? Where does it go? Or why does it not appear? What would be transgressed if it were to emerge? What would be imperiled if it were visible? What makes same-sex erotic feelings so dangerous in the consulting room? Is it experienced as too incestuous and is the closeness that can be generated between two women maintained at the cost of de-eroticization?

Questions such as these have led me to want to highlight the vacuum that exists in contemporary psychoanalysis with regard to the understanding of sexuality. While we have adequate accounts of construction of gender and for understanding reproduction, we do not really understand the erotic.

Perhaps we can get further in our thinking if we regard the erotic as an emergent property of the human species, a collective capacity akin to language and intelligence. Sex, the erotic—as opposed to sex, the reproductive—occurs in a relational context and is relationally constructed. If we consider for a moment the analogy between language and the erotic, ways of thinking that might be productive are opened up.

Language is created within culture and language acquisition is specifically transmitted within the mother-child relationship. Daniel Stern and Colwyn Trevarthen have demonstrated the proto-languages that exist between mother and child before the infant can enter into symbolization proper. Proto-language and language are expressions of relationship. The capacity and desire to verbalize in sounds that carry meanings speak to the essentially relational nature of language. We do not apprehend speech outside of relationship and it is only through the internalization of a relationship that we come to speak.

Language emerges from relationship. It is an instrument in the relationship for exchanging pleasure, for creating understanding or misunderstanding, for power, for transcendence and so on. We create words and ideas with one another. Language becomes a way we develop together and distinguish ourselves from one another. Language is a mechanism for self-expression and self-reflection in a world of other selves. It can be damaging or healing, an expression of closeness or of distance, of connection or separation.

So too with the erotic. It is apprehended in relationship. It is an instrument in the relationship for exchanging pleasure, for creating understanding or misunderstanding, for power, for transcendence and so on. We create a sexuality together through fusing, disidentification or a form of separated attachment. When we masturbate we do so with reference to an inner world of real or fantasized relationships. The erotic is a mechanism for self-expression and self-reflection. It can be damaging or healing, an expression of connection or a retreat from connection.

And this then is perhaps where the conundrum comes in. Insofar as a woman may experience difficulties in sustaining a sense of self, of her subjectivity, especially when she is a mother, such difficulties will have an impact on her erotic self. The erotic is not then an integrated aspect of her experience but almost an artifact of herself. We might argue that for many women the erotic is not an integral part of who they experience themselves to be but an attribute they can create in the right circumstances. There is an erotic that is employed rather than an organically occurring erotic. For many women such an erotic, which is culturally fashioned in particular ways crucial to the maintenance of a feminine identity, precludes the development of an authentic erotic.

To the extent that the taboo on female subjectivity constrains a woman, constrains a mother's capacity to experience herself as authentically sexual, in so far as sex is for her an instrument rather than an integral attribute of self, then sex, the erotic, is not necessarily woven into her experience of self and her experience of mothering an infant. It can be excluded, disassociated, absent or split off. While the mechanisms are in place in the infant to make the erotic a form of potential expression (just like language), a mother's discomfort with or disassociation from her own sexuality could be transmitted in such a way that her infant's and later her child's sexuality lies undisturbed. It is dormant. Thus when an adult intimacy that emotionally mirrors the ambience of early infancy occurs in analysis, or in a merged attachment between lovers, there is not so much a taboo on sex as rather that, with the re-evocation of infant-like states, sex, the erotic, fails to enter the picture.

To follow this argument, if in a woman-to-woman therapy the erotic is not stimulated, then it may well be that it is not so much repressed or taboo as that it was not part of the physical relationship of infancy and childhood. Because a woman's sexuality in motherhood has been disavowed or hidden until recently, sexuality is a source of deep tension for a mothering woman. This tension is transmitted from a mother to her daughter. The mother may seek to contain her daughter's sexuality much as she has contained her own. Or she may not have a way to introduce her daughter to a sexuality that is not laden with conflict or fear and so unwittingly becomes prohibited.

This prohibited, pre-emergent erotic within the mother-daughter relationship creates then the condition: The Impossibility of Sex. The issues that constrain the development of an authentic feminine subjectivity in turn constrain an authentic sexuality. While we have access to some aspect of the sexual, for many the erotic within an ongoing committed relationship, as with Carol and Maria's, proves hard to sustain. This is not because of boredom but because of fear of the deeper intimacies the erotic expresses and the tensions involved in maintaining a sense of each other as distinct individuals within the context of a committed loving relationship.

Body Countertransference

In trying to reformulate the relationship between the psyche and the soma, and to move away from a view in which the mind is seen as primary and the body as a mere psychological dustbin for what the mind is unable to contain, I have looked at the development of the individual's body sense of self and suggested ways in which it might be productive to view the development of a body self in relational terms.[2] Our bodies are made in culture, in relationship, in fantasy and even in the ambience of the caregiver-infant relationship every bit as much as our minds are.

The body, like the mind, is prewired to be a set of possibilities but those possibilities develop within relationship and within culture in as nuanced a way as our personalities do. To put it extremely: wild children fail to develop physically in ways which we associate with being uniquely human. Wild children do not have the physical capability of speech, they may not even walk upright, they do not eat in a way we recognize nor do they become sexual in a way we can understand. Everything about human physicality is influenced by our relationships. Certain human potentialities will not develop under certain conditions. Consider the fact that sighted children of blind parents need to be taught to organize the visual stimuli into the patterns of sighted people; otherwise they do not see. Now wild children do see, so it is not that we do not develop physically without relationship but that the catalyst for development and the form of development are relationally dependent. The wild child sees because it is imperative for her to do so. The sighted child of blind parents is introduced to other senses and need not see so urgently; thus she needs to be introduced to seeing if she is to develop that capacity outside her primary relationships. A Chinese-born baby brought up in the West in a Western family develops the body idioms, facial expressions, hand movements and physical stance of a European baby. Her body is formed in relationship in as significant a way as individual psyches are an expression of relationship. Furthermore, our bodies are created not simply by their biology but by the conscious and unconscious ideas we hold about babies' bodies depending upon their gender, their class and their ethnicity and by the emotional ambience in which they develop.

While biology and prewiring may preclude some possibilities and emphasize others, what a caregiver brings to the baby is not only her ideas about the baby's physicality and potential but also her own body as one to identify with, to ingest a body sense of, to locate itself by and so on. If, in addition, we think about how deeply physical the early life of a baby is—how much of its early life is involved with being held, being rocked, being fed, being burped, being sung to, being diapered— we can immediately recognize that there is very little pre-given about the physical development of the child. How she is held, how she is rocked, how she is changed, how she is fed, how she is sung to and how her physical expressions are interpreted are of tremendous significance. What the child is prewired with is the capacity to announce her presence, to enunciate in whatever ways she can her physical needs and to develop agency. This has implications for us at the level of psychoanalytic theory-making and a way into exploring some of these ideas is to take notice of the bodies in the room in the therapy situation.

The therapist's body, like the therapist's mind and heart, is part of the relational field. How I feel in my body, what is evoked in me at a bodily level, the nature of the body countertransference, the body or bodies I bring to therapy and the shifts in feeling between the bodies in the room are of enormous importance and are an extremely productive area for exploration and reflection, as I think the story of Edgar shows.

Body countertransferences can be understood in three distinct ways. The therapist can feel a demand or a request within the countertransference for a physical provision that may have been missing in the individual's development. The most striking example of this occurred many years ago when I was working with a woman who had suffered severe colitis, who had never felt "housed" in her body and hated her body. In the course of our work I became deeply aware of my own body, which felt wonderfully content during her sessions, almost as though it were purring. In analyzing this phenomenon, we understood it to be an act of creation on the part of the woman, who needed a stable, contented body in the room and thus evoked one in me so that she could begin the process of deconstructing her (hated) body and begin the process of taking in a body that felt nourishing and good.

A second way in which body countertransference can be seen and understood is through a patient's direct engagement with the therapist's body. It is a way of bringing physical distress into the therapy relationship, where it can be admitted and explored, and through its acceptance by the therapist in turn integrated into the patient's body. What has previously remained hidden and unexplored can then find shape in the psychotherapeutic relationship so that it can saturate the physical and psychological experience of the patient.

An easily understood example of this experience involves a woman of thirty-five who moved her chair and body so far into what I am accustomed to regard as my personal space that I found myself moving my chair back. The patient then inched her chair closer and I observed my desire to move away again, to create a physical distance between us that felt comfortable to me.

The chair-moving ensued over several sessions. I felt crowded out and as though I was being physically stifled. I felt nauseated. In trying to understand my response to the patient and to the physical ambience between us, I reflected on what I knew of her physical handling in infancy. The patient had vomited frequently in early childhood and then bed-wetted. She remembered being scolded for her vomiting and bed-wetting, and later had migraines.

We had already explored many of the symbolic meanings of vomiting, bed-wetting and migraines but it was through paying attention to the use of the interpersonal physical space in the room that we could focus directly on the patient's difficulties with living in and accepting her body. At one point in therapy I suggested that her body was to some extent unplotted, that she did not seem to know where it began and ended, and that it was only in its encounter with an *other* body, with its butting up against another body, that her own physicality could be experienced. She was always searching for a physical boundary in relation to another so that she could make that boundary her own.

In the therapy I understood the chair-moving as an attempt on the part of my patient to be physically recognized. My experience that she was pushy, that she evoked in me a desire to move back from her, was a hint about her possible body instability and her anxiety about physical connection. Our understanding of this led the way for the transformation of physical discomfort and disease, and for the emergence of a body within the therapy relationship that was both bounded and connected.

The third way in which body countertransference can be thought about is as a version of the physical distress the patient experiences. The patient's fatigue may provoke fatigue in the therapist. A patient's bodily symptoms may be felt by the therapist, enabling her to get closer to the patient's corporeal state.

Different experiences such as these with body countertransference have confirmed my sense that looking at the body and its development from this perspective can be extremely useful and together with other evidence it can provide entry points into new theory-making.

ALTHOUGH MY observations on both the erotic and corporeality do not make new theory, they do suggest some directions psychotherapists might want to take to advance our understandings and make sense of our current clinical findings. In showing what my thinking is on these topics, I have wanted to convey the sense that just as understandings in the therapeutic relationship are never set in stone but can always be revised and refined, so too the process of psychoanalytic theorizing is one of revision and refinement. The psychoanalytic inquiry, whether in theory-making or in clinical practice, is marked by questioning. I hope my stories and these last remarks have left the reader with a sense of what doing therapy is like from the therapist's point of view.

Thanks

For the past nine years I have been part of a seminar group involving Sally Berry, Margaret Green, Tom Ryan and Joseph Schwartz. Our wide-ranging discussions over many topics have been a forum for thinking through clinical and theoretical issues. The Women's Therapy Centre Institute in New York has also been a source of background support, and my conversations over the years with Luise Eichenbaum and Carol Bloom have helped my thinking greatly. An often unacknowledged discourse is that which occurs between a reader and the professional papers she reads. The journal *Psychoanalytic Dialogues* has been important to me in this way. I was also very fortunate in my own analysis to have as committed, generous, and gifted an analyst as Anne-Marie Sandler.

My thanks to Andrea Collett for being an enthusiastic first reader. Her response was crucial and extremely helpful, as was that of Lisa Appignanesi, who generously read the manuscript and understood what I was trying to do. Her encouragement has been very important to me. Thanks too to Luise Eichenbaum for reading "Belle," and deep appreciation to Gillian Slovo and Zack Eleftheriadou for carefully reading and commenting on Edgar's story.

One of the tricky things for me in writing the book is that I often suddenly encountered a need for information. I found myself reliant on a variety of extraclinical sources. In regard to the isolation hospital, many thanks to John Southgate and to Dr. Lesley Hall, the contemporary archivist at the Wellcome Institute. For information on Vancouver, many thanks to Patricia Kitchener. Thanks also to Robert J. Bloom of Kaiser Hospital in California, who read Jenny's story and thoughtfully discussed with me the possible medications, and to Caroline Pick, who talked me through a plot problem. Brett Kahr was always at the ready whenever I needed to check a Winnicott quote or a detail. I am extremely grateful to him.

My friends have lived with this project longer than they cared to. I have depended on their support, especially that of Gabrielle Rifkind, Gillian Slovo, Brett Kahr and Caroline Pick.

As always, Joseph Schwartz has read the manuscript as it was being written. He has been involved in far more conversations about it than I imagine he wished, but he has always maintained good humor and a high degree of interest in the project, for which I am deeply grateful.

I have found a uniquely thoughtful, energetic and understanding editor in Margaret Bluman. She has taken care over every detail of the book, from scrupulously reviewing the content, to finding the right copy-editor in Mary Ormond (who was fantastically patient and helpful), to thinking about the cover and design. It has been an absolute pleasure to work with her.

I've been blessed too with wonderful and enthusiastic U.S. publishers. Susan Moldow and Nan Graham saw the relevance of the book for North America, and Maria Guarnaschelli, its editor, has made sure that American readers will understand what I have wanted to say. It has been a lovely collaboration. Carodoc King has been my agent, my audience and my advocate. As ever, I thank him for his intellectual and emotional commitment to my work.

My greatest acknowledgment must go to my patients, who over many years have taught me all I know.

Notes

A Room with a View

1. The case studies brilliantly brought to popular attention in Robert Linder's *The Fifty-Minute Hour* and in Flora Rheta Schreiber's *Sybil* are evidence of the psychoanalyst's desire to show something about the struggles of often very distressed individuals to find a way to make a life for themselves with therapeutic help. More recently, Irvin Yalom's *Love's Executioner*, Lauren Slater's *Welcome to My Country* and Robert Akeret's *The Man Who Loved a Polar Bear* have used storytelling as a way for psychotherapists to talk about their patients and how they have been affected by them. Marie Cardinal's *The Words to Say It*, Hannah Green's *I Never Promised You a Rose Garden*, Emma Thrail's *Retrospect: The Story of an Analysis* and Nini Herman's *My Kleinian Home* are accounts of individual patients' analyses.

The Vampire Casanova

1. See, for example, Michael J. Tansey's "Sexual Attraction and Phobic Dread in the Countertransference" and Jody Messler Davies's "Love in the Afternoon: A Relational Reconsideration of Desire and Dread in the Countertransference," *Psychoanalytic Dialogues,* 4:2 (1994), and Freud's 1915 paper, "Observations on Transference Love," Standard Edition 12: 157–171 (London: Hogarth Press, 1968).

2. Thomas Ogden writes in *Projective Identification and Psychotherapeutic Technique* (Northvale, N.J.: Jason Aronson, 1982): "How much of the therapist's understanding of the patient's projective identification should be interpreted to the patient? The therapist's ability not only to understand but also to verbalise his understanding clearly and precisely is basic to therapeutic effectiveness . . . however the therapist's understanding may at times constitute a correct interpretation *for the therapist* but may not be at all well timed for the patient. In this case, the interpretation should remain a 'silent one' that is formulated in words in the therapist's mind but not verbalised to the patient."

Belle

1. J. Sandler and A. Sandler, "The Past Unconscious, The Present Unconscious and Interpretation of the Transference," *Psychoanalytic Inquiry,* 4: 367–400 (1984), and J. Sandler, "Countertransference and Role-Responsiveness," *International Review of Psychoanalysis,* 3: 43–47 (1976).

2. Lacan originated the idea of the significant moment in a session.

3. J. Butler, *Gender Trouble* (New York: Routledge, 1990).

4. S. Orbach, "Countertransference and the False Body," *Winnicott Studies,* 10 (London: Karnac Books, 1995).

5. D. W. Winnicott, "Ego Distortion in Terms of True and False Self," *Maturational Processes and the Facilitating Environment* (London: Hogarth Press, 1960).

6. Ibid.

7. Many therapists would not do this. They would see it as an intrusion, preempting an analysand's responses to an unanticipated break, but I felt it was necessary for me to make sure that Belle had received my message.

8. Many others too. See, for example, J. Sandler, *Projection, Identification, Projective Identification* (Madison: International University Press, 1987), and W. R. Bion, *Learning from Experience* (London: Heinemann, 1962).

Footsteps in the Dark

1. For a fuller discussion see, for example, C. Bollas, "The Expressive Use of the Countertransference," *The Shadow of the Object: Psychoanalysis of the Unthought Known* (London: Free Association Books, 1987), and E. Levenson, *The Fallacy of Understanding* (New York: Basic Books, 1972).

2. According to National Institute of Health estimates, 70 percent of breast cancer is environmental.

3. E. Person, *By Force of Fantasy: How We Make Our Lives* (New York: Basic Books, 1995).

4. The existence of the knife, the fact that it was in my consulting room, and my fear and fascination with it, allowed me to be more curious than I might have been if Joanna had simply reported that she cut herself. In taking the knife from Joanna, I took over some of the responsibility for it and for thinking about what it meant. I wondered, as well, whether the knife scared Joanna and thought that in taking it from her I might have taken on her fear. The menace lay in my lap now, not in hers, and in so easily handing the knife over to me she was relieved of it.

5. Ronald Fairbairn, the Scottish analyst, described this schizoid mechanism as creating a vertical split in the central libidinal ego in *Psychoanalytic Studies of the Personality* (London: Routledge & Kegan Paul, 1952).

6. If dissociated states break through the barricades that the psyche has erected to keep them out, they can be profoundly disruptive, confusing and overpowering. They fit no better now than they could before. Held separate for so long, they now, instead of being split off, take over. The dissociated self state that the individual creates to live through intensely horrific experience grips the person when it emerges. For example, if a child has been systematically abused, she may have managed this by "absenting" herself during episodes of active abuse by seeming to leave her body and looking down on it, as though from the ceiling, or seeing it as in a movie. It is as though the psyche literally divides off and becomes an observer of the experience. Then, both aspects of the event, both the child being done to and the child as observer, may become separated off and dissociated. If and/or when some stimulus forces these frozen states to emerge, they will do so in the form of performance. The child, now an adult, presents herself in one of the same self states that she was in when the abuse occurred. She is still on the ceiling or watching as in a movie; she is a spectator, not an inhibitor, dislocated from its totality. She embodies aspects of the experience, but she is not in it. She has the persona of the little girl watching or the persona of the little girl done to. If these personas appear in therapy, they will be rendered as they

were when they first developed. It will be the job of therapy to try to enable the individual to connect with and emotionally inhabit what has been severed.

7. R. K. Pitman, B. A. van der Kolk, P. O. Scott and M. S. Greenberg, "Naloxone-Reversible Analgesic Response to Combat-Related Stimuli in Post-traumatic Stress Disorders," *Archives of General Psychiatry,* 47: 541–544 (1990).

8. This finding and many others like it have helped psychotherapists understand what might be happening at a physiological level when patients are physically harmed in fights, by cutting themselves or by seeking violent situations. It explains that a psycho-physiological aspect of what Freud termed the repetition compulsion involves the search for soothing through physical release. At the same time as trauma may lead an individual to dissociate, their mechanisms for self-soothing develop a particular sensitivity whereby, unless there is extreme stress, they are inactive. Where there is a high level of stress or intensity, what psychologists call arousal, the individual's own internal (endogenous) opioids react rapidly to calm and soothe. So a person may seek out stressful situations in order to stimulate the action of endorphins.

9. J. Bowlby, *Attachment and Loss* (London: Hogarth Press, 1973).

10. My thanks to Penny Allen of Sheffield, who alerted me to this poignant detail.

11. F. Nakhla and G. Jackson, *Picking Up the Pieces: Two Accounts of a Psychoanalytic Journey* (London: Yale University Press, 1993), and S. Orbach, "Extending and Reconsidering Winnicott's False Self to the False Body," *The Legacy of Winnicott,* ed. B. Kahr (London: Karnac Books, 2000).

12. The symptom elaborates and symbolizes what we would normally think of as unconscious processes.

13. S. Orbach, "Countertransference and the False Body," *Winnicott Studies,* 10 (London: Karnac Books, 1995).

Fat Is a . . . Issue

1. S. Orbach, *Fat Is a Feminist Issue* (London: Paddington Press, 1978).

2. To regulate his blood sugar level, Edgar had been encouraged to eat complex carbohydrates at regular intervals.

3. A basic tenet of *Fat Is a Feminist Issue* is the idea that in order to eat with one's hunger it is necessary to remove restrictions and taboos against certain foods so that one can discover what foods actually satisfy and please. This tenet has to be modified for those with the low blood sugar of diabetes, but the basic idea remains: you try to match hunger with the food you desire rather than deprive yourself of the food you want that is deemed unhealthy and which is then eaten surreptitiously.

4. In a new friendship one has so many different ways to get to know someone that

there is a more organic fit between time spent together than can exist within the confines of a therapy relationship.

5. There have been valiant attempts to describe the transmission of feelings from patient to therapist, particularly in the work of Ogden, Sandler, Tansey and Burke, and Epstein. These are all plausible yet incomplete accounts of how the feelings of one person are engendered or evoked in another. The ubiquitous use in case reports of the word "got" as in "her feelings of rage got into me," seems sloppy. The *experience* is convincing while the *explanations* for it are inadequate.

6. The receiving of presents in therapy is a contentious issue. Many therapists will interpret the gift and then refuse it, or accuse the patient of undermining the therapy. See S. Orbach, "Psychoanalysis in the Twenty-first Century and the Agenda for the Next Hundred Years," Talk at the European Society for Communicative Psychotherapy, London, 3 June 1995.

7. J. Kareem and R. Littlewood, *Intercultural Therapy: Themes, Interpretation and Practice* (Oxford: Blackwell, 1992).

8. A. Metcalf and M. Humphries, *The Sexuality of Men* (London: Pluto Press, 1985); A. Samuels, *The Father* (London: Free Association Books, 1985); A. Samuels, *The Plural Psyche* (London: Routledge, 1989); E. Person, "Sexuality As a Mainstay of Identity: Psychoanalytic Perspectives," *Signs: Journal of Women in Culture and Society*, 5:4 (1980) and H. Formaini, *Men: The Darker Continent* (London: Heinemann, 1990).

Two Parts Innocent, Two Parts Wise

1. Although psychoanalysis is best known for its five-times-a-week, long-term analysis, Winnicott ran a "snack bar" consultation service at Paddington Green, where he saw many mother-baby couples for just one or two meetings in which he would endeavor to help restart processes that had become derailed.

2. This kind of worry has increased because of the concern about "recovered memory." In the space between what is recounted and "reality," there are many possible slips. What I want to emphasize here is that if the therapist picks up some kind of dissonance between a narrative and the affects, she holds in mind the tension between listening to the patient's account and trying to help her think into it more deeply.

3. C. Bollas, *The Shadow of the Object: Psychoanalysis of the Unthought Known* (London: Free Association Books, 1987); S. Orbach, "From Shoplifter to Drug Addict," *Guardian*, 18 March 1985 and S. Orbach, "The Psychological Processes of Consuming," *British Journal of Psychotherapy*, 10:2 (1994).

The Impossibility of Sex

1. I have sat in many sessions in which a very distressed woman confronts a quiet man whom she accuses of bullying behavior when they are alone. The woman uses the safety of therapy to talk about what she has been keeping inside and the man is quietened, reversing what usually happens in their relationship. It is for this reason that I often inquire whether what I am seeing in the therapy room is an accurate reflection of the relationship at home.

2. L. Eichanbaum and S. Orbach, *Outside In, Inside Out* (London: Penguin Books, 1982); L. Eichenbaum and S. Orbach, *What Do Women Want?* (London: Fontana, 1983) and L. Eichenbaum and S. Orbach, *Between Women* (London: Century, 1987).

3. See the three titles in the preceding note.

4. E. Person, "Sexuality As a Mainstay of Masculine Identity: Psychoanalytic Perspectives," *Signs: Journal of Women in Culture and Society*, 5:4 (1980).

5. S. Freud, "Three Essays on Sexuality," (1905), Standard Edition 7: 125–145 (London: Hogarth Press, 1968).

6. S. Freud, "Observations on Transference Love" (1915), Standard Edition 12: 157–171 (London: Hogarth Press, 1968).

7. When Freud was writing about transference love and entreating analysts to be wary of their patients' love for them, he was trying to address a phenomenon that had dogged analysis since its inception: the patient falls in love with the analyst, and the analyst takes this love as real rather than as a fit subject for analysis itself.

And So

1. My practice work has also included listening to and supervising the work of many other therapists in this country and abroad.

Reflections and Questions

1. Words whose technical meanings are often at odds with how these words are understood in ordinary conversation.

2. S. Orbach, "Working with the False Body," *The Imaginative Body,* ed. A. Erskine and D. Judd (London: Colin Whurr, 1993).

Index

INDEX